spring 2021

Mission

The *Community Literacy Journal* is an interdisciplinary journal that publishes both scholarly work that contributes to theories, methodologies, and research agendas and work by literacy workers, practitioners, and community literacy program staff. We are especially committed to presenting work done in collaboration between academics and community members, organizers, activists, teachers, and artists.

We understand "community literacy" as including multiple domains for literacy work extending beyond mainstream educational and work institutions. It can be found in programs devoted to adult education, early childhood education, reading initiatives, or work with marginalized populations. It can also be found in more informal, ad hoc projects, including creative writing, graffiti art, protest songwriting, and social media campaigns.

For us, literacy is defined as the realm where attention is paid not just to content or to knowledge but to the symbolic means by which it is represented and used. Thus, literacy makes reference not just to letters and to text but to other multimodal, technological, and embodied representations, as well. Community literacy is interdisciplinary and intersectional in nature, drawing from rhetoric and composition, communication, literacy studies, English studies, gender studies, race and ethnic studies, environmental studies, critical theory, linguistics, cultural studies, education, and more.

Subscriptions

Donations to the *CLJ* in any amount can be made with a check made out to "FIU English Department," with *Community Literacy Journal* in the memo line.

Send to:

> Paul Feigenbaum
> Department of English
> Florida International University
> DM462D
> 11200 SW 8th St.
> Miami, FL 33199

Donors at the $40 level or above will receive a courtesy print subscription of the academic year's issues.

Cover Artist and Art

Wendy Osterweil is a full-time fiber artist and printmaker in Philadelphia, PA. She is also a teaching artist/art educator with over 35 years experience in universities, schools, artist residencies, art centers, workshops, and out-of-school programs. She exhibits nationally and had a major installation exhibition at the Painted Bride Arts Center in

Philadelphia, 2012. MFA Graphics/University of Wisconsin-Madison, former Associate Professor Tyler School of Art/Temple University. www.wendyosterweil.com

The cover image is of Osterweil's woodcut print, *Birds Returning*. Of her inspiration for the piece, she writes, "I've been keenly aware of the birds during the past year of the pandemic. My husband and I have hiked almost every day on woodland trails near our home. One day in February I saw this amazing confluence of robins in a tree and realized they don't necessarily leave in the winter or perhaps they were returning early. The woodcut print was a response to this wonder which resonates with hope in 2021."

Submissions

Submissions for the articles section of the journal should clearly demonstrate engagement with community literacy scholarship, particularly scholarship previously published in the *Community Literacy Journal*. The editors seek work that pushes the field forward in exciting and perhaps unexpected ways. Case studies, qualitative and/or quantitative research, conceptual articles, etc., ranging from 20-25 manuscript pages, are welcome. If deemed appropriate, we will send the manuscript out to readers for blind review. You can expect a report in 8-10 weeks.

The *CLJ* also welcomes shorter manuscripts (8-12 pages) for two new sections:

Community Literacy Project and Program Profiles will discuss innovative and impactful community-based projects and programs that are grounded in best practices. We encourage community-based practitioners and non-profit staff to submit for this section. Profiles should draw on community literacy scholarship, but they are not expected to have the extended lit reviews that are customary in the articles section of the journal. If you are a community member wanting to submit, and it is your first time writing for an academic journal, we are happy to offer mentorship and answer questions. Pieces co-authored by multiple stakeholders in a project are also welcome.

Please submit using our online submission system. Contact the Project and Program Profiles Editor, Vincent Portillo, with questions at vportill@syr.edu.

Issues in Community Literacy will offer targeted analysis, reflection, and/or complication of ongoing challenges associated with the work of community literacy. Potential subjects for this section include (but are not limited to): building/sustaining infrastructure, navigating institutional constraints, pursuing community literacy in graduate school, working with vulnerable populations, building ethical relationships, realizing reciprocity, and negotiating conflicts among partners. We imagine this as a space for practitioners to raise critical issues or offer a response to an issue raised in a previous volume of the CLJ.

We encourage community-based practitioners and non-profit staff to submit for this section. If you are a community member wanting to submit, and it is your first time writing for an academic journal, we are happy to offer mentorship and answer questions. Pieces co-authored by multiple stakeholders in a project are also welcome.

Please submit using our online submission system. Contact the Issues in Community Literacy Editor, Cayce Wicks, with questions at cwick003@fiu.edu.

Coda: Community Writing and Creative Work welcomes submissions of poetry, creative nonfiction, short stories, and multigenre work on any topics that have ensued from community writing projects. This may be work about community writing projects, and this may be expressed in ways we have yet to imagine. We ask authors to include a personal reflection about the submission itself--information about your community writing group (if you belong to one); your personal journey as a writer; what inspired you to write your piece; and anything else you'd care to share about your life--as an invitation for the author and Coda's readers to consider writing and activism as intertwined.

Please submit using our online submission system. Contact the Coda Editorial Collective at coda.editors@gmail.com.

Advertising

Community Literacy Journal welcomes advertising. The journal is published twice annually, in the Fall and Spring (November and May). Deadlines for advertising are two months prior to publication (September and March).

Ad Sizes and Pricing

Half page (trim size 5.5X4.25): $200
Full page (trim size 5.5X8.5): $350
Inside back cover (trim size 5.5X8.5): $500
Inside front cover (trim size 5.5X8.5): $600

Format

We accept .PDF, .JPG, .TIF or .EPS. All advertising images should be camera-ready and have a resolution of 300 dpi. For more information, please contact Veronica House (housev@colorado.edu) and Paul Feigenbaum (pfeigenb@fiu.edu).

Copyright © 2021 *Community Literacy Journal*
ISSN 1555-9734

Community Literacy Journal is a member of the Council of Editors of Learned Journals.

Production and distribution managed by Parlor Press.

Publication of the *Community Literacy Journal* is made possible through the generous support of the English Department and the Writing and Rhetoric Program at Florida International University. The *CLJ* is a journal of the Coalition for Community Writing. Current issues and archives are available open access at https://digitalcommons.fiu.edu/communityliteracy/

Editorial Board

Jonathan Alexander, *University of California Irvine*
Steven Alvarez, *St. John's University*
April Baker Bell, *Michigan State University*
Kirk Branch, *Montana State University*
Stephanie Briggs, *Community College of Baltimore County*
Laurie Cella, *Shippensburg University*
David Coogan, *Virginia Commonwealth University*
Ellen Cushman, *Northeastern University*
Lisa Dush, *DePaul University*
Jenn Fishman, *Marquette University*
Linda Flower, *Carnegie Mellon University*
Beth Godbee, *Heart-Head-Hands.com*
Eli Goldblatt, *Temple University*
Laurie Grobman, *Pennsylvania State University Berks*
Shirley Brice Heath, *Stanford University*
Glenn Hutchinson, *Florida International University*
Tobi Jacobi, *Colorado State University*
Ben Kuebrich, *West Chester University*
Carmen Kynard, *Texas Christian University*
Paula Mathieu, *Boston College*
Seán Ronan McCarthy, *James Madison University*
Michael Moore, *DePaul University*
Beverly Moss, *The Ohio State University*
Steve Parks, *The University of Virginia*
Jessica Pauszek, *Texas A&M University Commerce*
Eric Darnell Pritchard, *University of Arkansas*
Jessica Restaino, *Montclair State University*
Elaine Richardson, *The Ohio State University*
Lauren Rosenberg, *University of Texas at El Paso*
Tiffany Rousculp, *Salt Lake Community College*
Iris Ruiz, *University of California Merced*
Donnie Sackey, *University of Texas at Austin*
Rachael W. Shah, *University of Nebraska-Lincoln*
Erec Smith, *York College of Pennsylvania*
Stephanie Wade, *Bates College*
John Warnock, *University of Arizona*
Christopher Wilkey, *Northern Kentucky University*

COMMUNITY LITERACY Journal

Editors	Paul Feigenbaum, *Florida International University* Veronica House, *University of Colorado Boulder*
Senior Assistant Editor and Issues in Community Literacy Editor	Cayce Wicks, *Florida International University*
Journal Manager	Erin Daugherty, *University of Arkansas at Fayetteville*
Book and New Media Review Editor	Jessica Shumake, *University of Notre Dame*
Consulting Editor and Project Profiles Editor	Vincent Portillo, *Syracuse University*
Coda: Community Writing and Creative Work Editorial Collective	Kefaya Diab, *Indiana University* Leah Falk, *Rutgers University, Camden* Chad Seader, *William Penn University* Alison Turner, *University of Denver* Kate Vieira, *University of Wisconsin, Madison* Stephanie Wade, *Bates College*
Social Media Editor	Christian Ruvalcaba, *University of Arizona*
Senior Copyeditor	Sarah Hughes, *University of Michigan*
Copyeditors	Adam Hubrig, *Sam Houston State University* Charisse Iglesias, *University of Arizona* Kelly Whitney, *The Ohio State University*

community literacy journal

COMMUNITY LITERACY *journal*

Spring 2021
Volume 15, Issue 2

1   *Editors' Introduction*
      Paul Feigenbaum and Veronica House, with Cayce Wicks

Talk

4   *The Complicity/Complexity Problem of Anti-Racism Work in The Academy*
      Natasha N. Jones

Articles

9   *Public Memory as Community-Engaged Writing: Composing Difficult Histories on Campus*
      Amy J. Lueck, Matthew V. Kroot, and Lee M. Panich

31   *Cultivating Legitimacy as a Farmer*
      Abby M. Dubisar

52   *(Re) Mixing Up Literacy: Cookbooks as Rhetorical Remix*
      Elizabeth J. Fleitz

Issues in Community Literacy

73   *Writing Group in an Emergency: Temporary Shelter*
      Alison Turner

84   *Rhetorical Curation of Patient Art: How Community Literacy Scholars Can Contribute to Healthcare Professions*
      Maria Novotny

97   *'I knew this was gonna be chaos': Voices Collide While Decolonizing Intersectional Injustice*
      Danielle Kubasko Sullivan and Mary L. Fahrenbruck

Book and New Media Reviews

106 *From the Book and New Media Review Editor's Desk*
Jessica Shumake, Editor

107 *My Life with Charles Billups & Martin Luther King: Trauma and the Civil Rights Movement* by Rene Billups Baker
Reviewed by Sherita Roundtree

112 *Researching Protest Literacies: Literacy as Protest in the Favelas of Rio de Janeiro* by Jamie D. I. Duncan
Reviewed by Catherine Compton-Lilly

116 *My Caesarean: 21 Mothers on the C-Section Experience and After* edited by Amanda Fields and Rachel Moritz
Reviewed by Cassie A. Wright

121 *Oral Literacies: When Adults Read Aloud* by Sam Duncan
Reviewed by Jamie D. I. Duncan

Coda: Community Writing and Creative Work

126 *A Word from Coda's Editors*
Kefaya Diab, Leah Falk, Chad Seader, Alison Turner, Kate Vieira, and Stephanie Wade

128 *Poesía para la Paz: Voces de Jóvenes Colombianos*
Introducción y comentarios por Juana María Echeverri Escobar y Rodrigo Aicardo Rojas Ospina

130 *Poemas*
Danna Samira Pérez Ramírez, María Fernanda Montoya Trujillo, y Mariana Ospina López

134 *Persistence and Creativity: EmersonWRITES Celebrates 11 Years with Young Poets and Writers of Boston*
Introduction by Mary Kovaleski Byrnes and Livia Meneghin featuring Rejeila Firmin, Star Igbinosa, Ebony Smith, Essence Smith, Winter Jones, Yaritza Santana, Paola Ruiz Manrique, Madison Lucchesi, and Zaryah Qareeb

147 *Moments*
Jessica Pisano

153 *Side Streets*
Eli Goldblatt

Editors' Introduction

Paul Feigenbaum and Veronica House, with Cayce Wicks

Occasionally, a scholar comes along and says precisely what is necessary for the political and cultural moment. As editors, we often feel that we miss the urgency of that moment because of the necessary peer-review and revision processes involved in academic publishing. As we try to find new ways to break down expectations of that academic timeframe while maintaining the quality of intellectual argument that *Community Literacy Journal* publishes, we are honored to open our Spring 2021 issue with a transcript of a talk by Natasha N. Jones, "The Complicity/Complexity Problem of Anti-Racism Work in The Academy," given on April 16, 2021 for the panel "Undoing BIPOC Erasure in the Academy: A Conversation about Race and Anti-Racism," which was hosted by the University of California Merced. We publish this talk because we believe it says what is precisely necessary for community literacy scholars, teachers, participants, and leaders "right now." In this talk, Jones demands of us a "radical honesty" and an interrogation of our complicity in racist systems. In her radically honest voice, she exposes her grief and rage at the broad historical moment and how the injustices writ large are also the injustices of the academy. This includes the extraordinary labor placed on people of color, particularly Black women. Jones urges us to move beyond a complicit focus on individual injustices toward dismantling complex, systemic, structural injustice. Ultimately, Jones argues that we must "do better."

As we write this introduction, COVID-19 has killed more than 581,000 people in the United States—and millions more worldwide—disproportionately ravaging Black, Brown, and Indigenous communities. Derek Chauvin has been found guilty of murdering George Floyd, and yet the process leading to that conviction has further illustrated the profound racism of the nation's legal system, in which unimaginably disturbing video footage is required to confirm that, legally speaking, Black lives do matter—and even then, right up until the verdict was read, we had good reason to think Chauvin would be acquitted. During and since the trial, many more Black and Brown people have been shot by police, including Daunte Wright, 20; Adam Toledo, 13; and Ma'Khia Bryant, 16. President Biden has supported and signed more progressive legislation than many of us would have believed, given his history, and yet we are no closer to establishing legal safety and security for the millions of undocumented people living in the U.S., let alone the tens of thousands more trying to escape the legacies of American imperialism. And despite the failure of the insurrection attempt on January 6, dozens of states are now curtailing access to the Constitutional right to vote and protest while also seeking to erase the existence of transgender communities. Meanwhile, as spring transitions to summer, the annual wait to see just how destructive climate change-accelerated forest fires and hurricanes will be this year is well under way.

There are countless reasons for skepticism and rage, though we reject despair. And a major reason we reject despair is that the *work* of community literacy, which was so vividly embodied in Carmen Kynard's Spring 2020 Conference on Community Writing keynote/*CLJ* essay, continues, and continues to inspire us.

Our first peer-reviewed article suggests one of the many important elements for us to consider as we work to do better. In **"Public Memory as Community-Engaged Writing: Composing Difficult Histories on Campus,"** authors Amy J. Lueck, Matthew V. Kroot, and Lee M. Panich dig into how universities can ethically and substantively reckon with settler colonialist and white supremacist legacies. Using their own institution of Santa Clara University as a case study, the authors leverage their positions and resources at the university to center and amplify the perspectives, experiences, and histories of local Native communities to ensure the history of colonization and Indigenous persistence are accurately reflected in various community-engaged writing projects on campus. Through their partnership with local Ohlone tribal members, Lueck, Root, and Panich demonstrate how community literacy scholars can use digital technologies to compose alternative public representations of their campus space and its history.

In our second article, **"Cultivating Legitimacy as a Farmer,"** Abby M. Dubisar introduces us to Lauren, a midwestern woman farmer navigating agricultural literacy work in a heavily gendered terrain. Running the largest woman-owned CSA in her state, Lauren's story is one of the fearless and exhausting literacy work women must do to break down stereotypes and assert not only their legitimacy but their leadership in shaping a narrative in an overwhelmingly male profession. Through investigation and interviews, Dubisar adds to a growing body of scholarship on the gendered struggles of women in agriculture.

Our third article studies the informal literacies practiced by home cooks in the pages of their cookbooks. In **"(Re) Mixing Up Literacy: Cookbooks as Rhetorical Remix,"** Elizabeth J. Fleitz pulls us into the pages of a 1950s cookbook as we look at the marginalia, notes, pasted-in clippings as remix – a scrapbook of sorts that Fleitz argues represents a food literacy practice. She looks at this authorial remix as a way to gain a voice in the domestic sphere. By studying this literacy practice as multimodal remix and applying de Certeau's theory of "making do," Fleitz opens a study of the ways female home cooks have asserted influence and authority as active makers rather than passive users.

For our Issues in Community Literacy section, we offer space for contributors to analyze, reflect, and/or complicate ongoing challenges associated with the work of community literacy. For this issue, concerns related to community health and the COVID-19 pandemic appeared across submissions, which focus on the authors' lived experiences with community literacy projects. In our first piece, **"Writing Group in an Emergency: Temporary Shelter,"** Alison Turner reflects on her experience working to build a writing group in a temporary "emergency shelter for women and trans folx experiencing homelessness during the COVID-19 pandemic." Using student creative writing from the group as a metaphorical frame, Turner crafts a poetic reflection on the constraints and affordances of implementing community literacy best practices in an emergency shelter, a fluid and dynamic context. Turner ultimately "suggests that while best practices can guide creation of a writing group during an emergency, an emergency, in turn, can generate innovation with these best practices."

In **"Rhetorical Curation of Patient Art: How Community Literacy Scholars Can Contribute to Healthcare Professions,"** Maria Novotny claims that "community literacy scholars are well poised to support challenges currently facing healthcare providers." Reflecting on her experiences with The ART of Infertility to curate an exhibit of patient art and stories to increase emotional literacy and empathy for healthcare providers, Novotny argues that through the act of "rhetorical curation," community literacy scholars can use their expertise to "design innovative public projects that contribute to improvements in healthcare."

Our final piece for the Issues section, **"'I knew this was gonna be chaos': Voices Collide While Decolonizing Intersectional Injustice,"** co-authored by Danielle Kubasko Sullivan and Mary L. Fahrenbruck, uses the paradigm of "indigenous-sustaining literacy" to analyze the events surrounding the One Book/One Community's "display of archival photographs depicting a Navajo Civil Rights march" at San Juan College in Farmington, New Mexico. Sullivan and Fahrenbruck argue that the paradigm "indigenous-sustaining literacy," a lens that foregrounds "racial literacy and orality," may be a useful tool to counter hegemony and enhance efforts to "decolonize community literacy practices." Each piece outlines a unique and interesting real-life experience with community literacy that asks the authors—and their readers—to reflect on what it means to apply best practices of community literacy in the real world.

We are especially proud to introduce a new section of the *Community Literacy Journal*, "Coda: Community Writing and Creative Work," and the founding editorial collective: Kefaya Diab, Leah Falk, Chad Seader, Alison Turner, Kate Vieira, and Stephanie Wade. Coda offers an inclusive space for the creative work ensuing from and about community writing projects, public engagement, and activism. We hope that you will enjoy the pieces selected for this section.

As always, we are grateful to Jessica Shumake for her work editing the Book and New Media Review section. We are likewise thankful to the scholars who contributed reviews for this issue.

Talk

The Complicity/Complexity Problem of Anti-Racism Work in The Academy

Natasha N. Jones

> This talk was given on April 16, 2021 as my contribution for the anti-racism panel "Undoing BIPOC Erasure in the Academy: A Conversation about Race and Anti-Racism." The panel was hosted by the University of California Merced. What follows is a transcript of this talk that incorporates some minor edits for print and publication in the *Community Literacy Journal*.

I'm going to talk about The Complicity/Complexity Problem of Anti-Racism Work in The Academy.

I draw on how Dr. Cecilia Shelton (2019) takes up Dr. Bianca Williams's (2016) concept of "radical honesty" in the technical communication classroom as I share with y'all today. Shelton demonstrates how a Black Feminist pedagogy approach creates a space for radical honesty that "allows for teachers (literal and figurative) to be whole humans with emotions who practice self-care; centers the significance of emotional labor and cost of transformative work; mitigates racial battle fatigue; and contextualizes and historicizes emotion, allowing for an analysis of power rather than a subjective truth" (22). So, here is my radical honesty.

So, when I was initially asked to participate in this panel, I had an idea of what I wanted to talk about. I thought originally that I might talk about mentorship and anti-racism in the university and in higher ed contexts. But, after this week, I've changed my mind because as a Black woman scholar, grief and rage are weighing heavily on me right now. And, because I am a Black woman scholar, I cannot and I refuse to separate who I am from what I have to say about anti-racism and the work that I do. As a Black woman academic, I can couch what I need to say in "scholarly" terms, but know that I'm not here for the performance of anti-racist work as it is understood by the academy.

I'm angry. I'm grieving. I'm enraged. As a Black woman I can say that I'm mad as hell. . .and I say that without any irony whatsoever. So, when I say that I wrote this presentation in anger and rage, you can clearly understand that my work is informed by who I am ... always.

On the heels of more murders at the hands of the police, Duante Wright, Adam Toledo, I am honestly in no position to mince words. And, even as I grieve, yet again this week with Black folks across the nation, I found myself seething that I had to log onto my computer, answer emails, RSVP for committee meetings, field questions from students, work on research presentations, and engage with all of the things that require my energy and attention in order for me to be called Dr. Natasha N. Jones, Associate Professor.

It's not the showing up to my job that I was enraged about. I love my job. I love the folks I work with. That's not the issue. It's the expectation that Black folk carry on, unphased, when our murders are played on a loop for the world to see. And, I know, I know that being Black in America means that I'm expected to swallow my grief, my anger, my sadness, my fear, and smile in the next department meeting. But my God, what kind of strength do y'all expect us to have? And, to be clear, it's not the being Black that is the problem. It's the pervasive refusal of this nation and its institutions to grapple with the continued oppression and attempted genocide of people who look like me that is the problem. It's the refusal of the nation and its institutions to account for and address its racially driven necro-politics.

As I told one of my white friends a few years back, think about this: On your hardest day--The day that nothing goes right. The day that you get the diagnosis from the doctor. The day you get the call from your kid's school. The day you get the rejection letter in the mail. The day your bills are due, your money is short, and you are just so tired. The day you see the flash of blue lights in your rearview mirror as you drive home alone.... On that day, your hardest day, try figuring out how to survive that day in Black skin, in a Black body, as a Black person.

In the context of this talk, I ask you ... try surviving the academy in Black skin, in a Black body, as a Black person. What do you think that looks like on a daily basis ... when we are answering emails, when we are responding to students, when we are serving on a mundane committee, and in the background, we are hearing the news reports of another state-sanctioned murder of a Black person?

I wholeheartedly acknowledge that yes, even our presence in the academy is resistance, but our resistance is labor and work ... Always.

And, it wasn't until sometime later, after I asked my friend to imagine her surviving her worst day as Black person that it occurred to me that survival and survivance is inextricably and intricately tied up in what it means to be Black. The academy is no different...

Just like the police that profile us in the streets, the academy expects complicity in exchange for the possibility (not the promise) of survival. And, when we think about the rhetoric of complicity as it relates to Black folks and other marginalized identities, it necessarily shifts how we think about diversity, equity, and inclusion efforts and initiatives from within academic institutions.

The focus on Diversity, Equity, and Inclusion (DEI) programs and initiatives and inclusion work in the academy is not focused on resistance at all. The focus is always on complicity. So, how do you work within a system, with the expectation of complicity, to change and resist the very system that you are working within? How exactly does that work?

Patricia Hill Collins provides us with a very useful conceptualization of power that allows us to see how DEI programs, initiatives, and inclusion work that originate and operate within academic institutions fall short.

In our 2019 book, *Technical Communication After the Social Justice Turn: Building Coalitions for Action*, Drs. Rebecca Walton, Kristen Moore, and I draw on Collins' work to understand power and the role of coalitions. Collins (1990) conceives of power through the matrix of domination. For Collins, power operates across four levels:

- Structural
- Disciplinary
- Hegemonic
- Interpersonal

Each domain of power provides insight into one way that power is enacted. But they are all connected!

- The structural focuses on infrastructure
- The disciplinary focuses on rules, regulations, policies
- The hegemonic focuses on ideology, culture, and consciousness
- The interpersonal focuses on individual actions

Collins cautions us to think *across*, not just within, domains and embrace complexity in our justice work in order to resist complicity in oppression.

If racism is structural, systemic, and interpersonal, then why isn't our anti-racism work also structural, systemic, and interpersonal.

In fact, most DEI work within the academy never rises to address the structural domain of power at all. Sometimes, we address the disciplinary, sometimes the hegemonic, often we address the interpersonal. But we need structural change so we need to engage the infrastructural power domain. This is almost never done, simply because addressing the structural domain of power means that we would necessarily threaten the very institution itself. Instead, DEI work focuses on the other domains of power, and most often, only on the interpersonal domain. So we end up asking questions like:

- How do we address race in our individual classrooms?
- Should we revise our syllabus to include more marginalized scholars?
- How can we recruit graduate students from marginalized populations into our programs?
- Who can we get to serve on this diversity committee?

My university implemented DEI training in which we were expected to view instructional modules about how to respond to racism and microaggressions. It was all focused on the interpersonal. Not to mention, the "instruction" centered largely on how the microaggressed should respond to the microaggressor … How those victimized must engage with the folks who were "insensitive" "unaware" or "uneducated." What should we say when we hear someone using a slur or acting "uncivilly"?

Now, this is all well and good. We SHOULD be doing these things and asking these questions. BUT … when will we ask the right folks questions about how they resist complicity embedded in the infrastructure of our academic institutions?

How do I enact anti-racist work in my classrooms or scholarship? Do you mean how do I show up as a Black woman and bring my whole self into my classroom? Or as Shelton notes: how do I center emotional labor and the cost of transformative work? How do I mitigate my racial battle fatigue? How do I contextualize and historicize my emotions and the emotions of folks that look like me? How do I do anti-racist work or how do I make it as a Black woman in the academy, where my complicity is expected in exchange for the possibility of survival? Collins reminds us that this resistance work is not *just* about institutional transformation, especially in the context of Black Feminist Thought. This work IS about survival for us. Collins tells us to remember that Black Feminist Thought is always oppositional and should remain so. So, who are we asking questions about anti-racist work and resistance? And from whom are we expecting answers? Those of us trying to survive? Or those of us who expect complicity?

Resisting complicity and embracing complexity means our DEI programs and initiatives would do fundamentally different work:

- We would diversify our syllabus AND question the very founding of how we teach and why we teach, like the work of April Baker-Bell on linguistic justice.
- We would recruit marginalized graduate students AND dismantle our programs that see these students as add-ons, instead of shaping our programs around their needs.
- We would support our faculty of color in their work, but also support our faculty in protests, walk-outs, unionizing, financial compensation, leaves, and other aspects that recognize ALL of our faculty as fully human.
- We would draft anti-racist statements and hold our deans, provosts, university presidents accountable when they refuse to push back against wealthy donors.

Our complicity will never do the anti-racist work that we think it will do. So, what now? What's next? We embrace that our anti-racist work is complex and oppositional and it should always be.

In her 2016 essay "Black Feminist Thought as Oppositional Knowledge," Collins asks "how might Black Feminist Thought remain oppositional, reflexive, resistant, and visionary in the context of contemporary intellectual and political challenges?" Collins talks about how, given the visibility of Black women, Black feminist work, and the political impulse toward surface level diversity that is now evident in our institutions, "visibility should not be mistaken for access, equality, or empowerment" (134). Instead, Collins calls for work that "aims to dismantle unjust intellectual and political structures" (134). Collins asks us to move past the "identifying and lamenting" in order to collectively create and innovate (136). In this way, complicity won't serve us and only offers us a short-lived illusion of inclusion.

I'll end here and say also that acknowledging the grief and trauma experienced by Black folks right now is something that we should demand from our institutions. And not, surface level acknowledgements; I mean material, tangible acknowledgements because the collective grief, trauma and rage that we feel impacts us in material and tangible ways. As my friend and colleague, Dr. Laura Gonzales reminded me: You can't have our discourse and our knowledge without acknowledging what we have to navigate in order to survive on a daily basis. Do better.

Works Cited

Collins, Patricia H. *Black Feminist Thought: Knowledge, Consciousness, and the Politics of Empowerment*. Routledge, 1990.

---. "Black Feminist Thought as Oppositional Knowledge." *Departures in Critical Qualitative Research*, vol. 5, no. 3, 2016, pp. 133-144.

Shelton, Cecilia. "Shifting out of Neutral: Centering Difference, Bias, and Social Justice in a Business Writing Course. *Technical Communication Quarterly*, vol. 29, no. 1, 2019, pp. 18-32.

Williams, Bianca. "Radical honesty: Truth-Telling as Pedagogy for Working through Shame in Academic Spaces." *Race, Equity, and the Learning Environment: The Global Relevance of Critical and Inclusive Pedagogies in Higher Education*, Edited by Frank Tuitt, Chayla Haynes, and Saran Stewart, 2016, pp. 71-82.

Author Bio

Natasha N. Jones is a technical communication scholar and co-author of the book *Technical Communication after the Social Justice Turn: Building Coalitions for Action* (winner of the 2021 CCCC Best Book in Technical or Scientific Communication). Her research interests include social justice and narrative. She holds herself especially accountable to Black women and marginalized genders and other systemically marginalized communities. As such, she strives to conscientiously center the narratives and experiences of those at the margins in her scholarship. Her work has been published in a number of journals and she has received national recognition for her contributions, being awarded the CCCC Best Article in Technical and Scientific Communication (2020, 2018, and 2014) and the Nell Ann Pickett Award (2017). She is the Vice President for the Association of Teachers of Technical Writing (ATTW) and is an Associate Professor at Michigan State University.

Articles

Public Memory as Community-Engaged Writing: Composing Difficult Histories on Campus

Amy J. Lueck, Matthew V. Kroot, and Lee M. Panich

Abstract

Colleges and universities across the United States are recognizing the public memory function of their campus spaces and facing difficult decisions about how to represent the ugly sides of their histories within their landscapes of remembrance. Official administrative responses to demands for greater inclusiveness are often slow and conservative in nature. Using our own institution and our work with local Indigenous community members as a case study, we argue that students and faculty can employ community-engaged, public-facing, digital composing projects to effectively challenge entrenched institutional interests that may elide or even misrepresent difficult histories in public memory works. Such projects are a nimble and accessible means of creating counter-narratives to intervene in public memory discourses. Additionally, by engaging in public discourses, such work helps promote meaningful student rhetorical learning in courses across disciplines.

Keywords

Ohlone; public memory; colonialism; California missions; digital; pedagogy; community engagement

Introduction

Communities across the United States are facing difficult decisions about how to represent their histories, as institutions and individuals doing memory work must grapple with the impacts of their historical frameworks and ideological claims in the public square (Epstein and Peck). The recent booms in scholarship on "memory" (Winter) and "difficult histories" (Attwood) across disciplines—and particularly within rhetoric and communication (see Greer and Grobman; Dickinson et al.; Crawford et al.)—have contributed to the growing acknowledgement that public memory, like all ideological claims about the past, does not merely reflect and preserve, but rather asserts and transmits conceptions of history, culture, and identity.

College campuses, whose present-day resources are at least in part products of the historical exploitation of marginalized and subjugated populations, are not exempt from these controversies (e.g., Clarke and Fine; Hart Micke). Indeed, because most institutions of higher education have instructors, scholars, and even units that work to interrogate hegemonic discourses and the production of new knowledge about the past, and because memory work is inherently educational work, colleges and universities are especially obligated to take on the challenge of historical representation proactively. Pairing the realities of campus histories and the cultural role of higher education with current trends in collaborative partnerships between academics and stakeholder communities (e.g., Colwell; Grobman; Heron; Israel et al; Kovach; Wallerstein et al; Wilson), we argue that campus public memory and public history work—particularly digital public memory projects—are an opportunity for community-engaged composition that is a powerful means for producing creative counter-narratives that challenge entrenched institutional interests, which may otherwise elide or even misrepresent difficult histories.

Using our own institution of Santa Clara University as a case study, we highlight how community-engaged digital public memory work can be both pedagogical and political, moving the needle on an otherwise often slow and highly conservative process of addressing historical wrongs on college campuses. We also emphasize how this community-engaged composition work can serve as a bridge between our different disciplinary backgrounds—archaeology and rhetoric—with our shared interest in collaborative research models, as well as the construction and deployment of public memories (Keene and Colligan; Wilson).

Santa Clara University's campus is an ideal case study because of its unique history. Our institution is the only university established at the site of one of California's twenty-one Spanish missions, being located on the former grounds of Mission Santa Clara de Asís. The California missions are highly charged sites of public memory, a fact that has only been exacerbated with the recent canonization of eighteenth-century Franciscan missionary Junípero Serra (Dartt-Newton; Helmbrecht; Kryder-Reid, *California Mission Landscapes*; Lorimer; Panich, "After Saint Serra"). Long seen as the anchors of European settlement on the Pacific Coast—Serra himself is often referred to as "California's founding father" (Hackel)—the missions occupy a foundational place in the public memory of the state of California (Figure 1). This is the interpretive frame employed by our institution, which has described the mission as the "anchor and spiritual center" of the university ("History"), a frame that effectively erases the experiences of the Indigenous groups associated with the mission and, in particular, the Ohlone whose ancestral territory the campus occupies. Similar narratives are replicated in culturally hegemonic settler colonial and white supremacist discourses on California history found in many educational contexts.

Figure 1. Plaque inside the Mission Church, commemorating the bicentennial of the founding of the first Spanish mission in Alta California in 1769, here defined by the Daughters of the American Revolution as the founding of California.

For many Native people, in contrast, the missions represent sites of profound loss. They are institutional agents of cultural suppression, coerced and uncompensated labor, corporal punishment, family separation, ecological degradation, and increased disease loads—historical injustices that are glossed over by the public interpretive programs at most California mission sites. At the same time, the hardships of missionization are just part of the story, and there is a risk that a single-minded focus on the horrors of colonialism only plays into settler colonialism's "logic of elimination" (Wolfe). Therefore, it is paramount for public memory rhetorics to provide what Sonya Atalay calls a "sense of the struggle," while also keeping the long-term persistence of Native Californians at the center of the narrative (Atalay, "No Sense"; Schneider et al).

As professors of anthropology and rhetoric, our intention in this work is to use our positions and resources at the university to center and amplify the perspectives, experiences, and histories of local Native communities in order to intervene in their erasure within our campus space. To ensure community-based sentiments about the history of colonization and Indigenous persistence are accurately reflected in our various community-engaged writing projects on campus, we partner with local Ohlone tribal members in order to disrupt California's hegemonic founding narrative, considering the particular role of digital technologies in helping to compose alternative public representations of our campus space and its history.

To introduce this case study as an example of community-engaged public memory work, we begin here by reviewing recent work on how US colleges have tackled difficult histories associated with their institutions as sites of cultural history and public memory. Next, we draw on scholarship in rhetoric and education to argue that assigning digital public memory projects as community-engaged writing in undergraduate courses can provide space for the knowledge-building, reflection, and engagement necessary for shifting public memory on campuses.

Turning to the case study of our university, we provide background into our campus's current commemorative landscape and recent developments towards re-examining its public memory works, particularly in relation to Ohlone history and culture. We explore the various sources of community-based engagement spurred by interests in campus public memory and activism, outlining the ways students at Santa Clara University—driven by their own identities, commitments, and coalitional goals—have been a central force in compelling reflection and enacting change on our campus. We then describe how the classroom-based digital projects and other grant-supported projects underway on our campus marshal those student-community connections and harness the potential of virtual space to publicly present counterstories that shape memory on our campus for more just and inclusive ends. We conclude with a discussion of the lessons of our community-engaged composition work on difficult campus histories, which are broadly applicable to other community-engaged projects.

Difficult Histories and Public Memory on College Campuses

In recent years, a number of colleges and universities across the United States have sought ways to reconcile their historical and contemporary perpetuation of systems of racial, economic, and political domination and exploitation with their claimed commitments to social justice and the creation of opportunity (Clarke and Fine 84; see also Wilder). For example, members of the Georgetown and Brown University communities have undertaken administratively sanctioned examinations of the colleges' histories in partnership with local stakeholder communities and used them to inform recommendations redressing the historical and contemporary legacy of slavery and racialized violence that helped shape these institutions (Clarke and Fine; Walters; Working Group).

However, universities too often forgo such a broadly inclusive communal approach to this sort of work in favor of official proclamations and representations that may reflect the identities and priorities of administrations, rather than students and other community stakeholders. This, in effect, makes public memory works on campuses "constructed for the people but not by the people" (Haskins 402). In these cases, faculty and students are often left filling the gaps in official memory with their own projects. For example, at Harvard University and the University of Alabama, individual faculty and their students drove the process of historical reckoning, with administrations responding to the publicity generated by this work (See Walters; Clarke and Fine). While Harvard's administration did eventually financially and rhetorically support the project, Alabama is cited as an example of a less successful case. There, agitation to address the legacy of slavery in that institution's past resulted in a lukewarm institutional apology in 2004 and little else in the way of recognition or reparations (Clarke and Fine). However, despite the lack of official change, Alabama faculty and students continue to take the lead in producing counternarratives, such as Professor Hillary Green and her student collaborators' Hallowed Grounds walking tour and After Slavery digital pop-up museum (Green, *The Hallowed Grounds Project* and "The Burden").

The legacies of chattel enslavement of Africans and members of the African Diaspora are not the only difficult histories with which members of campus communities are currently engaging. At Stanford University, faculty created the Chinese Railroad Workers in North America Project (CRRW) in part to explore the role of their institution's founding family in the exploitation of Chinese workers in the late nineteenth century (Chang and Fisher Fishkin; Voss). In addition to traditional, published scholarship, the Stanford CRRW project has generated digital galleries of documents and archaeological evidence to engage a variety of public audiences (Chinese Railroad Workers Project). Initiatives like those at Stanford and Alabama sidestep the challenge of institutional inertia or resistance, leveraging the affordances of ephemeral performance and digital space for intervening in public remembrance.

Just as slavery and exploitative labor practices are intertwined in the history of American universities, so too did such institutions benefit from the processes of settler colonialism, including the annexation and sale of tribal lands, the use of coerced Native labor, the erasure of cultural traditions, and the displacement and attempted genocide of Indigenous people (Lee and Ahtone; Hart Micke; Luke and Heynen; Nash). Higher education has only recently begun to address this legacy (Brasher et al.; Calloway; Hart Micke). For example, universities across North America have begun to bring the memory of Indigenous displacement and survivance into campus activities through the composition and circulation of land acknowledgement statements (Wilkes et al). In California, student activism is similarly forcing many campuses to reckon with how they commemorate Junípero Serra, founder of the Alta California mission system, with schools like Stanford making overtures to address their complicity in colonial domination by renaming buildings and other sites on campus (Gomez; Myers).

In light of these histories, memory scholars have theorized college campuses as "wounded" places fundamentally shaped by legacies of racialized, political, and cultural violence (Brasher et al; Till). Revisions to the campus environment, such as those described above, attempt to redress these historical violences, recognizing the fact that place names are political, and discursive violence has substantive impacts (Rios 63; Barnd). Still, many campuses have been slow to take up this call. Those universities without more obvious tributes to racist figures or traditions may not even recognize their campuses as sites of public memory construction, much less historical violence.

Of course, all universities do convey a sense of their own history and identity through their built environment, interpretive signage, and commemorative displays that become part of the "hidden curriculum" of their campus, communicating belonging and unbelonging to current and potential students and differently positioned community members (Jackson; Lueck et al.). As we will demonstrate, digital community-engaged composition projects represent a significant avenue for interrupting and contributing to this memory work, which can be engaged both within and beyond the classroom.

Campus Public Memory Work through Digital Community-Engaged Composition

Public memory scholars have widely acknowledged the "importance of involving multiple stakeholders in the processes of ethical decision making when public memory is being produced" (Greer and Grobman 3; also see Kryder-Reid, "Introduction"; Kryder-Reid et al.). Engaging students as stakeholders in community-engaged public memory projects can bring rhetorical and historical learning outside the classroom and into the public realm, where students can see themselves as participants in the construction of public remembrance, rather than merely passive consumers or inheritors of history. As Greer and Grobman argue, "Inviting students not only to analyse the arguments advanced by museums, archives, and memorials but also to invent those arguments themselves opens up significant opportunities for expanding their rhetorical repertoires as well as for deepening their understanding of the processes and powers of remembrance" (2). The understanding of processes and powers of remembrance is a key historical, communicative, and, ultimately, civic lesson for students. Whereas "relegating the task of remembering to official institutions and artifacts arguably weakens the need for a political community actively to remember its past", taking on this work with students and communities lays the groundwork for future critical engagement and civic action (Haskins 402).

As community-engaged compositions, the projects students produce can also move forward the political and cultural goals of community partners, contributing to their efforts in relation to public remembrance, the stakes of which many of them already deeply understand and experience daily. Sharing authority in the design of research, while centering marginalized perspectives and critically interrogating our own position as participants in domination and exploitation, are central goals of community-based research (CBR) (Stoecker). Striving towards decolonial models for university-community interaction, this work endeavors to not merely share authority but actually to cede it to stakeholder communities in the composition of public memory and historical representation (King; Kendi; Kovach; Lonetree; Lyons).

Appeals for a "place-engaged" approach to community-engaged learning similarly lay the groundwork for campus public memory projects. They pay special attention to the complex and multivocal histories of partner communities, as well as the role of an institution's own material, institutional, and cultural inheritances in the experiences and structural forces that continue to marginalize these communities in the present (Siemers et al.). Place- and community-engaged campus public memory projects can invite stakeholders into our own campus spaces to critique and improve what *we* are doing in terms of public remembrance and historical representation as part of our efforts to decolonize public remembrance, and to draw our attention to the colonial history of settler states and their component institutions.

Such collaborative efforts to revise public memory reflect Steinman's call to approach community-engaged work as "making space," which, "can be a vehicle for de-centering the perspectives of dominant social groups, for the creation of deeper and more community-oriented relationships, and heightening university/college participants' personal awareness of their location within, and participation in, social inequalities" (12). Campus public memory work engaged in partnership with diverse communities can "serve to identify, denaturalize, and replace hegemonic colonial power/knowledge regimes" (5).

In the case of community-engaged campus memory work, that change happens on several levels. The work of "making space" is as much about non-Native students and faculty listening and learning from communities as it is about *doing* or composing anything as a result. Learning from stakeholder communities' responses to campus's historical and cultural representations *is* part of a longer process of transforming public memory, as the conversations and compositions students and faculty produce as a result of these collaborations and reflections further contribute to that public memory work in circulating new models of historical remembrance to a broader public audience. Curricular practices are powerful ideological apparatuses that can reproduce or challenge existing power structure by creating popular discursive frameworks (Apple).

Of course, such community-engaged memory work is complicated, fraught with potential power differentials and needful of a careful personal and political approach. Grobman discusses some of these challenges in her cross-race work on a public history project with the NAACP branch of Reading, Pennsylvania. She reminds of the "complex web of interrelated issues that disappear from view only to reappear again" when working across difference and cautions that "theoretical understandings of hybridity, border-crossing, and blurring of group-based differences and identities do not necessarily occur in practice" (Grobman 131, 136). Responding to similar racial and political dynamics, Crawford et al. use their community-engaged historical writing as an opportunity for students to interrogate their own positionality and use their writing to provoke further conversation and inquiry that will disrupt damaging narratives in their residential community of Kansas City.

The possibility of perpetuating unequal power dynamics in the implementation of projects remains a reality, particularly when this work is engaged in by predominantly settler institutions, or within the disguised hegemonic ideologies of power at institutions rhetorically committed to social justice (La Salle and Hutchings; Shange). Practitioners must remain vigilant to this possibility by consistently striving to achieve the empowerment of community stakeholders on the collaborative level in rhetoric programs and on the societal level with careful consideration of how rhetorical products enter into broader fields of power.

While scholars have been rightly critical of overzealous claims about the democratic potentials of digital media for similar reasons (Haskins; Smith), digital public memory work has a number of advantages over other media when composing community-engaged public memory discourses on campus. It can be accessible to a wider audience and is a medium through which more people can operate than many physical or performance-based products. It also enables community-engaged writers and researchers to remain nimble and responsive to changing community priorities or needs as they emerge across cycles of iterative design and feedback. One of the major challenges recognized, for example, in planning and sustainability studies is what is commonly termed the "inertia of the built environment" (e.g., Haarstad and Oseland). Digital media, by contrast, are designed to be flexibly modified.

Thus, digital new media expands the "commemorative landscape" of the campus, providing opportunities for community collaboration and the sharing of memory work that do not exist within the more static and conservatively designed built environment (Aden 4; see also Greer and Grobman; Jay). Because of their easily revised nature, digital assets provide a flexible form of public commemoration and engagement that can accommodate new voices, changes in political context, and shifting rhetorical strategies among stakeholders. As Lueck and Panich have argued elsewhere, this flexibility is particularly important for work with communities, our relationships with whom are in process and unfolding and whose own interests and needs may shift over time.

Of course, digital projects are still no panacea for "democratic" memory practices. Haskins warns of the "twin dangers of ideological reification and amnesia" inherent in commemorative practices engaged online (405). These commemorative practices can also reflect the same disparities of power and access as other sites of public discourse and community engagement. This is why the use of collaborative approaches, with stakeholders driving the development, implementation, and revision of heritage programs, is so essential. The flexible, yet durable, nature of digital projects is only as valuable as the process through which they are enacted. In what follows, we examine the ways these factors are playing out in our own campus context.

Public Memory at Santa Clara University

Santa Clara University (SCU) is a prime example of a university that is beginning to grapple with its own difficult history. SCU is a Jesuit institution that was established on the grounds of a Spanish colonial mission originally founded in 1777 in the homeland of the Thamien Ohlone people. Like all 21 California missions, Santa Clara's primary purpose was to convert the local Indigenous population to Roman Catholic Christianity, indoctrinate them in European lifeways, and use them as the instruments and provisioners of the Spanish crown in the competition with other colonial powers for control of the Americas. The exact location of Mission Santa Clara changed over the course of the Spanish and Mexican colonial periods (ca. 1777-1840s) due to floods and earthquakes, and the remnants of three mission churches are on the grounds of the current SCU campus. The mission had a resident population of over 1,000 Native individuals in any given year, representing a diverse array of tribal communities from surrounding regions. The campus also covers the mission's large Native neighborhood, or *ranchería*, as well as two mission cemeteries that together hold the remains of more than 7,000 individuals, most of whom were Native Californians (Panich, "Mission Santa Clara"; Skowronek and Wizorek).

While in residence at the mission, Ohlone families endured the suppression of their culture, the theft of their lands, and the loss of loved ones. Yet, they eventually outlasted the mission system, regrouping in the second half of the nineteenth century in the hills of the southeastern Bay Area where they enjoyed a cultural revival despite the continuing pressures of settler colonialism (Milliken et al.; Panich, *Narrative of Persistence*). Today, their descendants are organized into several interrelated tribal groups, including the Ohlone Indian Tribe and the Muwekma Ohlone Tribe (Field et al.). Indeed, as Andrew Galvan, one of our community partners often underscores, "We are here, still! And, the Franciscans are not."

As the only institution of higher learning in the state to be located on a Spanish mission site, SCU uses various means to work the public's broad awareness of the California missions to its advantage. The mission church is the geographical focal point of the campus, and promotional materials tout the long tradition connecting the current university with the ostensibly educational purpose of the colonial mission. The central architectural theme of the campus is Mission Revival, complete with tile roofs and a color scheme meant to evoke adobe bricks. The likeness of the mission church is central to the university marketing materials, adorning everything from departmental letterhead to souvenir coffee mugs, while various sports teams proclaim to be "on a mission."

However, the complexity of the history behind this symbol is rarely explored. As of 2021, physical interpretive media related to SCU are limited to three venues. The university's art museum, the de Saisset, has a small California history exhibit. The mission church, operated by Campus Ministries, provides two brief interpretive panels dedicated to mission history. Outdoor media consist of a series of relatively unobtrusive markers and monuments, scattered across the campus, that fall under the purview of University Operations. All three entities—the de Saisset Museum, Campus Ministries, and University Operations—exist outside of the university's academic structure, a fact that limits student and faculty involvement in the creation of public memory at SCU.

SCU's efforts at public memory related to Mission Santa Clara are not meant to engage viewers in difficult questions about the past. Rather, they work together to present a relatively narrow interpretation of the colonial period that privileges the role of Euroamerican agents in creating the institutions that eventually became SCU and the modern city of Santa Clara, while being as visually unobtrusive as possible. In doing so, the current approach to public memory limits who exactly counts as part of the community being commemorated (Waterton and Smith). This framing, moreover, creates its own inertia against engagement with broader publics whose own histories may counter those currently being celebrated on our campus.

As revealed by a recent survey of undergraduates, a large proportion have little existing knowledge of our campus's difficult histories. However, a similarly large percentage are eager to learn more (Kroot and Panich). In fact, it has been students who have organized most effectively in support of incorporating Native history and culture in campus life. The sustained attention of students across courses, clubs, organizations, and public events has compelled the administration to pay attention to the issue of Native representation on campus. As a result of student pressure, SCU adopted a land acknowledgement statement and held its first formal Indigenous Peoples Day event in 2018. In the months that followed, SCU organized a formal Ohlone History Working Group to explore further actions. Following the model of Georgetown and others, then-President Engh charged the group to "review the current markers and monuments that honor the history of the Ohlone people on campus and particularly in the history of Mission Santa Clara de Asís de Thamien; consult with Ohlone representatives about their views on the most appropriate ways to honor their ancestors; consult/review commemorations of Native Peoples at other California Missions; and draft recommendations based on investigations and consultations" (Engh).

While this development is encouraging, it is important to recognize that it came about only as a result of sustained rhetorical action, particularly by students on behalf of Native stakeholders. President Engh even tacitly acknowledged the institutional inertia that otherwise prevailed, admitting that the need to better acknowledge Ohlone history had been clear "for some time." He also recognized the critical role pressure by Native communities and students—both Native and non-Native—played in moving the needle on this issue, giving "special thanks and praise" to leaders in the Ohlone community and the student group Native American Coalition for Change for their efforts (Engh). In what follows, we describe efforts to build on this momentum by employing digital public memory projects as community-engaged writing in and out of our classrooms. As we argue, such community-engaged writing projects are a way to support and extend the revision of public historical representation and remembrance on our campuses.

Digital Projects Engaging Difficult Histories at SCU

On our campus, we have partnered with local Ohlone tribal groups and engaged students with a range of digital composing projects—both inside and outside of courses—to begin to reconfigure the commemorative landscape and shift public memory. The collaborative research design and engagement with our tribal partners has come in several forms, all building on existing relationships our Anthropology department and campus museum had fostered for many years through consultations and collaborations on projects in the area. With this more focused turn towards questions of campus public memory, we have called on some of our established contacts as resources to help us think about how to proceed, obtaining several lines of funding to support deeply collaborative pedagogical and technological design projects as well as inviting tribal members into our classrooms more informally to share perspectives and guide student research projects such as those we discuss below. The resulting projects so far have included course websites showcasing student historical research, 360 tours built on Google Tour Builder, annotated 3D scans hosted online by the Sketchfab website, and digital exhibits designed on the open-source archiving platform, Omeka, all of which we have conceptualized as a process of asset-building in support of larger-scale, Ohlone-led public remembrance projects.

Our most focused community-engaged public memory work began in Spring 2019 in a course, co-taught by two of us, that focused on community-engaged digital writing projects related to the Indigenous histories at the mission. One of our projects was 3D modelling work to digitize and annotate Ohlone artifacts recovered archaeologically from our campus and surrounding areas. Ideally, students would have been free to choose from among the thousands of artifacts related to the rich archaeological history of our campus, covering precontact and colonial-period deposits related to the Ohlone and other Native American groups. However, given access restrictions, students chose from a limited number of artifacts that nonetheless offered various interpretive avenues.

Using a small internal grant to purchase an HP Pro S3 structured light 3D scanner, we worked with students to select and digitize artifacts that provide insight into Ohlone history and culture of our campus. Prior to the digitization process, students learned about the specifics of our campus history, the broader patterns of romanticization that have characterized public interpretation at California mission sites for more than a century (e.g., Kryder-Reid, *California Mission Landscapes*), and were taught contemporary Ohlone perspectives on the mission by Ohlone heritage professionals (e.g. Galvan; Galvan and Medina; Medina). Most crucially, students consulted with Andrew Galvan, member of the Ohlone Indian Tribe and curator of Mission Dolores in San Francisco, whose perspectives shaped students' digitization and composing choices. It is worth noting here that Andy and other Ohlone collaborators are always compensated for their time and expertise provided on these projects. Andy visited our class early in the quarter to share his perspectives on Native experience and history, reviewed student projects in development, and attended our final project exhibitions at the end of the quarter to discuss the work with the students.

In small groups, students researched their objects using the scholarly literature on local archaeology and ethnography. Based on their findings, they composed interpretive introductory texts for the artifacts and annotated key features of the artifact models.

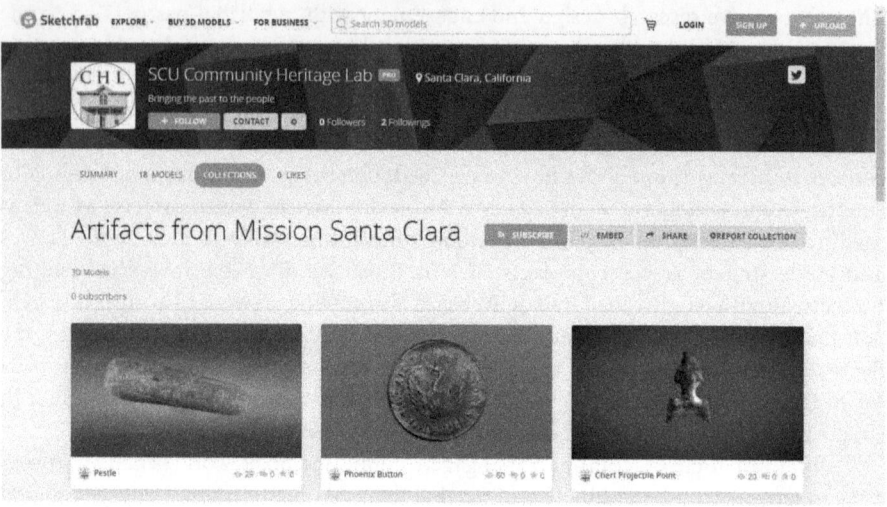

Figure 2. Screenshot of the Community Heritage Lab page on Sketchfab, with examples of 3D models of artifacts from the Mission ("Media").

Students then uploaded their scans to Sketchfab (Figure 2). By hosting the students' work on Sketchfab, we tried to extend the community-engagement and ensure that these projects connect to both the work of their peers and to others with an interest in Ohlone culture and archaeological research. This potential for public scrutiny produced incentives for students to both invest more thoroughly in their work and to critically think about the role of historical rhetorics in the world. Students opened themselves up to critiques on facts and frameworks from a much larger audience, a process that can both create risks, but also potential rewards through the forging of new relationships beyond the classroom (Greer and Grobman).

A consequence of this public audience is that students can become more critical consumers and capable producers of public remembrance. In this way, Collin Brooke observes that student blogs—and, we would add, other online projects—strike a balance between centripetal and centrifugal tendencies. Existing at the periphery of the classroom, they function to reflect and engage course concepts and networks, but also, and perhaps even more importantly, to engage the public. While we recognize that the platform may limit the audience to those with specialized interests, thereby falling short of the potential intervention into campus public memory that we envision, the Sketchfab platform is a temporary solution that allows us to build a shared repository of digital assets, meeting both short-term pedagogical and long-term public memory goals. In the meantime, being a publicly accessible online platform allows these models to be embedded in various university webpages. For example, the SCU Community Heritage Lab (CHL), the university's academic archaeology laboratory, includes several of these models on its media page, helping to reach a broader audience.

The success of the initial class has led others to use similar digital composing assignments in their own courses as well. For example, students in a summer archaeological class used the scanner to create a number of 3D models and annotations of archaeological artifacts associated with later Euroamerican residents who lived in the area of the SCU campus during the late 19th and early 20th centuries. Thus, while not limited to interventions in the difficult colonial heritage of our campus, assignments like 3D scanning and annotation of archaeological artifacts allow students to engage with the materiality of campus history, to think through how those histories might be told more inclusively, and to engage various community groups and stakeholders in the process.

Our second digital heritage program, using Omeka, has been more diverse in its coverage, with faculty and students focused primarily on uploading and cataloging high-quality digital assets. These include documentation of SCU's current efforts at public commemoration, scans of documents and ephemera housed in SCU's Archives and Special Collections, and still images of archaeological artifacts from colonial Spanish, Mexican, and American sites on and near the campus. This process provides students with tangible skills in various professional practices, from artifact photography to archival data entry to scientific illustration, while practicing critical rhetorical and writing skills, using these images and other file types, such as videos, audio recordings, and historical texts, to produce freely available, public-facing online digital exhibits (Figure 3).

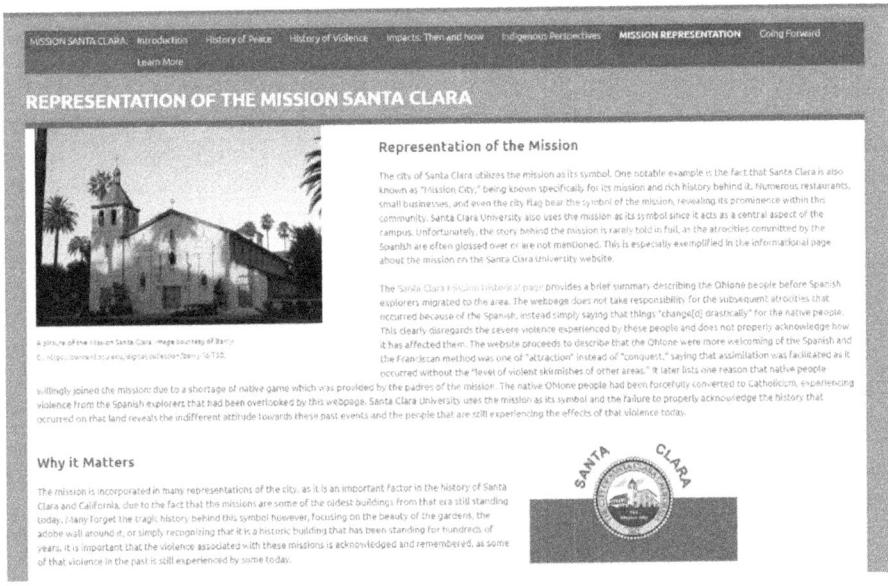

Figure 3. Screenshot of an Omeka page about the Mission, created by students in a general education course.

The first round of Omeka assignments using this model, during the 2019-2020 academic year, asked students to produce exhibits that advocated specific actions of the students' choosing for changing how SCU deals with mission heritage. The instructor for the course collaborated with Ohlone stakeholders to collate and develop the readings, videos, lecture frameworks, and supplementary resources used to provide students with the background they needed for the project. Future classes that will use Omeka include both lower level and upper level English and Anthropology courses using a similar collaborative process for instructional resources. The exhibits developed in these courses are to be featured on the CHL and SCU Digital Humanities Initiative websites. This program also serves to seed a continuously expanding digital archive and online exhibit space to be maintained by the CHL and to demonstrate to other faculty the potential for using the database and exhibit space—and the community-engaged writing these projects lend themselves to—in their classes across the disciplines.

Mobilizing Student Projects for Community Partnerships

Each class that contributes to our shared Omeka collection on local history or the Sketchfab collection will extend the work of public memory through their writing, engaging communities as both collaborators and potential audience members. Because the digital exhibits are public facing, students have to master content in such a way that they can thoughtfully and responsibly translate knowledge learned in the classroom and through engagement with community members into visual, audio, and textual narratives comprehensible to a non-expert audience. Though constrained by the assignments and presentation platforms, these choices are nonetheless significant, including choices of lighting effect, object orientation, terminology, and artifact selection itself, all of which substantially shape the way an audience understands the significance of an item and their own relationship to it. In this way, students working on digital memory projects grappled with the rhetorical choices inherent in language and detail selection, considering their consequences for readers' conceptions of Native people in both the past and the present. For example, what is the effect, in terms of how Native culture and history are remembered, of using the past tense or passive voice, or of highlighting the work of archaeologists in "discovering" a given artifact? Raising questions like these encouraged students to develop a more complex conception of both historical research and communication.

Within these constraints—and perhaps even *because* of them—students were able to learn historical content knowledge and practice rhetorical skills related to historical representation and public memory. Composing for public audiences encourages students to move beyond the conception of writing as reporting "facts" into a recognition of the persuasive work inherent in all composing. As Greer and Grobman argue in relation to other public memory work, "Students expand the range of their rhetorical repertoires in ways that they may deem more relevant to their lives beyond the university, and they become more flexible in their rhetorical practices" (12).

The representational insights and opportunities were equally spurred by the community engagement at the production end of student projects as well, where students learned about the lived experiences and material consequences of rhetorics of public remembrance for various communities, including the understanding of how rhetorics of Native "extinction" have contributed to a lack of federal recognition for many Native groups in California today, including the Ohlone (Leventhal et al.). In his class visit, Andrew Galvan provided a vivid image of the significance of federal recognition to many tribal members: that of a large hypothetical display case, empty, with a label designating the intent to someday enclose documentation of restored federal tribal recognition. This image of a dream deferred, framed by the technologies of public memory and museum curation, was a powerful idea that stuck with many students and faculty alike.

In the process, such community-engaged writing projects make student research and labor useful for more than just the learner and the instructor, giving students a greater sense of ownership over their work. Their investment in the work itself contributes to the public memory function of their projects, as they continue to discuss and share research findings and compositions with their own networks as well.

But it is equally important to note that students are not "experts" in Ohlone history and public representation at the end of any of these courses or experiences. Instead, having been grounded in the attempt to understand and represent just one artifact or site, we hope that they are left with the sense of only being able to tackle one small part of the question, leaving the larger questions of commemoration and representation to Ohlone representatives themselves. Ultimately, we hope that lesson is one of the most lasting insights: that is, the recognition among non-Native students and faculty of when it is *not* our place to shape public remembrance, and we strive to devise structures in our own classroom and research to support more decolonial approaches. This has been a challenge, given the existing paradigms of expertise and privilege that determine who is at the front of the classroom and produce the need to seek outside funding to support Native contributions. Still, it is a goal we continue to strive for in our shared work with tribal members as we move forward.

Discussion and Conclusion

The focus on digitization of Ohlone artifacts was a shared interest of both Ohlone collaborators and us as professors. A significant number of Ohlone individuals work in Cultural Resource Management (CRM) as consultants and monitors of construction job sites to protect their cultural heritage and participate in the work of advancing knowledge about their ancestors. These artifacts are an important way they connect to their past and learn about their own history, and some individuals have an even more direct connection to the artifacts, having been involved in their recovery and preservation. Recognizing the value of having Ohlone individuals drive the public memory process but unable to embark on the development of a large-scale project without funding to support Ohlone contributions, we were interested in having students preserve these artifacts as a means to incrementally build a repository of digital assets to support later project development.

Designing student projects in this way, we are able to do double duty: engaging students in the analysis and production of historical and interpretive exhibits while also contributing to a shared repository of digital assets that will move the broader initiative forward incrementally, providing the raw material on which future large-scale digital public memory projects can draw. By working on small public-facing projects, students were able to engage in questions of representation and remembrance while minimizing the risk of inserting their own colonial perspectives on the end product. Crucially, for the purposes of our own campus, this strategy will allow us to work more effectively with our Native partners to have them lead the design of the eventual large-scale projects with a better sense of what kinds of materials and resources we have available to contribute to the process. In keeping with anti-racist methods of activist-scholars such as Ibram X. Kendi, Kenneth Jones, and Tema Okun, we question our own impulses towards perfection and our desire to leap towards final products, attending to the process of knowledge building, asset development, and, thus, political organizing as key metrics of success for this ongoing community-engaged memory work. In this process, students in our courses are positioned not only as learners but also as contributors to a political and cultural movement. Many archaeologists and historians are leading projects with highly engaged student and community collaborations. As writing studies professionals, we can leverage this existing community-engaged public memory work to advance the cause of community-engaged writing and, together, compose more just and equitable historical representation on campuses. As sites of public memory construction, colleges and universities have a particular opportunity to use their own campuses and histories to engage students in meaningful, community-engaged public memory composing work, and decades of community-based archaeology and related heritage work has already helped to nudge a variety of institutions to acknowledge their obligations to communities and stakeholder groups (Atalay, "Can Archaeology"). In our case, students have collaborated with community stakeholders to bring new voices into the remembrance of campus histories. Without these partnerships, the central role of Native life and labor for our campus could remain silenced, distorted, or at the very least, truncated.

Because these projects are meant to combat the pervasive lack of knowledge and appreciation of Ohlone culture and history among students and the broader public, the primary audience of these projects is not Ohlone individuals themselves. Nonetheless, given the general lack of opportunities to interact with and learn about Ohlone culture, our Ohlone collaborators have also expressed interest in these projects for their own learning and that of their families, as they continue to engage themselves in a process of unlearning harmful historical narratives and replacing them with historically rich understandings of their own ancestors and heritage. As several of our collaborators have emphasized throughout this work, there is still a lot more for *all* of us to learn about Ohlone history and culture.

While many administrations remain conservative in their strategies for addressing their own complicated histories and revising their public commemorative landscapes, we have found that digital community-engaged writing projects have the ability to intervene in this process. Through the composition of digital projects as part of an ongoing and changing public conversation, students were able to conceive of their writing as civic engagement and a contribution to public historical discourse, and could share their work with their friends, classmates, and a broader public interested in the local, national, or global stories with which our campuses intersect.

Public memory is a particularly useful frame for thinking about this kind of community-engaged writing work because both enterprises encourage us to see—and to seek—ways that our pedagogies are always already political, our histories are positioned and provisional, and our educational and composing work affects both students and communities in a deeply connected way. The explicit move to engage the public in both memory work and community-engaged writing also comes with a shared set of risks and responsibilities, requiring us to continually reflect on our relationships and the needs and interests of our stakeholders. As Gabriela Raquel Rios suggests, "Instead of assuming that our disciplinary standards define our commitment to communities, we might consider how our commitment to communities challenges our disciplinary norms" (63). We see the interdisciplinary insights afforded by community-engaged public memory work such as we have done as a fruitful example of challenging disciplinary norms and practices, in response to the specific exigencies on our campus and in working with our stakeholder communities. Through an incremental, iterative, and responsive process of digital asset building in our community-engaged classrooms, we hope to continue to challenge assumptions and commitments and move the needle on campus historical representation in ways that are responsive to the stakeholders with whom we are working. We are continually challenged and even chastened by this process, which is how we know that good community-engaged historical work is happening in our classrooms and, in time, beyond them.

Works Cited

Aden, Roger C. *Rhetorics Haunting the National Mall: Displaced and Ephemeral Public Memories.* Lexington Books, 2018.

Apple, Michael. *Ideology and Curriculum.* 4th ed., Routledge, 2018.

Atalay, Sonya. "Can Archaeology Help Decolonize the Way Institutions Think? How Community-Based Research is Transforming the Archaeology Training Toolbox and Helping to Transform Institutions." *Archaeologies*, vol. 15, no. 3, 2019, pp. 514-535.

———. "No Sense of the Struggle: Creating a Context for Survivance at the NMAI." *American Indian Quarterly,* vol. 30, no. 3&4, 2006, pp. 597–618.

Attwood, Bain M. "The International Difficult Histories Boom, the Democratization of History, and the National Museum of Australia." *The International Handbooks of Museum Studies*, edited by Sharon Macdonald and Helen Rees

Leahy, *Volume 4: Museum Transformations*, edited by Annie E. Coombes and Ruth B. Phillips, John Wiley & Sons, Ltd., 2015, pp. 61-83. DOI: https://doi.org/10.1002/9781118829059.wbihms403

Barnd, Natchee Blu. *Native Space: Geographic Strategies to Unsettle Settler Colonialism*. Oregon State UP, 2017.

Brasher, Jordan P., et al.. "Applying Critical Race and Memory Studies to University Place Naming Controversies: Toward a Responsible Landscape Policy." *Papers in Applied Geography*, vol. 3, no. 3-4, 2017, pp. 292-307.

Brooke, Collin. "Weblogs as Deictic Systems: Centripetal, Centrifugal, and Small World Blogging." *Computers and Composition Online*, 2005. http://cconlinejournal.org/brooke

Calloway, Colin G. *The Indian History of an American Institution: Native Americans and Dartmouth*. Dartmouth College Press, 2010.

Chang, Gordon H., and Shelley Fisher Fishkin, editors. *The Chinese and the Iron Road: Building the Transcontinental Railroad*. Stanford UP, 2019.

Chinese Railroad Workers Project. Stanford University. https://exhibits.stanford.edu/crrw.

Clarke, Max and Gary Alan Fine. "'A' For Apology: Slavery and the Collegiate Discourses of Remembrance--the Cases of Brown University and the University of Alabama." *History and Memory*, vol. 22, no. 1, 2010, pp. 81-112.

Colwell, Chip. "Collaborative Archaeologies and Descendant Communities." *Annual Review of Anthropology*, vol. 45, 2016, pp. 113–127.

Crawford, Anne E., et al. "Drawing Hope from Difficult History: Public Memory and Rhetorical Education in Kansas City." *College English*, vol. 82, no. 3, 2020, pp. 255-280.

Dartt-Newton, Deana. "California's Sites of Conscience: An Analysis of the State's Historic Mission Museums." *Museum Anthropology*, vol. 34, no. 2, 2011, pp. 97-108.

Dickinson, Greg, et al. *Places of Public Memory: The Rhetoric of Museums and Memorials*. U of Alabama P, 2010.

Engh, Michael. Email Communication, May 29, 2019.

Epstein, Terrie and Carla L. Peck. *Teaching and Learning Difficult Histories in International Contexts: A Critical Sociocultural Approach*. Routledge, 2017.

Field, Les, et al. "A Contemporary Ohlone Tribal Revitalization Movement: A Perspective from the Muwekma Costanoan/Ohlone Indians of the San Francisco Bay Area." *California History*, vol. 71, no. 3, 1992, pp. 412–3.

Galvan, Andrew. "Old Mission Dolores Under New Management: An Open Letter." *News from Native California*, Summer 2013, pp. 11-13.

Galvan, Andrew and Vincent Medina. "Indian Memorials at California Missions." *Franciscans and American Indians in Pan-Boarderlands Perspective: Adaptation, Negotiation, and Resistance*, edited by Jeffrey M. Burns and Timothy J. Johnson. The Academy of American Franciscan History, 2018, pp. 323-331.

Gomez, Mark. "Stanford University to Remove Junipero Serra Name from Buildings, Mall." *The Mercury News*, Sept 14, 2018. https://www.mercurynews.com/2018/09/14/stanford-to-remove-Junípero-serra-name-from-buildings-mall/

Green, Hillary. *The Hallowed Grounds Project: Race, Slavery, and Memory at the University of Alabama*. University of Alabama, 2017. https://hgreen.people.ua.edu/hallowed-grounds-project.html

―――. "The Burden of the University of Alabama's Hallowed Grounds." *The Public Historian*, vol. 42, no. 4, 2020, pp. 28–40. https://doi.org/10.1525/tph.2020.42.4.28

Greer, Jane and Laurie Grobman. *Pedagogies of Public Memory: Teaching Writing and Rhetoric at Museums, Archives, and Memorials*. Routledge, 2015.

Grobman, Laurie. "'Speaking With One Another' in Community-Based Research: (Re)Writing African American History in Berks County, Pennsylvania." *Reflections*, 2009, pp. 129-161.

Haarstad, Håvard, and Stina Ellevseth Oseland. "Historicizing Urban Sustainability: The Shifting Ideals Behind Forus Industrial Park, Norway." *International Journal of Urban and Regional Research*, vol. 41, no. 5, 2017, pp. 838-854.

Hackel, Steven W. *Junípero Serra: California's Founding Father*. Hill and Wang, 2013.

Hart Micke, Sarah. "Sustainability, Place, and Rhetoric; A Levinasian Pedagogy of Responsibility." *Reflections*, vol. 16, no. 1, 2016, pp. 126-139.

Haskins, Ekaterina. "Between Archive and Participation: Public Memory in a Digital Age." *Rhetoric Society Quarterly*, vol. 37, no. 4, 2007, pp. 401-422. DOI: 10.1080/02773940601086794.

Heron, John. *Co-Operative Inquiry: Research Into the Human Condition*. Sage, 1996.

Helmbrecht, Brenda. "Revisiting Missions: Decolonizing Public Memories in California." *Rhetoric Society Quarterly*, vol. 49, no. 5, 1996, pp. 470-494. DOI: 10.1080/02773945.2019.1668048.

"History." *About SCU, Santa Clara University*. https://www.scu.edu/aboutscu/history/

Israel, Barbara A. et al. "Review of Community-Based Research: Assessing Partnership Approaches to Improve Public Health." *Annual Review of Public Health*, vol. 19, 1998, pp. 173-202.

Jackson, Philip W. *Life in Classrooms*. Teachers College Press, 1968.

Jay, Gregory. "The Engaged Humanities: Principles and Practices of Public Scholarship and Teaching." *Imagining America*, vol. 15, 2010.

Jones, Kenneth, and Tema Okun. *Dismantling Racism Works: A Workbook for Social Change Groups*. https://www.dismantlingracism.org/

Keene, Arthur S., and Sumi Colligan. "Service-Learning and Anthropology." *Michigan Journal of Community Service Learning*, Summer 2004, pp. 5-15.

Kendi, Ibram X. *How to be an Antiracist*. One World, 2019.

King, Lisa. *Legible Sovereignties: Rhetoric, Representations, and Native American Museums*. Oregon State UP, 2017.

Kovach, Margaret. *Indigenous Methodologies: Characteristics, Conversations, and Contexts*. University of Toronto, 2009.

Kroot, Matthew V., and Lee M. Panich. "Students are Stakeholders in On-Campus Archaeology." *Advances in Archaeological Practice*, vol. 8, no. 2, 2020, pp. 134-150. DOI:10.1017/aap.2020.12

Kryder-Reid, Elizabeth. *California Mission Landscapes: Race, Memory, and the Politics of Heritage*. U of Minnesota P, 2016.

———. "Introduction: Tools for a Critical Heritage." *International Journal of Heritage Studies*, vol. 24, no. 7, 2018, pp. 691–93.

Kryder-Reid, Elizabeth, et al. "'I Just Don't Ever Use That Word': Investigating Stakeholders' Understanding of Heritage." *International Journal of Heritage Studies*, vol. 24, 2018, pp. 743-763.

La Salle, Marina and Rich Hutchings. "What Makes Us Squirm--A Critical Assessment of Community-Oriented Archaeology." *Canadian Journal of Archaeology*, vol. 40, 2016, pp. 164-180.

Lee, Robert, and Tristan Ahtone. "Land-Grab Universities: Expropriated Indigenous Land is the Foundation of the Land-Grant University." *High Country News*, March 30, 2020.

Leventhal, Alan, et al. "The Ohlone: Back from Extinction." *The Ohlone Past and Present: Native Americans of the San Francisco Bay Region*, edited by Lowell John Bean, Ballena Press, 1994, pp. 297-336.

Lonetree, Amy. *Decolonizing Museums: Representing Native America in National and Tribal Museums*. U of North Carolina P, 2012.

Lorimer, Michelle M. *Resurrecting the Past: The California Mission Myth*. Great Oaks Press, 2016.

Lueck, Amy, et al.. "Inclusivity in the Archives: Expanding Undergraduate Pedagogies for Diversity and Inclusion." *Diversity, Equity, and Inclusivity in Contemporary Higher Education*, edited by Rhonda Jeffries, IGI Global, 2019, pp. 1-12. doi:10.4018/978-1- 5225-5724-1.ch001.

Lueck, Amy J., and Lee M. Panich. "Representing Indigenous Histories Using XR Technologies in the Classroom." *Journal of Interactive Technology and Pedagogy*, vol. 17, 2020.

Luke, Nikki, and Nik Heynen. "Abolishing the Frontier: (De)Colonizing 'Public' Education." *Social & Cultural Geography*, 2019. DOI: https://doi.org/10.1080/14649365.2019.1593492.

Lyons, Scott Richard. "Rhetorical Sovereignty: What Do American Indians Want from Writing?" *College Composition and Communication*, vol. 51, no. 3, 2000, pp. 447-68.

"Media." *Community Heritage Lab*, SCU Community Heritage Lab. https://www.scu.edu/community-heritage-lab/media/.

Medina, Vincent. "Tips for Teaching California History to Kids." News from Native California, Winter 2014/15, pp. 48-58.

Milliken, Randall, et al. *Ohlone/Costanoan Indians of the San Francisco Peninsula and their Neighbors, Yesterday and Today*. Report to the National Park Service, Golden Gate National Recreation Area, San Francisco, 2009.

Myers, Alex. "LMU Needs to Respect Native Californians." *The Los Angeles Loyolan.* Oct. 24, 2018. -http://www.laloyolan.com/opinion/lmu-needs-to-respect-native- californians/article_3accaa63-107d-5cee-b5d4-f9662735e45c.html

Nash, Margaret A. "Entangled Pasts: Land-Grant Colleges and American Indian Dispossession." *History of Education Quarterly*, vol. 59, no. 4, 2019, pp. 437–67.

Panich, Lee M. "Mission Santa Clara in a Changing Urban Environment." *Boletín: Journal of the California Mission Studies Association*, vol. 31, no. 1, 2015, pp. 36-45.

———. "After Saint Serra: Unearthing Indigenous Histories at the California Missions." *Journal of Social Archaeology*, vol. 16, no. 2, 2016, pp. 238–258.

———. *Narratives of Persistence: Indigenous Negotiations of Colonialism in Alta and Baja California*. U of Arizona P, Tucson, 2020.

Rios, Gabriela Raquel. "Cultivating Land-Based Literacies and Rhetorics." *Literacy in Composition Studies*, vol. 3, no. 1, 2015, pp. 60-70.

Schneider, Tsim D., et al. "Scaling Invisible Walls: Reasserting Indigenous Persistence in Mission-Era California." *The Public Historian*, vol. 42, no. 2, 2020, pp. 97–120.

Shange, Savannah. *Progressive Dystopia: Abolition, Anti-Blackness, and Schooling in San Francisco*. Duke UP, 2019.

Siemers, Cheryl K., et al. "Engaging Place as Partner." *Michigan Journal of Community Service Learning*, 2015, pp. 101-104.

Skowronek, Russell K., and Julie C. Wizorek. "Archaeology at Santa Clara de Asís: The Slow Rediscovery of a Moveable Mission." *Pacific Coast Archaeological Society Quarterly*, vol. 33, no. 3, 1997, pp. 54–92.

Smith, Kevin. "Negotiating Community Literacy Practice: Public Memory Work and the Boston Marathon Bombing Digital Archive." *Computers and Composition*, vol. 40, 2016, pp. 115-130.

Smith, Laurajane. *Uses of Heritage*. Routledge, 2006.

Steinman, Erich. "'Making Space': Lessons from Collaborations with Tribal Nations." *Michigan Journal of Community Service Learning*, 2011, pp. 5-18.

Stoecker, Randy. "Community-Based Research: From Practice to Theory and Back Again." *Michigan Journal of Community Service Learning*, 2003, pp. 35-46.

Till, Karen E. "Wounded Cities." *Political Geography*, vol. 31, no. 1, 2012, pp. 3-14.

Voss, Barbara L. "The Archaeology of Precarious Lives: Chinese Railroad Workers in Nineteenth-Century North America." *Current Anthropology*, vol. 59, no. 3, 2018, pp. 287-313.

Wallerstein, Nina, et al. *Community-Based Participatory Research for Health*. Jossey-Bass, 2018.

Walters, Lindsey K. "Slavery and the American University: Discourses of Retrospective Justice at Harvard and Brown." *Slavery and Abolition*, vol. 38, no. 4, 2017, pp. 719–44.

Waterton, Emma, and Laurajane Smith. "The Recognition and Misrecognition of Community Heritage." *International Journal of Heritage Studies*, vol. 16, no. 1, 2010, pp. 4-15.

Wilder, Craig Steven. *Ebony and Ivy: Race, Slavery, and the Troubled History of America's Universities*. Bloomsbury Press, 2013.

Wilkes, Rima, et al. "Canadian University Acknowledgment of Indigenous Lands, Treaties, and Peoples." *Canadian Review of Sociology*, vol. 54, no. 1, 2017, pp. 89–120.

Wilson, Shawn. *Research is Ceremony: Indigenous Research Methods*. Fernwood Publishing, 2008.

Winter, Jay. *Remembering War: The Great War Between Memory and History in the Twentieth Century*. Yale UP, 2006.

Wolfe, Patrick. "Settler Colonialism and the Elimination of the Native." *Journal of Genocide Research*, vol. 8, no. 4, 2006, pp. 387–409.

Working Group. *Georgetown University: Slavery, Memory, and Reconciliation*. Georgetown University, 2016. http://slavery.georgetown.edu/

Author Bios

Amy J. Lueck is Assistant Professor of English at Santa Clara University, where her research and teaching focus on histories of rhetorical instruction and practice, women's rhetorics, feminist historiography, and public memory. She is the author of *A Shared History: Writing in the High School, College, and University, 1856-1886* (SIU Press 2020), and her work has also appeared in journals such as *College English*, *Rhetoric Review*, *Composition Studies*, *Peitho*, and *Kairos*.

Matthew V. Kroot is an anthropological archaeologist at Santa Clara University. He studies the growth of political and economic inequalities, as well as the development of egalitarian institutions in the deep past and recent history of the Middle East and West Africa. His work also focuses on community collaborative methods.

Lee M. Panich is an Associate Professor of Anthropology at Santa Clara University. His research employs a combination of archaeological, ethnographic, and archival data to examine the long-term entanglements between California's Indigenous societies and colonial institutions, particularly the Spanish mission system. Working with members of local tribal communities, he has conducted collaborative investigations of Indigenous life at Mission Santa Clara de Asís and Mission San José in Alta California, as well as at Mission Santa Catalina in Baja California, Mexico. Panich is the co-editor of *Indigenous Landscapes and Spanish Missions: New Perspectives from Archaeology and Ethnohistory* (University of Arizona Press, 2014) and the author of *Narratives of Persistence: Indigenous Negotiations of Colonialism in Alta and Baja California* (University of Arizona Press, 2020).

Cultivating Legitimacy as a Farmer

Abby M. Dubisar

Abstract

Beyond growing and selling food, women farmers perform literacy work to establish and maintain legitimacy. As part of a larger interview-based dataset, this article analyzes the literacy practices that one woman farmer, Lauren, undertakes in relation to her legitimacy as a farmer. Informed by literacy studies research and feminist rhetoric scholarship, as well as interdisciplinary studies on women in agriculture, the analysis here illustrates how Lauren performs specific literacy practices. Audiences' gendered expectations necessitate such practices, which Lauren performs in order to be understood as a farmer in a masculine, patriarchal landscape shaped by her family, customers, and broader farming community. These literacy practices include crafting an image visually, interacting intentionally through verbal conversations, adapting to audience assumptions, and taking on community leadership roles.

Keywords

farmer, woman farmer, agriculture, food, food literacy, legitimacy

"My grandparents [on both sides] were farmers, but I didn't know women could farm. There's a whole story there, that I can tell you," Lauren says with a brief laugh during the first three minutes of our research interview. Her laugh signals the irony of how even though her ancestors farmed she could not imagine that women could farm, either on their own or otherwise, due to the ways sexism shapes agriculture. Lauren's life is populated with sexism, as I have come to learn through multiple interactions with her, and she navigates agriculture with particular attention to its gendered landscape. A midwestern farmer in her early thirties, Lauren is committed to making sure people know that women can farm. Our interview took place during the winter between her eighth and ninth farming seasons. Her farm is thriving. She uses organic practices to farm eight acres of rented land, growing over thirty different vegetable and herb crops in over 150 total varieties during the June-September growing season and about a dozen other vegetables in October and November. She runs the largest woman-owned CSA (community supported agriculture) in her state. Lauren defines a CSA as "basically a subscription service that people sign up [for] for the year and then get vegetables each week." Her CSA—the second largest overall in her state—feeds over two hundred families and is evidence of the fact that women can farm.

Making sure that people know that women can farm requires a range of literacy work, labor performed to address constraints that women farmers encounter. These farmers experience unique challenges not only in running their farms but in being interpreted as legitimate farmers. At times they face hostility and must justify their existence to audiences who are unfamiliar with or threatened by a woman farming. At other times they are welcomed, especially by those who are alarmed by the thousands of farms that close each year in the United States. Although fewer than 1.5% of the United States population engages in agriculture (Bureau of Labor Statistics)—and women make up only 14% of that 1.5% (USDA, "Women Farmers")—women are increasingly entering farming. The National Sustainable Agriculture Coalition describes women farmers as "one of the fastest growing sectors of American agriculture." Due to this recent increase, and how this change in population sheds light on gender in agriculture, literacy scholars who participate in interdisciplinary food studies have an opportunity to research how this farmer population harnesses past literacy experiences and develops new ones as they start and sustain their farms.

In this case study with Lauren, I join scholars who have examined the perspectives of women farmers to position them as literacy workers (Gollihue; Greer; Wolford). Based on the data I gathered by listening to and interacting with Lauren on multiple occasions, I argue that Lauren, as an independent woman farmer, performs specific literacy practices in order to contend with audiences' gendered expectations and be understood as a farmer in a sexist landscape shaped by her family, customers, and broader farming community. These literacy practices include crafting an image visually, interacting intentionally through verbal conversations, adapting to audience assumptions, and taking on community leadership roles. My analysis of Lauren's literacy work provides scholars with a model of the strategies that a woman farmer can use to meet various audience expectations and be recognized as an expert in agriculture.

First I review the literature on constraints faced by the current generation of women farmers, including the ways that literacy researchers have recently highlighted women farmers' work amidst such constraints. Then I describe my methods for conducting this research before explicating my argument that gender shapes Lauren's literacy performances in multiple ways as Lauren acquires and maintains her legitimacy as a farmer. To support my argument about Lauren's literacy practices and the impact of gender, I analyze examples of her efforts to access legitimacy, including visual and verbal strategies. Finally, I discuss some conclusions and limitations of my study as well as its implications for future studies.

Constraints Facing Women Farmers: Literature Review

In both multiparticipant and single case studies, scholars have exposed the sexist infrastructures of agriculture and American agrarianism[1] as well as the resulting constraints that women farmers face. I rely on the work of scholars from a variety of fields invested in women's contributions to agriculture, including sociology, history, and literacy studies. As scholars have shown, some of these constraints faced by this farmer population arise from the fact that, despite the recent growth in women running their own farms as new farmers, they still make up a small percentage of farmers in the United States overall, just 14% (USDA).[2] They also lack access to land (Pilgeram and Amos). The USDA indicates that women farm only 6.9% of U.S. farmland ("Women Farmers"). The invisibility of women's labor on farms is another constraint, shown in Andrea Rissing's ethnographic study of eleven women farmers in Iowa. Even though women have been farming for generations, they report that they are not considered "farmers" (128). Infrastructural discrimination is another constraint faced by these farmers, including racist and sexist treatment by the USDA and other gatekeepers that prevent women and other historically marginalized farmers from accessing loan applications and other resources (Penniman; Schell). Julie Keller's results from ethnographic field research with twelve Wisconsin farmers show how USDA representatives did not "read" women and racial minorities as farmers (76), enabling them to withhold resources from these farmers. Interviews with sixteen women farmers in Colorado reveal additional challenges they faced, including tokenism, harassment, and resistance from their own families (Shisler and Sbicca 881). Lauren, too, faces these challenges in her work as a farmer, and they shape her interactions with various audiences.

Compounding the material challenges women face as farmers, the literacy landscape is also fraught with constraints that prevent them from being understood as legitimate farmers. Jane Greer analyzes Myrtle Tenney Booth's 1985 autobiography, showing how women like Booth, who lived from 1906-1999, performed undervalued farm labor in the early twentieth century. Greer's analysis reveals how Booth's farming required technical expertise, advanced reasoning skills, intellectual flexibility, and rhetorical sophistication. Booth's writing enabled her to "fix the meaning ascribed to her lifetime of labor" (95). Her writing to secure meaning to her labor and gain recognizability as a farmer aligns with Lauren's literacy work to attain legitimacy in the present.

Highlighting a woman a generation younger than Booth, Rachel Wolford studies Annette, born in the 1920s and in her mid-eighties when Wolford interviews her in 2011. Annette inherited 160 acres of farmland after her husband died in 1994, suddenly finding herself in charge of all farm decisions. The main constraint Annette faced arose from attitudes long held by her husband's family. Before becoming widowed, she was not allowed access to any farm knowledge, a position held by her in-laws that her husband maintained. Annette's experiences show how resilience is a crucial characteristic of women who attempted "to build meaningful lives despite difficult circumstances" (np). As I examine below, while Lauren works in a different farming context, her experience still retains some of the constraints Annette faced over a generation earlier.

Featuring a participant another generation younger than Annette, Krystin Gollihue uses first-person videoethnographic methods to capture the farming work of her mother, Wendy, who became the sole caretaker of their family's twenty-two-acre farm and apiary when her husband died unexpectedly in 2017. Gathering data using GoPro video cameras attached to her and Wendy's bodies as they farm, Gollihue analyzes how Wendy enacts literacy through her farming body as she expertly attends to bees on her land and talks through her intimate knowledge of the landscape. Gollihue addresses the constraint of the invisibility of women's integral farm labor, showing how farm work is "constructed through technological and institutional systems to be a masculine activity" (25). By positioning agricultural labor and knowledge as relational practices that take place within built infrastructures designed for men's bodies (31), Gollihue helps us understand how Lauren's literacy work and farmwork include negotiating interactions and spaces not designed with her in mind.

To be read as a farmer and avoid some of these constraints, some women farmers choose to engage in "alternative" agriculture and sustainable practices, which are more likely, in Rissing's terms, to "empower" these women's identities as farmers. That is, they participate in sustainable or regenerative farming practices to address the constraint of working in a masculinized occupation by undertaking a completely different type of farming that does not directly reject the masculine norms of conventional, industrial agriculture (Sachs et al.). By growing diversified crops such as vegetables and flowers and selling them directly to local consumers at farmers' markets and through CSA memberships, often called "direct marketing," they are read as farmers in those contexts and are not competing with established men farmers in their communities who sell to commodity markets (DeLind and Ferguson; Trauger). As a direct marketing farmer, Lauren works to be recognized and known by her community, establishing relationships that sustain her business and preserve her reputation. By investigating how farmers navigate those relationships and the role that gender plays in doing so, this study contributes to other work that increases the readability of women as farmers and highlights the legitimizing literacy work these women perform along with that of farming.

Methods

My case study, approved by my institutional review board, features the literacy practices that Lauren uses to be read as a farmer. I selected Lauren for this case study because she is a member of the rising generation of women farmers, and her gender brings attention to her farm, a fact she both resents and invites. Lauren was chosen from a larger pool of interview participants that includes thirty-three other members of this population because her strategies for contending with gender show a range of proactive and nuanced approaches that made her stand out among the participant group. Further, Lauren is committed to bridging two points on the wide spectrum of farming practices. She brings together farmers like her who grow vegetables using organic practices on smaller parcels of land in order to sell this food to their local community and larger-scale commodity growers who use chemical inputs and rely on expensive machinery to grow crops on several thousand acres of land. These commodity crops will be manufactured into ethanol and other food and non-food products in order to be sold on the multinational market. While often represented as a binary, contexts for agriculture in the United States are far more complex than overly-simplified constructions of big vs. small, local vs. international, etc. That said, the boundaries Lauren crosses are also gendered borders for many in her community, with *big* commodity farming led by white men while farmers who are women lead *small* vegetable farms. Among my participants, Lauren is the only farmer who detailed the ways she deliberately seeks out interactions with commodity growers. She is not meant to be representative of all farmers.

The design of my larger study follows in the tradition of scholars who insist that women's literacy experiences have worth (Al-Salmi and Smith; Bean; Leonard; Moss; Royster; Simon; Solberg; Vaughn, Harrell, and Dayton; Vieira; White-Farnham). My intention is to listen to women farmers who create and adapt strategies that address a range of audiences who meet them with a broad spectrum of responses to their work and status as farmers. In the interviews, farmers draw upon their experiences and generate knowledge that I then analyze and amplify in order to offer farmers' perspectives in farmers' own terms. Farmers' own views can be unfamiliar to those outside agricultural communities since food systems are increasingly obscured and hidden from those not directly engaged in farming. Additionally, like other scholarship engaged in studying women's roles in agriculture, my study is oriented from the perspective that gender is socially constructed and shapes individual and community experiences. I agree with Rissing that a "social constructivist understanding of gender [frames]…the ways women farmers conceptualize their gendered identities alongside their professional identities [and that] agriculture is not a gender-neutral field" (129). To that end, listening to Lauren's opinions and experiences regarding why and how gender matters to farming prompt me to place the farm as a literacy context with gendered implications.

To gather data, my study draws on several experiences listening to Lauren, initially during a field trip to her farm in 2017 and months later at a 2018 farmer conference where she spoke as part of a panel on land access. While listening to Lauren, my eagerness to speak with her one-on-one for a research interview grew. In 2018 I traveled back to Lauren's farm for the interview. On a sunny, icy January morning, we sat together at her kitchen table, in a building she lives in on the land she rents to farm. In our seventy-minute conversation, Lauren spoke about her literacy practices. I took handwritten notes while listening to Lauren speak to the audience on her farm and at the conference, as well as at her farm when we spoke one-on-one. Rev.com transcriptionists transcribed the interview audio recording into text for me to read and analyze. Lauren is a pseudonym, and all identifying information has been removed. Lauren was given an opportunity to member check this write-up. Appendix A lists my interview questions.

To analyze Lauren's speeches and interview transcript, I use a grounded theory approach (Charmaz) to explore how being a woman affects Lauren's life as a farmer and how she uses literacy practices and strategies to address audiences' gendered expectations for farmers. As Melanie Birks and Jane Mills note, "grounded theory is the preferred choice when the intent is to generate theory that explains a phenomenon of interest to the researcher" (17). By asking Lauren open-ended questions I encouraged her to describe how and why gender and farming intersect and how she communicates in her work. That is, these questions were intended to gather knowledge about how Lauren makes meaning of the intersections of farming and gender that occur in the communicative contexts she experiences in her work life. In my analysis, I initially looked for recurring themes in my notes and the interview transcript, paying particular attention to Lauren's descriptions of written and spoken interactions, and how her identity as a woman mattered during these interactions. One recurring theme was access, and a major subtheme of that was legitimacy. My analysis illustrates how Lauren must both acquire legitimacy because she needs to prove herself as a farmer, a burden that she says farmers who are white men do not have, and maintain legitimacy because it is always at risk.

My findings show how Lauren's literacy practices are essential to her acquiring and maintaining legitimacy. It joins other literacy studies scholars' findings that increase knowledge of agriculture as a unique literacy context, including Gollihue's evidence that shows how farming involves a network of making practices that are co-animated relationally with others (22), such as Lauren's visibly gendered identity that matters to those with whom she interacts. My findings also contribute to the growing group of scholarship that reveals how an evolving understanding of literacy must view literate practices as enacted and lived (Ehret and Hollett; Pink; Schmidt and Beucher; Shivers-McNair; Swacha; Walker; Woodcock; Work-Slivka). As this case study shows, Lauren is both put into situations by others in which she must work for legitimacy and puts herself in situations with the intention of enhancing her legitimacy. She offers examples that show how her experiences as a farmer are rich with opportunities to effect change through her lived literacy work, especially in the minds of those who do not see her as a legitimate farmer.

Acquiring Legitimacy

Lauren's efforts to be understood as a legitimate farmer occur through visual and verbal strategies that occur in two ways: by crafting a legitimate farmer image and by interacting intentionally through verbal conversations in order to gain status as an insider. I provide examples of how Lauren obtains and attempts to obtain legitimacy with audiences to argue that the literacy strategies under consideration here demonstrate how her farmer work involves much more than growing and selling vegetable crops. She must make herself readable as a farmer to the audiences she interacts with as a farmer.

Crafting an Image

Appearance matters for acquiring legitimacy. Lauren describes that within farming and other physically-demanding work contexts, her appearance as a woman is delegitimizing. Normative expectations of white femininity, which Lauren visibly presents, do not align with her appearance after a day of farming when she has visible dirt and sweat on her work attire, as is typical of those who do manual labor. In other words, Lauren's look as a woman in dirty jeans and a sweaty t-shirt does not signify to audiences that she is a farmer or even a respected worker in a phyiscally-demanding job. She said, "I have a burden [of] explaining myself. A man who's a farmer has [no] need to explain himself. You walk into a room with a plaid shirt and overalls on [as a man and] people think you're a hard worker." This notion that the visual cue of a man wearing overalls signifies that he is "a hard worker" represents the unearned legitimacy Lauren has noticed others receive. To not be misread, she must create strategies so that people know who she is and recognize her work.

Lauren also describes how the type of labor-intensive vegetable farming she does delegitimizes her. Even when her labor is recognized as agricultural work, she is still not granted the legitimacy that her men peers seem to be granted automatically, especially if they do commodity farming on large acreages. As Lauren describes, "I constantly get told that I'm a gardener and not a farmer, and sometimes I don't know if that's because I'm a woman or because it's vegetables." Lauren explains that men farmers are granted legitimacy because of both their masculine appearance and their status as commodity growers using expensive, specialized equipment on large parcels of land. These farmers, both in their appearance and their crops, fit normative expectations for the definition of farmer.

Lauren further describes the gendered expectations related to physical labor and how even her own farming grandmother tells her "you can't physically do that" in regard to the farm work Lauren is actively accomplishing. She proves her grandma wrong over and over again. Lauren said, "I constantly get told that the amount of physical labor I'm doing is not sustainable whereas a guy wouldn't be told that. They're expected to work that hard on a farm, if you're a guy. If you're a woman, it's considered, you know, not sustainable." Such denials of her ability to do farm labor serve to repeatedly delegitimize her farmer status merely because of her gender, not her physical capability.

One strategy Lauren uses to respond to these delegitimizing constraints and acquire legitimacy is to craft an image by agreeing to be featured in publications of nonprofit organizations and government agencies that work with farmers. She expressed mixed feelings about her participation with these organizations: Although she welcomes these opportunities for the way they both publicize her farm and legitimize her as a farmer, she dislikes the added labor and time they require of her. She also expressed concern that she is participating in the tokenization of women farmers. She asks herself what it means to be featured as a *woman farmer* when she is working for legitimacy as a farmer without the gendered qualifier. But Lauren thinks the benefits of these opportunities outweigh the drawbacks. For example, she tells about two separate occasions when she was photographed for two different organizations, noting how the respective photographers each had a different way of photographing her, which she did not fully realize until the photographs were published:

> [Organization A] sexualized me in the photographs. [Organization B] made me look like a working woman, in a positive way. And just talking to [Organization B's] photographer about her concept behind [securing my identity as a woman doing farm labor] and how important that is…I didn't even see it until she pointed it out and I was like, wow. [Organization A] showed my butt and not my head, you know—and then [Organization B] has these pho-

tos of my muscles that are just huge, you know, and the way she took the photo was just trying to show strength.

When Lauren agrees to features of her and her farm in food and farming publications, she thinks that doing so will be good publicity for her business and the wider community, helping to legitimize her individually as a farmer and normalizing the broader notion that women farm. In these photos she is always wearing her normal work attire for the growing season: jeans and a t-shirt or plaid button-down flannel shirt. But she has to rely on choices made by the photographer, editors, and others who work at the sponsoring organization, so not being able to control how the images will be used or where they will travel is a risk that comes with those rewards.

As a result of these experiences, Lauren directs the photographers regarding how they feature her body. Lauren describes how one photographer traveled to her farm from Washington, D.C., to take her photo for a government organization's profile of her. The photographer downplayed the importance of women's contributions to agriculture, and Lauren details her response as it aims to secure legitimacy: "I had a conversation with the photographer about why it's a big deal for women to be in farming, and I had to convince him that this project [he was hired for] is legit, and I had to talk him down from his 'women are just whining' kind of mentality." Lauren details how tiring and time-consuming it can be to repeatedly do this work to acquire legitimacy, but then she explained again how she benefits from the resulting projects: "And granted, I get benefits from it, like, when my name appears in the paper, there's a benefit to that, but... It gets kind of exhausting being the token woman farmer, even though I simultaneously love it. Like, I do love it, right?" Lauren, then, continues to question her participation in these campaigns and what impact such profiles yield, both for her farm operation and women's noticeable prominence on farms.

Relating to these concerns about photographers' choices, cutesiness is a recurring term that Lauren used when talking about these opportunities to craft an image. By *cutesiness*, Lauren is referring to the trend in profiles of women farmers to dwell on the farmer's conventionally attractive looks, such as by positioning her with a bouquet of flowers or other displays of beauty. Although Lauren knows that such representations do not increase women's legitimacy in agriculture, she understands why they continue to be perpetuated. She says that one factor motivating these images is the attempt to elevate the plummeting legitimacy of farming writ large at a time when farms are closing: "Conventional agriculture doesn't know what [to] do with the fact that farmers are going away. They don't know what to do with this new trend of alternative agriculture coming in, and so their antidote is this really poor attempt at cutesiness." But when agriculture organizations feature Lauren or any woman farmer in an objectifying, cutesy way or by only showcasing her image and not her farm, these portrayals limit viewers' understandings of women who farm. That is, such representations position farmers like Lauren not as decision makers and hard workers, but instead as physically attractive feminine objects.

To better secure legitimacy, then, Lauren makes sure publications feature her story along with her photograph. Commenting on Organization A, which objectifies Lauren as it does others in its visual campaign, she says, "That was the thing (being cutesy) that [Organization A's leader] did, and she never connected it to people's stories." Lauren details that she notices that some other women Organization A features in their campaigns are no longer even farmers, yet their images are on display to lead viewers to believe they still farm: "A lot of those women [Organization A features] aren't still farmers, and their pictures are still being used whereas [Organization B] connected [the farmer photos] to a story, [the farmers'] work, which I think is really important, that you can't just separate the image from the farmer." So to acquire legitimacy for herself and others, Lauren wants the image she crafts via these organizations to include detail and description in order to communicate who she is as a farmer, not just display a feminine image of her as one.

Interacting Intentionally through Verbal Conversations

Another practice that Lauren uses to acquire legitimacy is to interact intentionally through verbal conversations, especially by introducing herself to specific audiences. To participate in organizations that farmers in her community traditionally engage in, Lauren attends her county and state meetings for an agriculture organization that is not necessarily known to include vegetable farmers. She describes how those attending the meetings introduce themselves: "[You] go around the circle and explain yourself, and most of the women pass and let their husbands explain them, which is annoying as hell." But Lauren, breaking the tradition that women do not speak in these introductions, introduces herself and talks about her farm. As a single woman, she is also an exception in the room of married pairs of men and women or men attending alone. She explains how she carefully chooses her words in these contexts in which independent women farmers who grow vegetables are not likely attendees, much less speakers during meetings:

> I think very hard about how to craft my words so that the men in the room will hear me. And I do that ... I'm successful at it. I'm highly successful at it, which is fascinating. But I think about the way I dress, I think about the way I speak, I think about the way I talk about my operation. I try to put it in their terms, and I constantly am doing that, because ... And I'm aware that I'm doing it, but I'm also not going to stop doing it, even though I hate that I have to do it, because it's, I feel, like the only way to move across those barriers of change.

As Lauren put it, effectively moving across barriers means that the men in the room who farm large commodity operations, including growing soybeans and corn or keeping animals in confinement facilities, have an opportunity to understand and respect farmers like her who grow food for the local community. The words she chooses show that she understands their operations, such as connecting their farm to the types of farming her grandparents did, bringing up antique tractors with fellow farmers who like them, finding common ground through challenges all farmers face with weather, among other verbal strategies. She sees herself as highly successful because these other farmers remember her and her name at subsequent events, they attend events that she hosts, and they ask about her farm. They also ask her for advice as some of them consider adding vegetables to the crops they grow. Regarding her appearance, she dresses for off-farm meetings and activities in clean work boots, jeans, t-shirts or flannel shirts, and baseball caps that bear the logos of non-profit organizations that support farmers. When she describes her appearance in these interactions she mentions another woman vegetable farmer in her community who has a *hippie* style of dress. While Lauren deeply respects this farmer and praises her farm, Lauren describes how she herself would never dress in styles that evoke a hippie identity since doing so would not yield respect from the famers with whom she is trying to connect. While working to acquire her own legitimacy as a farmer, she tries to bridge boundaries between those practicing industrial agriculture and those using sustainable, regenerative, *alternative* practices. So in legitimizing herself through her appearance, words she uses, and topics she speaks about with these farmers, she is also legitimizing the type of farming that she and other women in her surrounding community do, including those who would never go to the meetings that Lauren attends with commodity farmers.

Maintaining Legitimacy

Maintaining the legitimacy Lauren acquires is an ongoing aspect of her life as a farmer and her continuing literacy labor. She maintains her legitimacy by adapting to known audiences' assumptions and by both creating and taking on leadership roles through hosting community events and mentoring other farmers. It took years for Lauren to reach acceptance by audiences she encounters, and gaining insider status is an ongoing process that recurs each time she meets and explains herself to new audiences. Having farmed for eight years, however, she can rely on her established legitimacy.

Adapting to Audience Assumptions

Lauren explains a range of strategies she uses to maintain her legitimacy with audiences she has built rapport with in the early years of her farming. While she is now beyond being the unfamiliar face at farm organization meetings, she still does the communicative work to maintain her insider status with those groups—partly because even after years of being involved with these organizations, she remains the only woman who is vocal at these meetings and runs her own farm. To maintain her status within these contexts, she learns as much as she can about her fellow farmers' operations and demonstrates that knowledge to show that she values their farms and understands the conventional farming on large acreages in her area. She avoids the label of a person who is critical of industrial agriculture despite being personally and politically invested in changing certain aspects of conventional practices. She has been successful with her efforts, shown by the fact that she wins leadership awards from an organization not known for its inclusion of vegetable farmers or women and also now serves on the organization's county-level board.

One example she provides in our interview is how she navigates in-person conversations, specifically in how she adapts her words to meet known audiences' assumptions: "[I try to] always find the fine balance of where to put [my] words and in what context...when I'm talking to a large [acreage] farmer....I'm always thinking about [how to be taken seriously] especially if I'm going into an environment with other farmers. I also have a way of speaking to male farmers, making sure that I know some of the lingo of the equipment that they're using." By showing her familiarity with other farmers' operations, she shows that she respects them and—even though her farm is quite different from theirs—that she understands and values what they do. Although she now has an established farm, she still does not want to alienate herself. She explains how she would adapt her vocabulary and conversation topics when talking to a customer and others at the farmers' market. She illustrates all the different ways she meets audiences' assumptions and expectations:

> So, I'm going to talk about the beautiful vegetables [with a customer at the farmers' market] and how I cook them and how healthy they are and things like that. If I'm talking to a farmer, I'm going to talk about the soil, I'm going to talk about the cultivation, I'm going to talk about my antique tractors, I'm going to talk about the horse power of my tractor. I'm going to make a self-deprecating joke about how my tractor is small, but I can still produce a lot per acre.

Lauren's use of self-deprecating jokes about her equipment and yield demonstrates her evolving status as both an insider and an outsider farmer in these contexts. She shows that she values yield, like other farmers, and understands soil science and engine size, all ways that farmers compare their operations and demonstrate expertise. And with the confidence of an insider she can make self-deprecating jokes, connecting with her conversation partners through humor. Instead of feeling threatened by not being taken seriously, Lauren feels she can now balance her performance of farmer literacies, such as about soil content and antique tractors, with levity. She can participate in a normative farming discourse that maintains her legitimacy in that particular interaction and builds friendships with other farmers. Whether this respect is fully reciprocated on an individual level is difficult to assess, but could be partially shown, from her view, by the friendly relationships Lauren now has with these farmers and the fact that she feels more welcome around them now than when she first started attending meetings and introducing herself and her farm to them.

Additionally and more specifically, to maintain her legitimacy during in-person interactions with conventional farmers who are men, Lauren takes great strides to connect with these audiences and intentionally find common ground, which she further details as being an effort on the conversational level: "I'm going to make sure that I ask good questions about their operation, make sure I praise their operation, make sure I don't say anything that's dissenting to who they are, even if I don't personally believe in hog confinements, I'm never going to say that to them because I'm going to try to make sure that they like me. I'm going to spend a lot of time making sure that they like me." She must perform this conversational work in order to be read as an insider even though her farm and the choices she makes for it are quite different from these other farmers who grant legitimacy in her community. Lauren deliberately works to not only depoliticize her interactions but also connect with these other farmers. She understands that these intentional habits of hers are unique among others who practice sustainable agriculture. She notices that other vegetable farmers who choose to be publicly political about the food system as it exists in her surrounding community can alienate themselves from the established farming community led by men who practice conventional farming.

But beyond communicating with other farmers about farming, Lauren takes on a new kind of personal embodiment when she pays particular attention to how she communicates significant news to her audience of CSA members in order to maintain legitimacy as their farmer. In this particular occasion, she makes public an evolution of her embodiment by describing her heterosexual relationship and future marriage. She wants to be the person who breaks the news to her customers because she knows her personal life matters to them, and she wants to be specific about how they receive the news. Concerns that her customers would assume she would quit farming or that her future husband would take over the farm motivate her worries that the news would put at risk the legitimacy she works so hard to secure.

Marriage includes embodying new roles, so when planning to deliver this message and maintain her legitimacy, Lauren knows to use and define the new term *farm husband* to delineate that her future spouse would not be a farmer on her farm. But her first step in articulating this new role to CSA members was to explain it to her fiancé. Because she anticipates that his role will require articulation to those outside the relationship and that many would assume that he will become the lead farmer, she wants to first make sure he understands his role: "I've had a lot of conversations with my fiancé…in a not unkind way, [making sure he knows] he will be my farm husband, because he is not going to be doing primary labor on the farm. And I want to … I believe that term, that farm wife, was used well for a long time, and then was misused for a while, depending on what era you're in and how much work women were doing on the farm." The use of terms is important to her, and she trusts that "farm husband" will designate that her fiancé is not the primary farmer—she is. Lauren wants her new status as a woman marrying a man to not compromise her legitimacy as the primary operator on her farm, and she anticipates that her fiancé will get immediate, unearned, unwarranted credit as a contributor to her farm. She intends to make sure that he knows his role. She specifically describes this role, framing it in a historical context:

> But I feel that that concept [of farm spouse] is important to reclaim and the beautiful part of it [is that] farm wives, even if they weren't doing physical labor on the farm, there was this huge support role that they were in. There are women, like my grandmother, who should've been called farmer, because she was farrowing the hog, she was milking the cows. But in my situation, my fiancé isn't going to be doing those things. He might be helping me with equipment and things like that. He will be in a support role, so, we joke a lot about it [and] we actually had a long conversation last weekend about what does that mean, and what does that mean to both of us, that I'm the farmer and he's the farm husband.

Securing her fiancé's understanding of her autonomy over the farm is essential before she can articulate the news to her CSA members.

Lauren's specific vocation as a farmer necessitates her articulation of her new role as a woman planning to marry. Other jobs would not require her to write such an explanation. She names being a hairdresser in town as an example and points out, "no one would think twice of me getting married" if she held other occupations. Continuing, Lauren illustrates, "one of the reasons I feel like it's really important to talk about [my fiancé's role as a support person] is because if we're going to talk about women farmers and women ... all aspects of that need to be talked about." Lauren estimates that once she is read as a wife and no longer as a single woman farming independently, her legitimacy as a farmer is at risk. Thus, Lauren articulates her transition from being a single, independent farmer to being a married, independent farmer as important to the broad, inclusive understanding of women's lives and their efforts toward legitimacy. Farmers should be able to choose marriage without sacrificing their farmer status and Lauren explicitly rejects the assumption that women are only truly independent as farmers if they are single.

After talking about her discussions with her fiancé about his role on her farm, Lauren details her strategies for communicating the news to her CSA customers. She wants to strike an informative yet joyous tone so that her customers would take seriously the boundaries she is describing for her future husband's minimal, supportive role in the operation, and simultaneously celebrate her happy news. She reads the email to me after describing her process in composing it. Before sending the email, she recruits her sister, a marketing professional, and other friends as readers to assess its effectiveness. In the message, she refers to how her readers have heard of farm wives, but they might not have heard of a farm husband. She introduces him in the email message and briefly describes their courtship. After reading the introductory part of the message to me, she stops and says, "This is the important part." Then, she starts reading the details about how her farm would continue to operate the way it always had in the past. When she finishes reading the email to me, she explains her customers' viewpoint to further justify why such a message is necessary to maintain her legitimacy: "It was really important [to write to my customers with this information, in this manner] because a lot of people had said, 'Oh, are you moving?' Every time I said I was getting married, people asked me if I was moving." I ask whether people respond to her engagement news by assuming that she was going to quit farming. Nodding, she answers, "I got asked that a lot. So I was like, We're going to nip this in the bud with my customers and just say, 'This is how it is.'" Customers also express assumptions that she would not do a fall CSA since she would be busy wedding planning, which Lauren gently rejects when it comes up. In multiple ways, Lauren anticipates and responds to reactions from customers who assume her entire life and business would change in the context of her future marriage, an experience, she emphasizes, that would not happen to men farmer colleagues when they announce an engagement. Lauren feels that men's multiple identities as farmers and husbands do not put their legitimacy at risk, whereas this new role of wife risks delegitimizing her as a farmer.

Taking on Community Leadership Roles

Another strategy Lauren uses to maintain her legitimacy is to create and accept leadership roles, such as hosting events that all farmers in her community will enjoy and feel welcome to attend and mentoring aspiring vegetable farmers. For example, she tells about co-hosting a farmer documentary screening with a woman farmer friend. She intends that hosting such events makes her a recognizable member of the community, someone who brings people together. Lauren expresses why she would much rather create these open, farmer-focused events than events aimed at women: "I happen to be a woman farmer, and I believe in female farmer issues and all that kind of stuff, but really who I want to reach are the people that control the strings, and I don't want to get bogged down in this cutesy kind of like thing." Lauren assumes that if her public persona seems relevant to women only, she will not maintain her legitimacy among all farmers. For the film event, she reaches out to farmers with operations different from hers in order to be intentional about the event's inclusivity: "I personally invited a friend of mine who's the largest farmer in the county. He and his family farm ten thousand acres, and I've worked really hard to be respected by him because I think it's important." This importance to Lauren stems from the fact that she believes all farmers need one another, and they should thus actively transgress boundaries across their different farming practices. She sees herself as an ambassador for vegetable farmers who successfully gains the friendship of a farmer who is quite different from her when it comes to farm choices and the types of farms they lead. This man validates her and her farm by coming to her event, in her view.

Lauren also takes on community leadership roles by agreeing to mentor women pursuing vegetable farming and who are also married to men who farm large, conventional operations. By answering the call to perform as an expert who is trusted by men farmers who do not know how to grow vegetables or run a CSA operation like Lauren's, she further secures her legitimacy as a successful, independent woman vegetable farmer. She agrees to volunteer in this capacity when men farmers ask her to mentor their wives. In this role she feels pressure not only to show that she knows every detail of her farm operation, but also to speak on behalf of all vegetable farmers working small parcels of land. This role is high stakes for Lauren because her success in it can both maintain the legitimacy of vegetable farming and support the ambitions of the women she is mentoring. Although the men are often skeptical of vegetable farming, they know and respect Lauren, so she is aware that she has a lot to prove in these mentoring roles. She explains two of these opportunities: "Both [women] are part of large family operations. One's five thousand acres; one's ten thousand acres. Both have hog confinements in the family and large row crop operations, and both have either started or are considering starting vegetable operations." Thus, both of these women are familiar with one type of farming and want to start a much different type, looking to Lauren as the expert. "[For] the first one, who's already started her vegetable operation," she continues, "I drive down [a few hours to their farm] and I have this very uncomfortable lunch where her husband comes in and basically grills me about my business. And you know, I feel like I'm having to talk for all of vegetable farming, and be this legit vegetable farmer. So, I better know my numbers, I better know my business. So, I'm always feeling like I'm having to be this perfect person because if I show a crack, then it's going to bring down the whole thing." Performing such mentorship means putting her legitimacy on the line, and those that ask her to take on this work rely on her expertise as a farmer as well as her identity as a woman, assuming their wives will be able to learn from her.

Lauren's description of the multiple roles she has to fulfill while doing such mentoring work—an arrangement she agrees to, uses her own time and money to drive to, yet dislikes in many ways—shows her commitment to her broader community and the ongoing legitimacy of women leading vegetable farms. Here Lauren has to not only demonstrate her own farmer legitimacy and the value of her farming choices but she also bears the burden of this other woman's persuading her husband that her ambitions are legitimate too, which is a lot of pressure. Thus, to maintain her legitimacy, in this case, Lauren must rely on enacting her knowledge about farming, which she does to meet the expectations of mentoring and communicate effectively as an expert. Doing so means continuing to foster trust with established, conventional farmers while validating new farmers' pursuits to farm differently.

Conclusions, Limitations, and Future Studies

In their 2010 article on "civic" agriculture in Pennsylvania, Amy Trauger and her coauthors ask, "Do women express a connection between their practice of agriculture and particular articulations of gender identity?" (44). Their findings show that the majority of respondents affirmed that their gender affected their decisions and choices, particularly concerning "barriers and problems they had faced" (51). My case study on Lauren pushes the conversation on the significant role gender plays in women farmers' lives by analyzing one farmer's literacy work, including the strategies she uses to navigate constraints and cross boundaries.

While my findings from this analysis are not meant to be generalizable, the details of Lauren's literacy life described here, especially the literacy work she does to acquire and maintain legitimacy, provide one dynamic case study on the complex literacy work of a woman farmer and how gender is a critical factor in her literacy life. These findings support my argument that Lauren, as an independent woman farmer, faces a range of audiences' gendered expectations, which elicit the necessary legitimizing literacy work she performs to maintain and grow her farm business and influence in her community.

But this study has several limitations. To follow IRB protocol and maintain the farmer's anonymity, I could not interview any of Lauren's customers or members of her community to get their perspectives on the status of Lauren's legitimacy as a farmer. Lauren's farm, however, remains a thriving business, a strong indicator that her communication with customers is meeting its goals. Since I am also unable to interview men farmers who grow commodity crops in Lauren's community, I cannot claim that her strategies are successful with them. However, as she describes, they attend events she hosts. Further, the agriculture organizations Lauren joins, organizations not known for being inclusive of vegetable farmers or women farmers, ask Lauren to speak at their events and feature her farm on their website and other venues, showing they at least trust her to represent the organization, which she also does on the county-level board. In one photo on their website, with an accompanying story about her farm, Lauren is pictured standing in a field and holding a CSA box of vegetables. She is wearing a shirt with a slogan the organization uses as well as a hat that bears the logo of a well-known clothing brand also worn by commodity farmers, visibly demonstrating her affinity with conventional farmers who are members of the organization.

Case studies like this one with Lauren can be expanded in the future by collecting other types of data. For example, understandings of Lauren's legitimacy-building work could be enhanced by combining interviews with other ethnographic approaches, such as working an entire farmers-market season with a farmer to observe interactions with passersby. That said, farmers may be hesitant to consent to a research study that includes allowing the researcher to interact with customers. Doing so would also present challenges for anonymity, an aspect of the study that empowers farmers to be transparent and honest about information they do not necessarily disclose to customers and fellow farmers.

More research is needed in order to better understand the literacy practices of women farmers, both in their local communities and in food systems writ large. Future literacy-based studies could investigate what strategies are necessary for women to obtain land access, such as negotiating leases with landowners, obtaining grants and loans to buy land, or even challenging local norms and laws that prevent smaller parcels of land from being defined as farms. Lauren, for example, said she actually hated vegetables when she first started her farm, but growing vegetables made the most sense because she rented a smaller plot of land. Now she appreciates vegetables in a new way, but growing what is accessible for a few acres of rented land was key to her farm's success, especially initially. Thus, instead of assuming women make certain farm decisions because of their gender, such as connecting sustainable practices to nurturing stereotypes, we can ask them how constraints and access shape their choices.

Ultimately, literacy scholars could more actively apply a gendered lens to studying agriculture and participate in this multidisciplinary field of inquiry, contributing our findings to the growing efforts of interdisciplinary food studies. While many in food studies commit their work to demystifying agricultural labor and promoting eaters' knowledge about the conditions under which food producers work, more can be done to better understand the literacy labor that goes into such oft-obscured and intentionally hidden roles within food production. Listening to practitioners describe the strategies they use to negotiate the sexist and racist infrastructures that undergird our food systems and analyzing these findings contributes to building the knowledge that can change these systems and the intersecting oppressions they perpetuate. One effort toward doing so includes taking a both/and approach that invites practitioners to speak about both farming and gender. We cannot expect women farmers to only be experts on gender. They are eager to talk about their farms and their expertise on farm-related literacies, all efforts that normalize women as agriculture experts.

The findings I feature here illustrate a range of examples regarding how one farmer applies her literacy skills to acquire and maintain her legitimacy. The observations and experiences Lauren provides portray complex terrain for why and how gender and farming interlink in rich literacy contexts. Further, they show how her interactions with others create opportunities for her to articulate her own narratives beyond those based on statistics and gendered stereotypes. While sitting in Lauren's home on the cold and sunny January day of our interview, I became struck by how much she thought about how gender matters to her interactions with others. It permeates her farm life. She expresses gratitude to me for my attention to her experiences and the validation she feels from our interaction, demonstrating that farmers are eager to tell their stories to those invested in learning more about the hidden and obscured aspects of women's work in food systems. Interviews with women farmers showcase the literacy work they do in order to be read as legitimate farmers who shape the cultural context of agriculture and offer opportunities to expand our access to their literacy lives and the ways that gender is critical to their literacy work.

Acknowledgments

Without the farmer's willingness to do an interview with me, this study would not exist. I appreciate her generosity with her time and expertise. I am also grateful for the feedback provided by Jane Greer, Rasha Diab, and anonymous reviewers of this article, which strengthened, narrowed, and clarified it considerably. A research award from the Center for Excellence in Arts and Humanities at Iowa State University provided funding for this project.

Appendix A

Food, Farming, and Feminism Interview Questions

General

1. What has been your past experience with being a farmer or food worker?
2. In what ways do you see gender making a difference to farming and food?
3. What do you see as the status of women farmers and food workers in your community?
4. What do you see as the status of women farmers and food workers within the food system, both as it currently exists, and in future iterations?
5. In the academic field of feminist rhetoric, researchers study how gender matters to persuasion and communication. Please describe some occasions in your working life when gender mattered as you communicated and persuaded others.
6. What communication strategies do you use in your job?

7. How did you learn to communicate effectively in your work? For example, are there any mentors you have as models? Or ways you've learned about how to communicate differently in different aspects of your work?
8. Organizations like the Women, Food, and Ag Network claim that networks are important to women in food and farming. Please respond to this idea.
9. Some people claim that food is a feminist issue. Please respond to this idea.

Questions for farmers only

1. Some academic researchers connect sustainable agriculture to women. For example, the book *The Rise of Women Farmers and Sustainable Agriculture* shows the work that women are doing in this area. In your experience as a farmer, in what ways do you see women making contributions to sustainable agriculture as well as conventional agriculture and agriculture policymaking?
2. How do you define the word farmer?
3. Have you noticed organizations and individuals claiming that women are the future of agriculture and farming? What do you make of these claims?
4. What do you wish nonfarmers knew about what it's like to be a farmer? And what do you wish nonfarmers knew about what it's like to be a woman farmer?

Notes

1. According to American Masculinities: A Historical Encyclopedia, agrarianism is a "complex set of ideas that celebrates the moral, spiritual, and political superiority of men who cultivate the soil, was a central cultural theme of early American society, and it has heavily influenced American understandings of manhood" (Hartman 20). Lynn Harter defines American agrarianism as rooted in Thomas Jefferson's writings, which positioned farming as important since it prompted democratic citizenship as a revolutionary virtue. As they evolved, Jefferson's ideas about farmers have taken on mythic qualities and been coupled with "frontier images and hegemonic constructions of masculinity (i.e., the privileging of a patriarchal, managerial masculinity guided by technical rationalities)" (91). Janet Galligani Casey shows how the agrarian ideal is predominantly masculinist and its lead reformers linked farming to "authentic" American pasts that aspired to a "eugenics-inspired, racially sanitized future" (25). As Wolford summarizes, "Much of the research concerning women in agriculture over the past thirty years from social sciences and feminist and women's studies scholarship in Europe and North America concludes that conventional industrial agriculture in Western countries is a hegemonic, male-gendered institution that has obscured women as ancillary helpers with little or no decision-making power regarding the farm" (np). The masculinist agrarian tradition can also be located in other texts

and practices from American history and current popular culture, such as children's books that primarily depict farmers as men.

2. More recent statistics exist, but deserve qualification. Between 2012 and 2017, the USDA Census of Agriculture indicates that the percentage of farm operators who are women increased from 13.66% to 29.13%, a statistic used to argue that women farmers have doubled when, in fact, such a significant increase may be partially due to a change in how farmers are counted, obscuring the actual growth in numbers of women running farms. In the new census, respondents could indicate that multiple people make decisions on individual farms, so women who may have been farming for generations with a partner or other individuals now show up in the data. (https://www.agdaily.com/insights/usda-releases-2017-census-of-agriculture-data/)

Works Cited

Al-Salmi, Laila and Patrick Smith. "Arab Immigrant Mothers Parenting Their Way into Digital Biliteracy." *Literacy in Composition Studies,* vol. 3, no. 3, 2015, pp. 48-66.

Bean, Janet. "Critical Literacy for Older Adults: Engaging (and Resisting) Transformative Education as a United Methodist Woman." *Literacy in Composition Studies,* vol. 6, no. 2, 2018, pp. 59-75.

Birks, Melanie and Jane Mills. *Grounded Theory: A Practical Guide.* Sage, 2011.

Bureau of Labor Statistics. https://www.bls.gov/emp/tables/employment-by-major-industry- sector.htm#3. 2017.

Casey, Janet Galligani. *A New Heartland: Women, Modernity, and the Agrarian Ideal in America.* Oxford University Press, 2009.

Charmaz, Kathy. *Constructing Grounded Theory: A Practical Guide through Qualitative Analysis.* Sage Publications, 2006.

DeLind, Laura and Anne Ferguson. "Is this a Women's Movement? The Relationship of Gender to Community-Supported Agriculture in Michigan." *Human Organization,* vol. 58, no. 2, 1999, pp. 190-200.

Ehret, Christian and Ty Hollett. "Embodied Composition in Real Virtualities: Adolescents' Literacy Practices and Felt Experiences Moving with Digital, Mobile Devices in School." *Research in the Teaching of English,* vol. 48, no. 4, 2014, pp. 428-452.

Gollihue, Krystin. "Re-Making the Makerspace: Body, Power, and Identity in Critical Making Practices." *Computers and Composition,* vol. 53, 2019, pp. 21-33.

Greer, Jane. "Women's Words, Women's Work: Rural Literacy and Labor." *Reclaiming the Rural: Essays on Literacy, Rhetoric, and Pedagogy,* edited by Kim Donehower, Charlotte Hogg, and Eileen Schell. Southern Illinois UP, 2012, pp. 90–106.

Harter, Lynn. "Masculinity(s), the Agrarian Frontier Myth, and Cooperative Ways of Organizing: Contradictions and Tensions in the Experience and Enactment of Democracy." *Journal of Applied Communication Research,* vol. 32, no. 2, 2004, pp. 89-118.

Hartman, Rebecca. "Agrarianism." In *American Masculinities: A Historical Encyclopedia*, edited by Bret Carroll, Sage, 2003, pp. 20-22.

Keller, Julie. "I Wanna Have My Own Damn Dairy Farm!" Women Farmers, Legibility, and Femininities in Rural Wisconsin, US." *Journal of Rural Social Sciences*, vol. 29, no. 1, 2014, pp. 75-102.

Leonard, Rebecca Lorimer. *Writing on the Move: Migrant Women and the Value of Literacy*, University of Pittsburgh Press, 2019.

Moss, Beverly. "'Phenomenal Women,' Collaborative Literacies, and Community Texts in Alternative 'Sista' Spaces." *Community Literacy Journal*, vol. 5, no. 1, 2010-2011, pp. 1-24.

National Sustainable Agriculture Coalition. "Farming Opportunities." https://sustainableagriculture.net/our-work/issues/farming-opportunities/#4 Accessed 1 April 2020.

Penniman, Leah. *Farming While Black: Soul Fire Farm's Practical Guide to Liberation on the Land*. Chelsea Green, 2018.

Pilgeram, Ryanne and Bryan Amos. "Beyond 'Inherit It or Marry It': Exploring How Women Engaged in Sustainable Agriculture Access Farmland." *Rural Sociology*, vol. 80, no. 1, 2015, pp. 16-38.

Pink, Sarah. "From Embodiment to Emplacement: Re-thinking Competing Bodies, Senses and Spatialities." *Sport, Education, and Society*, vol. 16, no. 3, 2011, pp. 343-355.

Rissing, Andrea. "Iowan Women Farmers' Perspectives on Alternative Agriculture and Gender." *Journal of Agriculture, Food Systems, and Community Development*, vol. 3, no. 2, 2013, pp. 127-36.

Royster, Jacqueline Jones. *Traces of a Stream: Literacy and Social Change among African American Women*. University of Pittsburgh Press, 2000.

Sachs, Carolyn, et al. *The Rise of Women Farmers and Sustainable Agriculture*. University of Iowa Press, 2016.

Schell, Eileen. "Racialized Rhetorics of Food Politics: Black Farmers, the Case of Shirley Sherrod, and Struggle for Land Equity and Access." *Poroi*, vol. 11, no. 1, 2015, pp. 1-22.

Schmidt, Kimberly and Becky Beucher. "Embodied Literacies and the Art of Meaning Making." *Pedagogies: An International Journal*, vol. 13, no. 2, 2018, pp. 119-32.

Shisler, Rebecca and Joshua Sbicca. "Agriculture as Carework: The Contradictions of Performing Femininity in a Male-Dominated Occupation." *Society & Natural Resources*, vol. 32, no. 8, 2019, pp. 875-92.

Shivers-McNair, Ann. "Mediation and Boundary Marking: A Case Study of Making Literacies Across a Makerspace." *Learning, Culture, and Social Interaction*, vol. 24, 2020, pp. 1-7.

Simon, Kaia. "Daughters Learning from Fathers: Migrant Family Literacies that Mediate Borders." *Literacy in Composition Studies*, vol. 5, no. 1, 2017, pp. 1-20.

Solberg, Janine. "Taking Shorthand for Literacy: Historicizing the Literate Activity of US Women in the Early Twentieth-Century Office." *Literacy in Composition Studies*, vol. 2, no. 1, 2014, 1-28.

Swacha, Kathryn Yankura. "'Bridging the Gap Between Food Pantries and the Kitchen Table': Teaching Embodied Literacy in the Technical Communication Classroom." *Technical Communication Quarterly*, vol. 27, no. 3, 2018, pp. 261-282.

Trauger, Amy. "'Because They Can Do the Work': Women Farmers in Sustainable Agriculture in Pennsylvania, USA." *Gender, Place, and Culture*, vol. 11, no. 2, 2004, pp. 289-307.

Trauger, Amy, Carolyn Sachs, Mary Barbercheck, Kaithy Brasier, and Nancy Ellen Kiernan. "'Our Market is Our Community': Women Farmers and Civic Agriculture in Pennsylvania, USA." *Agriculture and Human Values*, vol. 27, 2010, pp. 43-55.

USDA. "Direct Farm Sales of Food." *2012 Census of Agriculture Highlights*. 2016, www.nass.usda.gov/Publications/Highlights/2016/LocalFoodsMarketingPractices_Highli ghts.pdf.

---. "Women Farmers." *2012 Census of Agriculture Highlights*. 2014, https://www.nass.usda.gov/Publications/Highlights/2014/Highlights_Women_Farmers.pd f.

Vaughn, Jennie, Allen Harrell, and Amy Dayton. "Digital Literacy in Rural Women's Lives." *Community Literacy Journal*, vol. 9, no. 2, 2015, pp. 26-47.

Vieira, Kate. "On the Social Consequences of Literacy." *Literacy in Composition Studies*, vol. 1, no. 1, 2013, pp. 26-32.

Walker, Clay. "Composing Agency: Theorizing the Readiness Potentials of Literacy Practices." *Literacy in Composition Studies*, vol. 3, no. 2, 2015, pp. 1-21.

White-Farnham, Jamie. "Rhetorical Recipes: Women's Literacies In and Out of the Kitchen." *Community Literacy Journal*, vol. 6, no. 2, 2012, pp. 23-41.

Wolford, Rachel. "When a Woman Owns the Farm: A Case for Diachronic and Synchronic Rhetorical Agency." *Enculturation*, 2016. http://enculturation.net/when-a-woman-owns- the-farm

Woodcock, Christine. "'I Allow Myself to FEEL Now...': Adolescent Girls' Negotiations of Embodied Knowing, the Female Body, and Literacy." *Journal of Literacy Research*, vol. 42, no. 4, 2010, pp. 349-384.

Work-Slivka, Julie Anne. "A Rhizomatic Exploration of Adolescent Girls' Rough-and-Tumble Play as Embodied Literacy." *Jeunesse: Young People, Texts, Cultures*, vol. 9, no. 1, 2017, pp. 37-56.

Author Bio

Abby M. Dubisar is an Associate Professor in the English Department at Iowa State University, where she is also an affiliate faculty member in women's and gender studies and sustainable agriculture. She teaches graduate and undergraduate classes on rhetoric, gender, activism, and popular culture analysis. Most recently her publications include analyses of students' critical agrifood literacies and activist cookbooks as well as teaching ideas to address the issue of food waste. Her work has appeared in such venues as *College English, Rhetoric of Health and Medicine, Rhetoric Review, Computers and Composition, Present Tense,* and *Peitho*.

(Re) Mixing Up Literacy: Cookbooks as Rhetorical Remix

Elizabeth J. Fleitz

Abstract

Exploring literacy practices of home cooks, this article analyzes how cookbooks are remixed by users (with writings, clippings and other ephemera added to the text throughout its use). The practice of remixing the text with further editing by its user/audience illustrates the multilayered literacies at work in establishing authorship within the domestic space. The article builds its argument around one remixed cookbook as a case study, describing the remix-literate practices of the user, as the woman who used this cookbook remixed the text and genre to fit her needs and interests. This literacy practice is argued as a remix, which results in a transformation of the text itself and of the authority of the user. Both the original authorship (the act of compiling recipes from the church community) and the remixed authorship (the added ephemera and handwritten editing done by the user of this particular copy) are analyzed in tandem.

Keywords

remix, literacy, community cookbook, recipe, rhetoric

> To love and honor is O'kay
> And one might promise to obey;
> But what makes wives turn slowly gray,
> Is what to cook each blessed day
> —OUR FAVORITE RECIPES,
> Ladies Aid Society of Hope Lutheran Church

Penciled-in notes. Dog-eared page corners. Pasted-in newspaper clippings. Annotations mark the well-worn cookbook on my shelf. Page stains indicate the most frequently used recipes. Crossed-out ingredients show substitutions, or personal preferences. Ephemera stuck between pages, like a scrapbook, tell of user interest: we are what we collect. One of my cookbooks, *OUR FAVORITE RECIPES* of 1950, demonstrates this scrapbooking practice, as the user has handwritten recipe edits in the margins, taped newspaper clippings on top of each other, and collected cooking tips on blank pages. I employ the term "cookbook user" intentionally here to indicate an active participant in the text's development. One "uses" a cookbook—one does not passively "read" or "observe" the text. As a home cook, I also engage in this same annotation practice. The cookbooks on my shelf bear marks of use—the good ones, anyway. Like a textbook, my cookbooks are annotated to indicate which recipes, techniques, and ingredients work, and which do not. This process of marking up cookbooks is ongoing: an endless search for improvement.

This practice of textual annotation, the marking up of recipes, the margin notes and pasted in clippings, is a common literacy practice for home cooks as they refashion and remix their cookbooks to better suit their lives. The act of marking up a recipe is a practice of food literacy, which enables a home cook to participate in a community of cooks by building a multimodal archive of their domestic needs and aspirations, leading them to create an original contribution to share. Jennifer Sumner defines food literacy as the ability to understand and apply knowledge about food and nutrition to one's own habits (83). Lauren Block et al. describe three components of food literacy: (1) conceptual or declarative knowledge, which includes the reading or acquiring of knowledge about food; (2) procedural knowledge, which applies knowledge about food to decision making, such as shopping for or preparing food; and (3) the ability, opportunity, and motivation to use this knowledge about food (7). Thus, food literacy involves not just the traditional concept of literacy—reading and interpreting information—but also the embodied practice of applying this knowledge to life. This act of marking up cookbooks is a multimodal process contributing to food literacy. Home cooks regularly engage in these literacy practices to improve their knowledge and skills involving food preparation.

While women have been participating in these literacy practices for generations, until recently there has been little scholarship to acknowledge their role in rhetorical history. Cheryl Glenn explains the historical silence of women in the history of rhetoric, noting that throughout Western culture, women have been disciplined by cultural codes restricting them to the private domain of the home, pushing them out of the public sector and thus out of history. Women were assumed to be caretakers of the home and of the family, and efforts outside of that realm were not considered appropriate to their role. However, since rhetorical history is written by those in public spaces, women were silenced from being part of that history due to their gender. Thus, rhetorical history has replicated the same kind of power dynamic as gender, pushing women aside due to their assigned role.

The past few decades of scholarship have demonstrated that women did, in fact, have a voice, and they used it frequently in the public sphere throughout rhetorical history. Glenn reminds us that even though women were invisible and silent throughout the history of rhetoric, that is not the same thing as being absent from it. Women found their own avenues to express themselves, going outside of domestic space and into history. This work of "remapping" women into rhetorical history, as Glenn describes it, allows women's voices to be heard and illuminates their presence (3). As a "resisting reader" (Bizzell 51), scholars of women's rhetorics have challenged the patriarchal retelling of history and have instead worked to insert women back into the historical narrative.

While much scholarship focuses on women who have gained a public voice in history, there are indeed just as many, if not more, women who expressed their voice within the private sphere. These voices, while more difficult to locate than those of women speakers and writers in the public domain, are just as vital to constructing our history with a gendered viewpoint. This article explores one specific literacy practice within the domestic space: the act of marking up a cookbook into a useable text to suit a home cook's needs and budget and finds that the literacy practices women use when interacting with the cookbook are valuable to study in order to remap the role of women into the history of rhetoric.

My claim, then, is to identify this marking-up practice as remix. Naming this act of annotating a recipe as "remix" allows for greater insight into the level of skill that amateur home cooks practice to gain literacy. This insight offers a better way to describe the transformative power this literacy practice offers the user as she claims authority within the text and within the larger community of home cooks. While most scholarship on remix involves digital technology, Jody Shipka reminds us that "multimodal" literacy exists in more forms than just digital (12). She notes that "If we acknowledge that literacy and learning have always been multimodal … the challenge becomes one of finding ways to attend more fully … to the material, multimodal aspects of all communicative practice" (21). If we only consider the topic of remix as applied to digital forms, we lose its potential for uncovering new insights, new ways to look at texts. As Shipka warns, "a narrow definition of technology fails to encourage richly nuanced, situated views of literacy" (31). To avoid this problem, Shipka suggests focusing on the composing process. In fact, remix effectively describes the composing process of home cooks interacting with their well-loved cookbooks, and thus is the reason I have chosen it as the lens through which to view this literacy practice. Additionally, there already exists a valuable body of scholarship on the process of remix in digital forms; therefore, using this scholarship will allow for a detailed observation of the user's composing process within the cookbook.

Much of the existing scholarship on cookbooks explores the ongoing revision process of recipes common to the genre. Cookbooks are unfinished works. Social historian Janet Theophano notes that "Cookbooks, as they are used in daily life, are works-in-progress" (187). It's a common practice to alter recipes, to revise amounts or oven temperatures, or to substitute ingredients for those more readily available. To better suit the user's current and future needs, annotations are made in the margins or between the lines of print. This is true for any cookbook, to be sure. In fact, Theophano reminds us that "Cookbooks invite editorializing" (188), explaining that for any cookbook or recipe, revisions are expected and even encouraged. For example, the author might recommend a different method or a substitution if preferred, encouraging the reader to decide what is best to suit her own needs. Other times, the editorializing might be unstated. In any case, cookbooks are frequently revised and edited to fit the user's own kitchen and preferences, as well as her own budget and resources.

This editorializing comes from the form of the genre itself. Rhetorical scholar Anne Bower explains that "[a] community cookbook is a subtle gap-ridden kind of artifact, that asks its reader (at least the reader who seeks more than recipes) to fill those gaps with social and culinary history, knowledge of other texts (such as commercial cookbooks), and even personal knowledge" (143). Bower argues that these gaps help invite the reader to become part of the text and engage with it, to insert her own knowledge and her own preferences, to interpret the recipes as she sees fit. In scholarship, cookbooks are generally considered as a genre that necessitates perpetual revision. The sub-genre of community cookbooks, in particular, are themselves a remix: a collection of recipes shared by a local community of home cooks. My contribution to this conversation, then, is to describe how a user constructs a multimodal text within a community of home cooks: to do so, I name this process as remix as a way to home in on the technical practice a user engages in with the text. Through the use of remix, the home cook can offer new insight on the text, making an original contribution to share within the domestic space.

This article looks at the user's interaction with the community cookbook, exploring how the manipulation of the physical space of the printed page is in itself a literacy practice. This practice is impacted by the contexts of gender and community. These contexts inform the user's practice of collecting and arranging texts within the pages of the community cookbook—a cookbook which itself is also an arrangement of texts, an archive. In this resulting literacy practice, users collect and arrange the text in the most effective way to serve their purposes, according to their interests, ability and budget as well as that of their family. Users remix their cookbook to serve their own kitchen the best way they can. Women, due to the expectations of their gender role, gravitated towards literacies that have been highly adaptable and flexible. They had to be practical in all ways, literacy practices included.

In the following sections of this article, I begin by introducing the cookbook under discussion, using it as a case study to illustrate remix. I then define the concept of remix, explain how remix is motivated by Michel de Certeau's concept of "making do," and use examples from the cookbook to describe how a user remixes the text as they seek to empower themselves through making an original contribution as part of a community of home cooks.

The Cookbook

Clad in robin's egg blue, the laminated paper cover worn at the edges, the title declares in all-caps: "*OUR FAVORITE RECIPES*" (see Fig. 1). Compiled in 1950 by the Ladies Aid Society of Hope Evangelical Lutheran Church in Bowling Green, Ohio, this community cookbook shows much shelf wear. The printed black and white photograph of Hope Lutheran on the back cover has mostly faded, leaving an almost indecipherable image. On the side, a rainbow of paper tab dividers label the sections, from "CAKE" and "PIE" to "VEGETABLES SOUPS" and "DRINKS." Overall, this community cookbook is a simple, text-based document designed for daily use in the kitchen. The comb-binding, which helps it lie flat on the counter, as well as the laminated cover and cardstock tabbed section dividers help to make it sturdy and easy to use.

Figure 1. Front cover of *Our Favorite Recipes*

While the original user of this cookbook is unknown, the content of the added text and ephemera gives some hints. While it is impossible to know for sure, based on context clues, the owner was most likely female. The fact she owned a cookbook published by the Ladies Aid Society of Hope Lutheran Church would indicate she was either a member of that church or had friends who were; being from the same town as this group, she likely had similar Midwestern values. She was a homemaker and added not just recipes, but also cleaning tips, gardening notes, and even medical reminders. She creates a text similar to Isabella Beeton's *Book of Household Management*, an 1861 reference guide known for its inclusion of domestic tips along with recipes. I was given this cookbook by a friend from my hometown, Bowling Green, Ohio, who knew of my interest in collecting cookbooks, so I know little more of its origins than the town and the church it came from. Nor can I be sure these annotations were done by only one person (though the handwriting is consistent throughout). Considering that lack of information, all I can do is observe how this user, whomever she may have been, interacted with this text.

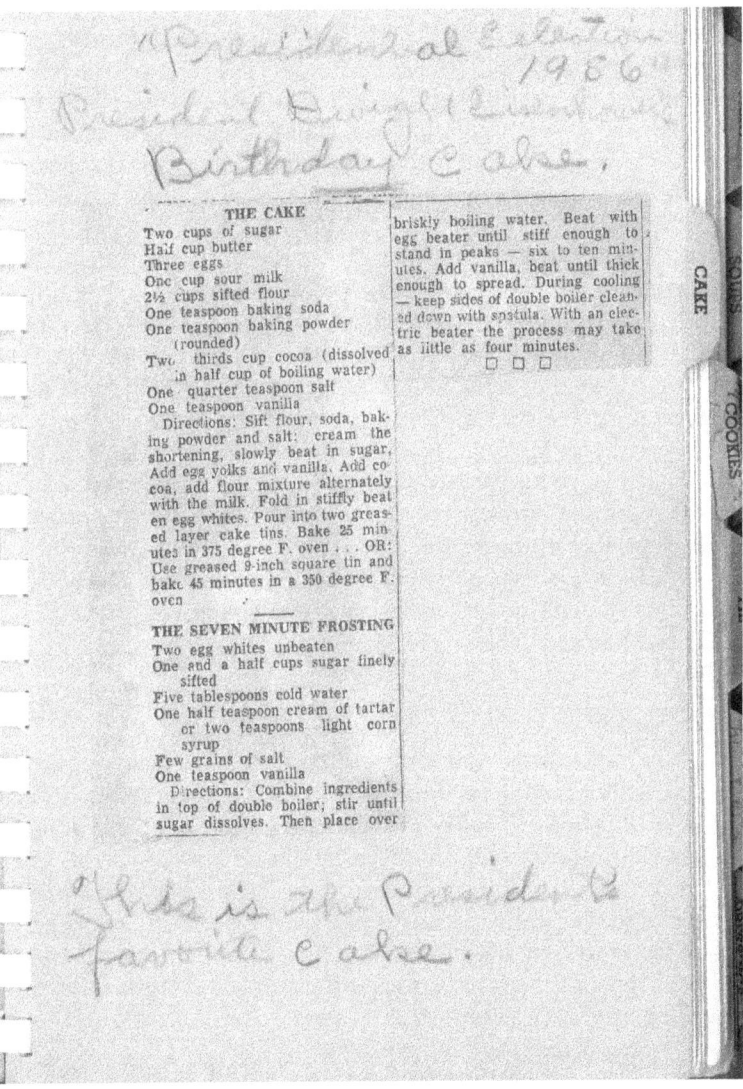

Figure 2. The front of the CAKE divider with Eisenhower's birthday cake recipe & handwritten notes

This particular copy of OUR FAVORITE RECIPES illustrates how a cookbook may be used to suit its owner, and how it can be adapted for remix. The shelf wear and stains on the cookbook are not the only evidence of its frequent usage: this copy contains many newspaper and magazine clippings, handwritten notes, and index cards to enhance the original publication. As the user remixed this text to suit her own needs, she used it as a scrapbook to collect more recipes, gardening tips, medical information, and other household notes. In the margins, in blank spaces, and even over top of existing printed recipes, she wrote, or glued, taped, and pinned the ephemera, fashioning a more useable cookbook to fit her own purposes.

Most of the ephemera are included on the tabbed section dividers located between each chapter, though the taped recipes also spill over into the printed pages as well. She uses each blank page to the limit, fitting in clippings in addition to handwritten text. In one example, on the front side of the "CAKE" section divider, a newspaper clipping of a recipe titled "The Cake" and "The Seven Minute Frosting" is pasted in (see Fig. 2). Above the clipping is a handwritten caption in pencil: "Presidential Eelection (sp) 1956" / "President Dwight Eisenhower's Birthday Cake." Below the recipe is a comment: "This is the President's favorite cake." Other pages throughout this cookbook follow suit, serving as a container for the ideas she couldn't forget. On the back of the "COOKIES" divider (see Fig. 3), words written in pencil ("Yellow [...] Freestone") are obscured by a pasted-over recipe for Lemon Drops from the September 1958 issue of *Better Homes & Gardens*. Also pasted on the page are a magazine clipping for "Strawberry-Pink Punch," as well as "Holiday Fruit Cookies," the latter of which she edits in pen with her own preferences for ingredients and oven temperature. In her process, she compiles relevant materials together first, which is her process of putting together the collection. Then, she organizes and arranges them within the text, which is her process of creating the remix. Within this cookbook, this user remixes the text to design--quite literally, in terms of visual design as well as choice of content--her own text and to best serve her own kitchen.

Remix Culture and the Cookbook

Let us pause for a moment to gain a better understanding of the concept of remix. Lev Manovich, writing in "Who is the Author?," observes "Remix culture has arrived" (8). Focusing on its origins in audio mixing, Manovich defines remix as the "systematic re-working of a source" (6-7). Lawrence Lessig goes further with his definition of remix, as he ties the rise of remix culture to the rise of Web 2.0, with the use of ranking, tagging, and sharing links on blogs in the early 2000s (85). Lessig notes, "Whether text or beyond text, remix is collage; it comes from combining elements of RO [read-only] culture; it succeeds by leveraging the meaning created by the reference to build something new" (76). Lessig's definition involves the act of combining, gathering, and juxtaposing of elements, in particular as part of social interaction. Lankshear and Knobel, focusing on digital culture, define remix as "the practice of taking cultural artefacts and combining and manipulating them into a new kind of creative blend" (1). Similar to Lessig, this definition identifies combining as having the effect of creating something new; again, a type of collaboration or collage.

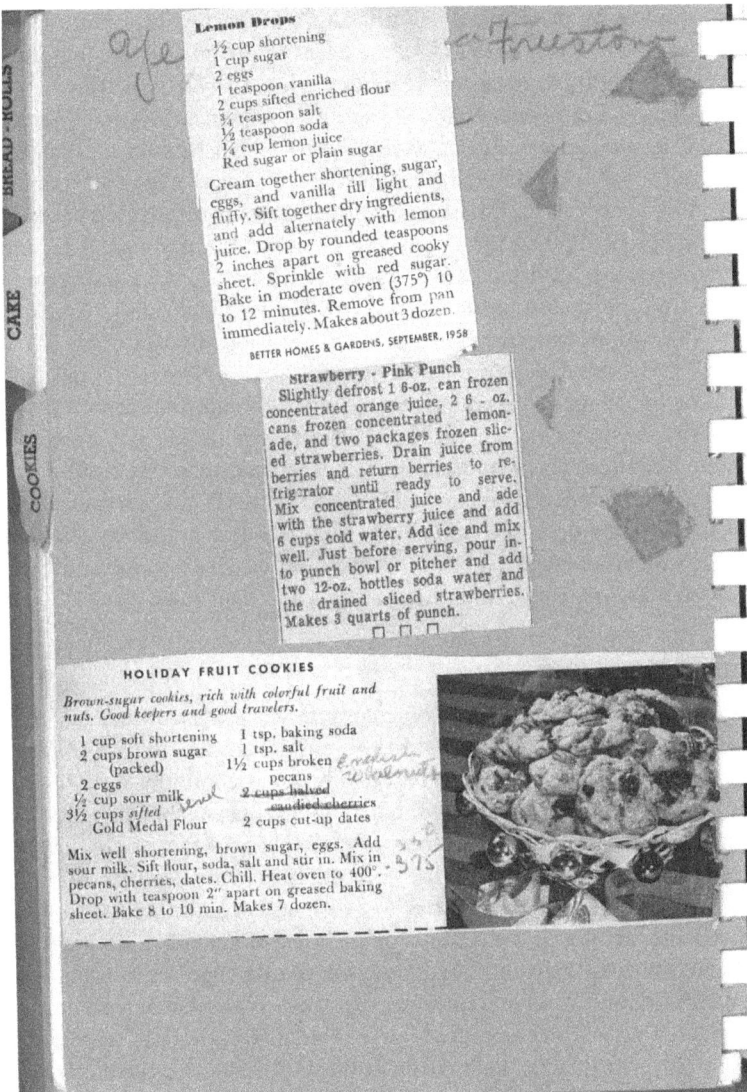

Figure 3. The back of the COOKIES divider with handwriting obscured by magazine recipes

Interpreting remix as collage is useful in an educational sense—as Lessig explains, we "learn by remixing" (81). Lessig cites scholar Henry Jenkins, who explains that the retelling and appropriation of elements from existing stories is an important step in the process by which children develop cultural literacy (81). Remix isn't just a step leading to learning, though; it is also a marker of understanding: "It takes extraordinary knowledge about a culture to remix it well" (Lessig 93). These margin notes and taped-in cooking tips in this cookbook aren't placed there at random. This act of remix is a demonstration of the user's level of knowledge—knowing what details are relevant to be placed in the best location in the text for optimum usability. This cookbook remix is also evidence of the user's future goals, including the literacy skill they want to improve, or aspect of domestic life they want to perfect.

At first glance, a remixed cookbook can look like a mess of pencil marks, paper scraps, and dog-eared pages. This messiness isn't limited to a time period, either—the 1950s-era OUR FAVORITE RECIPES illustrates the same messy habits I use in my own cookbooks. Deborah Brandt, in her article "Accumulating Literacy," writes about the present moment's "piling up and extending out of literacy and its technologies" (651). Today's readers "find themselves having to piece together reading and writing experiences from more and more spheres, creating new and hybrid forms of literacy" (651). New forms of literacy "pile up" as they are added to the old (651). Literacy "spreads out" as we are expected to use these skills in more aspects of our lives (652), with domestic life being no exception. According to Brandt, "Being literate in the late twentieth century has to do with being able to negotiate that burgeoning surplus" (666). While Brandt writes of an era several decades later than this cookbook, her observations can fit the messy literacy of OUR FAVORITE RECIPES. It makes sense then to negotiate the piling up of responsibilities and spreading out of expectations in the kitchen that women manage via remix. Women experience a practical benefit of remixing cookbooks, improving both their cooking and their lives.

Remix as Community

Cookbooks themselves are an act of community. Lessig reminds us that remix wouldn't exist without community; as part of internet culture, the act of sharing with an audience is vital. Today, sharing a link to a recipe is common: websites, blogs, social media pages, and apps are devoted to the practice. Lessig explains that "[r]emixes happen within a community of remixers … [m]embers of that community create in part for one another. They are showing each other how they can create" (77). While we might initially presume home cooks to be isolated working in their own individual kitchens, the fact is that the act of cooking is a shared culture. To Janet Floyd and Laurel Forster, recipes "exist in a perpetual state of exchange," as they are often being shared, evaluated, and modified between women (6). The kitchen has for centuries been a gendered place of community, a site of exchange between generations of women. Miriam Meyers explains: "as the communication center for the entire household, the kitchen serves as the locus of communication between mother and daughter" (37). Women's relationships are created and maintained in the kitchen, the central domestic space of the home. Even though a kitchen is often home to only one woman, it is still a social space. While the woman may cook alone, she uses skills taught to her by her mother, recipes given to her by a neighbor, ingredients recommended to her by a friend. The communality of food and the dinner table may be enjoyed by everyone, but the discourse involved in food preparation identifies a woman's community. Cookbooks, therefore, are texts that both define and perpetuate community. Kennan Ferguson notes that "cookbooks *intensify*" a sense of belonging within a community (698).

While the user of this particular church cookbook may have remixed alone, she did so within a larger culture of home cooks, gathering hints and tips from other women she may have never met. As a participant in print cooking culture, particularly aimed at housewives of the 1950s, she gained ideas about what was good, affordable, or delicious from this context, remixing it to suit her own interests, desires, or skill level. Therefore, remix is not only useful as a practical benefit for gaining food literacy, but also as an empowering benefit. Remix aids the user in gaining a voice within the rhetorical space of the cookbook, albeit privately, like a diary.

Cookbook scholars describe the space of the cookbook as an active, empowering one. Andrea Newlyn, writing about nineteenth-century manuscript cookbooks, calls them "scrapbooks of women's lives" (41). She argues that cookbooks "record women's efforts toward legitimating themselves and authenticating the spaces they inhabited, demonstrating both the diverse mediums in which female artists worked and their attempts to control their own stories, histories, and traditions" (37). Women use these texts to empower themselves and have control over their lives, at least as much as they can control within the domestic space. Sarah Walden, writing about the cookbook as gendered space, asserts, "The rhetorical acts [cookbooks] embody … -the authority to define, act, own, and subvert--expand women's abilities to actively participate in their own construction: as women, as citizens, as rhetors" (171). Women use these texts to claim their voice—albeit in a socially-acceptable form. Ferguson reminds us that the user, not the text itself, is the real creator of the content: "Cookbooks do not preach directly. They allow the cook to design her own ways of making of this community what she will" (713). It is this concept of design, the idea of user as designer, that makes remix so relevant to describing this process of marking up a cookbook, as the user is an active participant in composing the text. Newlyn describes the cookbook as a design space, saying that "[t]he cookbook is both literally and metaphorically a canvas (often containing actual drawings and sketches), a frame in which to situate and arrange forms to evoke both artistic and social meaning" (37).

Within the space of the cookbook, women design their lives. They compose their ideal home through collecting and piecing together recipes, ingredients, and tips to attain what they desire: a well-run home. This is reminiscent of when Geoffrey Sirc, in his article "Box-Logic," describes the act of composing as collecting or curating, like a designer: "It's the writer not only as selector (Duchamp) but as collector, where the choosing is suffused with desire. The personally associational becomes key criteria. A kind of idio-aesthetic or idio-connoisseurship" (118). As the home cook desires a better-tasting meal, or more efficient home, she selects and arranges texts to pursue that desire. Of these users, Sirc says, "These are artists whose material concerns are guided by their strong visionary needs, their desires to recreate the deeply felt images that excited them" (121). The home cook has a vision for her home and uses remix to progressively attain that vision. Sirc reminds us that collection is never complete (122)—just like domestic work. Thus, the home cook relies on remix to continually design her life and get ever closer to her desired ideal.

The Literacy Practice of Making Do

Individuals in culture are not passive consumers but are instead active users. This use of remix to design a more useable text is supported by Michel de Certeau's concept of "making do." de Certeau explains that in mass culture, users refashion their experiences with culture and with cultural objects as a way to have control over them and claim their own identity in a mass-produced society. Similarly, home cooks remix a recipe or, like here, even entire cookbooks to help fit their needs. This reappropriation of the text not only provides the user a voice, but also adds another layer of intertext to the recipe.

Women are especially suited to developing a literacy of "making do." Having been pushed out of the public sphere whereby access to mainstream modes of literacy is limited, women had to work with the means available to them. In order to make their voice heard, they needed to create their own literacy, their own rhetorical practices, and their own discourse. Feminist rhetorical scholarship on women's diary writing (Gannett; Carr), needlepoint samplers (Goggin), signs and banners (Carter), clothing (Mattingly), as well as other modes, have been previously argued as being rhetorical practices unique to women. Because women's literacy was devalued, women had to develop a practical literacy that would permit their communication practices to continue while fulfilling the duties of their gender role. This type of literacy needed to be adaptable, with the ability to create and sustain strong networks of women, to "affirm this female sense of self as linked to others" (Gannett 133). Thus, because of gender constraints, women developed literacy practices that relied on a wide variety of modes, creating flexible, open texts that are dialectic in nature and work to maintain bonds with others in the community.

In discussing these flexible aspects of women's texts, Jacqueline Jones Royster exemplifies how author Alice Walker engages in "writing across genres" (20). This multi-genre writing, Royster claims, evidences Walker's desire to not let her voice be defined by a single expressive form. Because Walker and others are able to work within this "fluid space," they are not limited by the boundaries set by public, male-dominated genres and in effect can ignore convention. As women have been ignored by the dominant discourse, it is not surprising that women find it easy to ignore convention, as the convention marks a style they have largely not had access to. Remix, then, is women's alternative. Using remix, women may create their own voice through textual adaptation, taking and revising a text to suit their own purposes, and create their own narrative (Mastrangelo 83).

The act of remixing is reminiscent of the commonplace book or scrapbook. Commonplace books were popularized in the late Renaissance period, though Quintilian is thought to have been the first to reference the use of the commonplace book. In a commonplace book, scholars, which in this period would have been largely limited to men, would compile useful words, ideas, and quotations together to preserve them as an aid for future speaking and writing. It was used as a way to preserve memory, as the book or tablet functioned as a mnemonic device for writing. Just like any act of compiling, it was never completed, and the user would continue to add to his commonplace book, as it was a work-in-progress. Scrapbooking, which came about during the Victorian era, was billed as a way to preserve memories—this time, specifically memories of family. Because of this focus on family and home, scrapbooking was marketed to and became a popular activity for women. Women picked up this commonplace method, collecting quotes, recipes, newspaper clippings of births, deaths, and wedding announcements, letters, postcards, poetry, Bible verses, photos, and other ephemera, for their own uses. They might put these textual objects into a bound book created just for this purpose or insert them into the pages of a Bible or diary, in a favorite novel, keepsake box, or in a cookbook.

It is no surprise that women were attracted to the commonplace book, as it was a literacy adaptable enough to fit their own lives and needs. Despite having limited access to formal education, women were able to use these commonplace books to build their own literacy skills and construct their own identities through texts. Women used the available means to create persuasive texts of their own voices. Additionally, as Theophano points out, the act of compiling a commonplace book puts emphasis on shared, not individual, knowledge, just as women come together in groups and clubs to affirm and sustain community. This act of compiling is also collaborative: the user relies on others for texts to collect, such as a friend's recipe written on an index card or a winning bake-off recipe cut out of the newspaper. This act of compilation particularly applies to cookbooks, as much of a woman's job in the home revolves around food. This act of compilation also applies to cookbooks because such a high volume of cookery texts exist, more so than texts that handle any other domestic role. Thus, cookbooks function in many ways as women's commonplace books. Community cookbooks, those particular culinary texts written by one's friends and family members, chatty and personal in tone, are perhaps the best fit for a choice of commonplace book. What other cookbook is more likely to be used, as it contains the best recipes from church potlucks, family dinners, and school bake sales? What other cookbook is closer to home and one's own foodways practices? Certainly not today's glossy-paged, magazine-perfect, aspirational-lifestyle celebrity chef cookbook. Instead, a community cookbook reflects real life, bringing together the many texts and voices of women in a group, and thus is an archive itself.

Remix in the Community Cookbook

Community cookbooks, perhaps more than any other genre of cookbook, invite remix. I chose OUR FAVORITE RECIPES because it is doubly interesting in terms of remix: not only does it demonstrate user remixing through annotations and scrapbooking, it also is a compiled cookbook of user-generated recipes, a sort of remix in itself. One way community cookbooks invite remix is in their practicality. Community cookbooks are a text built for use, the very model of "making do." Far from the glossy, full-page color photographs of beautiful dishes in other cookbooks, this is a text to be used, not browsed. Its features point to ease of navigation (table of contents, tabbed sections, index) and ease of active use (comb or spiral binding to lay flat on the counter). In OUR FAVORITE RECIPES, there are no photographs, save one of the Hope Lutheran Church of Bowling Green, Ohio, on the first page of the book.

The lack of photos or special features that might otherwise be found in professional cookbooks also point to this cookbook's frugality: this is a cookbook sold for charity. Nonprofit groups selling cookbooks like these likely didn't have extra funds for color printing or extra pages. Community cookbooks are never much to look at; they are an utterly practical genre.

Community cookbooks invite remix, as well, as they invite the user to be an editor. The reader's active participation is encouraged through the cookbook's inclusion of multiple similar recipes. Instead of editing and selecting only the best recipe for nut bread, the Ladies Aid Society women chose to include four of them, respecting the fact that some women make their nut bread with brown sugar, others with white, and still others with both. Rather than dismissing this feature as a mistake or editing oversight, these women had a purpose in including these recipes, so as to value multiple perspectives. Instead of naming a single method as the "correct" way to make nut bread, the clubwomen choose to value each woman's perspective and include a range of "best" recipes for the dish. In community cookbooks, diversity of voices is valued over what is the "best" recipe. The inclusion of multiple similar recipes allows the user the freedom to choose between possibilities, thus encouraging her to participate as an editor of the text, remixing the text to suit her own purposes.

A familiar feature of community cookbooks (and, occasionally, commercially-published cookbooks) is the inclusion of blank pages at the end of chapters or at the end of the book, in which a user can write or paste additional recipes or notes, constructing herself as a co-author of the text, engaging with community through remix. These pages, usually titled "Recipes" or "Notes," are a feature of community cookbooks that help aid in the text's development as a remix, as users will take up more space in the book to write notes or recipes, insert newspaper clippings or other ephemera. *OUR FAVORITE RECIPES* includes blank pages at the end of each section, as well as blank dividers between each section, which the user has filled with handwritten reminders ("1/4 lb. Butter = 1/2 Cup" being one example) or taped in newspaper clippings of recipes (a recipe for "Out-Of-This-World Pumpkin Pie" is pasted over an advertisement for a body shop in town, within the pages of the Pie section), or both at once (a recipe for Mamie's Pumpkin Pie, a pumpkin chiffon pie favored by First Lady Mamie Eisenhower, is pasted on the divider to the "PIE" section (see Fig. 4). Surrounding the clipping is a handwritten recipe for Elderberry Pie, in pencil, with edits over top of the handwriting in pen. Here again, the user becomes editor of the text via remix, selecting the elements that help her build her food literacy to improve her domestic life.

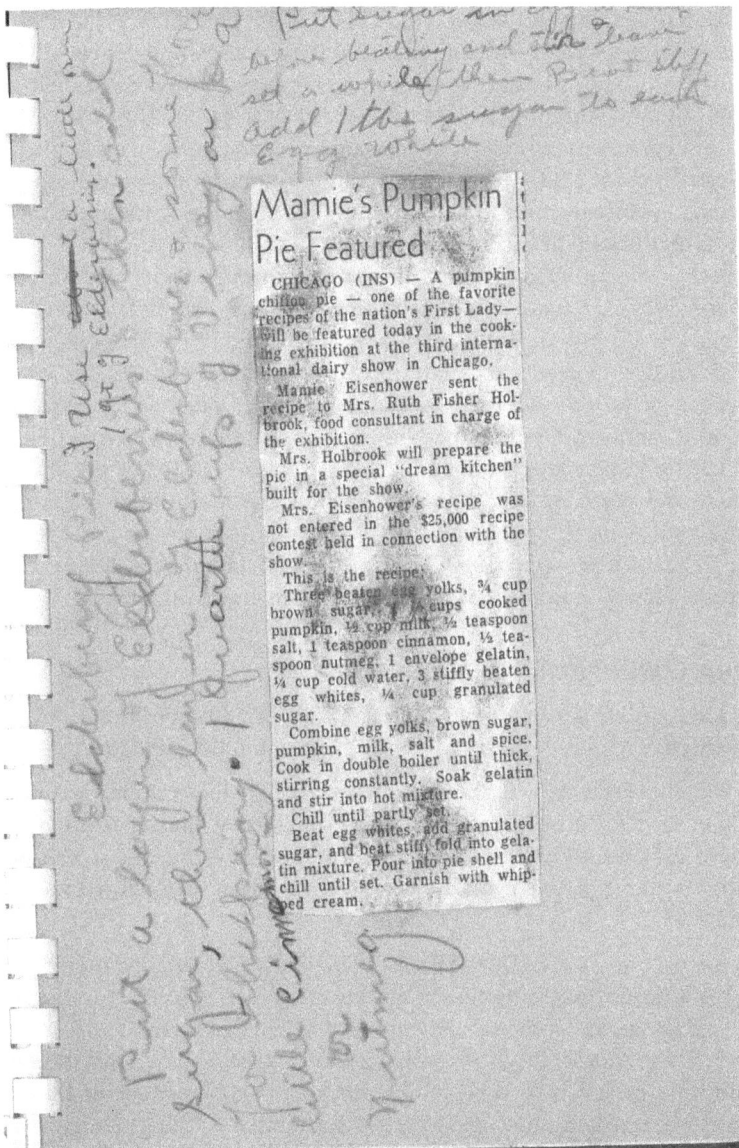

Figure 4. Front of PIE divider with newspaper clipping and handwritten text

Community cookbooks invite remix through their tone. The authors of these recipes frequently offer substitutions or alternative variations, encouraging the user to remix the recipe to suit their own taste or budget. By offering alternatives, the recipe writer's tone is one of possibility. By suggesting these options, the writer adds humility to their recipe. While substitutions or variations are a common occurrence in recipes in general, community cookbooks, authored by home cooks, seem to give these alternatives more frequently. These authors don't claim that their recipe and ingredients list is the best solution; without judgment, these authors suggest equally effective options, such as giving alternatives for butter, suggesting revisions to their recipe if margarine, lard, or shortening is used instead. For example, a recipe for Hot Pineapple Eggnog suggests serving "with grated orange peel if you like," noting that the beverage is also excellent cold. These offers of substitutions or alternatives open up the text to remix, inviting the user to make changes based on their own preferences. Here again, she is encouraged to become editor of the text.

Similarly, community cookbooks invite remix through their tone with their use of pronouns. While pronouns are usually scarce in most commercial cookbook recipes, second-person pronouns are often used in community cookbooks, in order to rhetorically engage the reader within the text through direct address. The inclusion of pronouns in a recipe indicates the presence of authentic women in the process of food preparation. Command-type instructions may be more direct (such as "Fold in the cheese") but using personal pronouns such as "I" and "you" explicitly acknowledge the women who participate in a recipe's creation and re-creation. These pronouns perpetuate a dialogue between the reader and the contributor, as if the writer were speaking to the reader personally. The use of direct address emphasizes the active participation necessary on the part of the reader to interact with the text.

The Home Cook as Remix Literate Composer

Kyle Stedman, in his article "Remix Literacy and Fan Composition," discusses the habits of effective remix composers in online fan communities. Stedman states:

> An effective remixer will show proficiency using the technical skills and tools needed for a task, an astute understanding of the expectations and generic considerations of a chosen discourse community, and a well-practiced system for internally and externally evaluating the quality of a given text. (109)

Just like the user of OUR FAVORITE RECIPES, remix literate composers are capable of using the tools involved in remixing (in this user's case, pencil, tape, scissors). They are aware of the genre (recipes), audience (family, guests, themselves), and purpose (taste, efficiency, affordability) of remixing the domestic space, and of identifying texts worthy of inclusion to achieve this purpose. Stedman observes that remixers do "inventional research": they explore texts for remix by asking the question "what could I *do* with this?" (114). For anyone who has searched a cookbook, magazine, blog, or Pinterest board looking for a recipe, this is the question in their mind. A remix literate composer searches for text with an eye towards how they will be used, like curating a collection.

Stedman identifies several skills of remix literate composers to describe how users engage in the process of remix, which are relevant here to describe how the user of OUR FAVORITE RECIPES illustrates remix literate skills. One skill he identifies is: "Attends meticulously to the details needed to achieve compositional goals, refusing to be satisfied with anything but the most effective delivery possible for a given audience" (119). Remixing the cookbook is reliant on details, as she edits recipes to suit her own tastes and improve upon them. She engages directly with the printed text and edits the recipes. For example, on page 44, she corrects a typo, from "cook" to "cool." On page 51, she adds a line missing from the ingredients list for "Ice Water Cake," including the essential ingredient of four egg whites. She also comments on some recipes, marking some with an "X," its meaning unclear to anyone other than the original user (51, 72), or writing "Good" next to the ingredients list (such as for "Rolled Oats Drop Cookies" on page 79), aiding her memory for future use.

Another skill Stedman describes is that the remixer "Is community- and collaboration-minded, following an ethic of content reuse developed along with others and attending to the demands of genre, audience, and purpose that make the most sense in a given discourse community" (119). As previously discussed, cookbook users (in particular, community cookbook users) consider themselves part of the authorship of the text, feeling comfortable writing in notes and edits, adding their own recipes or ones they've collected to enhance the text, or marking recipes that they prefer. A cookbook user becomes an editor, curator, and remixer. Often, she will write notes in the page margins. For example, on the divider tab of the "SALADS DRESSINGS" section, she writes a recipe for cranberry relish, fitting it in below and beside the taped-in recipe that takes up most of the open space (144-145). At the end of the "COOKIES" section in the space at the bottom of the page below the final recipe, she fits in a handwritten recipe for a faux meringue made with jarred marshmallow creme (108).

The remix literate composer "searches widely for inspiration, integrating remixing into [her] everyday life to such an extent that it seems natural to find new artistic and rhetorical possibilities in any area of life" (119). Remixing the cookbook is part of domestic life—those women with an interest in gaining food literacy and improving their home will attend to these skills regularly, finding relevant texts anywhere. I myself have a pocket folder stuffed with magazine and newspaper clippings, as well as handwritten recipe cards that I've collected based on my taste preferences over the years, not to mention several Pinterest boards, several Saved folders on Facebook, as well as bookmarks and notes in my cookbooks to mark my future cooking goals. In *OUR FAVORITE RECIPES*, along with the previously mentioned handwritten recipes, a wide variety of clipped recipes from different publications are taped or glued into the book, indicating an ongoing remix occurring over time, rather than a one-time edit. This ephemera includes magazine clippings from different publications, handwritten notes in multiple colors of ink, and different dates noted. On the front of the "BREAD - ROLLS" section divider alone (see Fig. 5), the "piling up" of literacy is shown in multiple pieces of ephemera as well as several handwritten notes. Pinned to the top of the divider with a straight pin, at the top of the pile, is a small note in pencil listing spices to avoid for those with ulcers. Underneath is a black and white magazine clipping for "Juicy Meat Loaf" from *Farm Journal*. Beneath that is a piece of lined paper with a recipe for "Rice Meat Loaf" in pencil. Under all of these items is the divider itself, on which is written a series of quick notes in different pencils and inks. "House Hold Hints" is at the top, about how adding salt to a candle's wick will prevent it from dripping. Below these lines is a series of "X"s as a visual divider in red pencil, plus a note about using potatoes to remove refrigerator odor, also in red. A note in plain pencil reminds the original user about a flower's bloom and a date. At the bottom of the page, in black ink, is a note about stain removal. This series of ephemera and handwritten notes indicates a process of adding to this text over time—a constant process of remix.

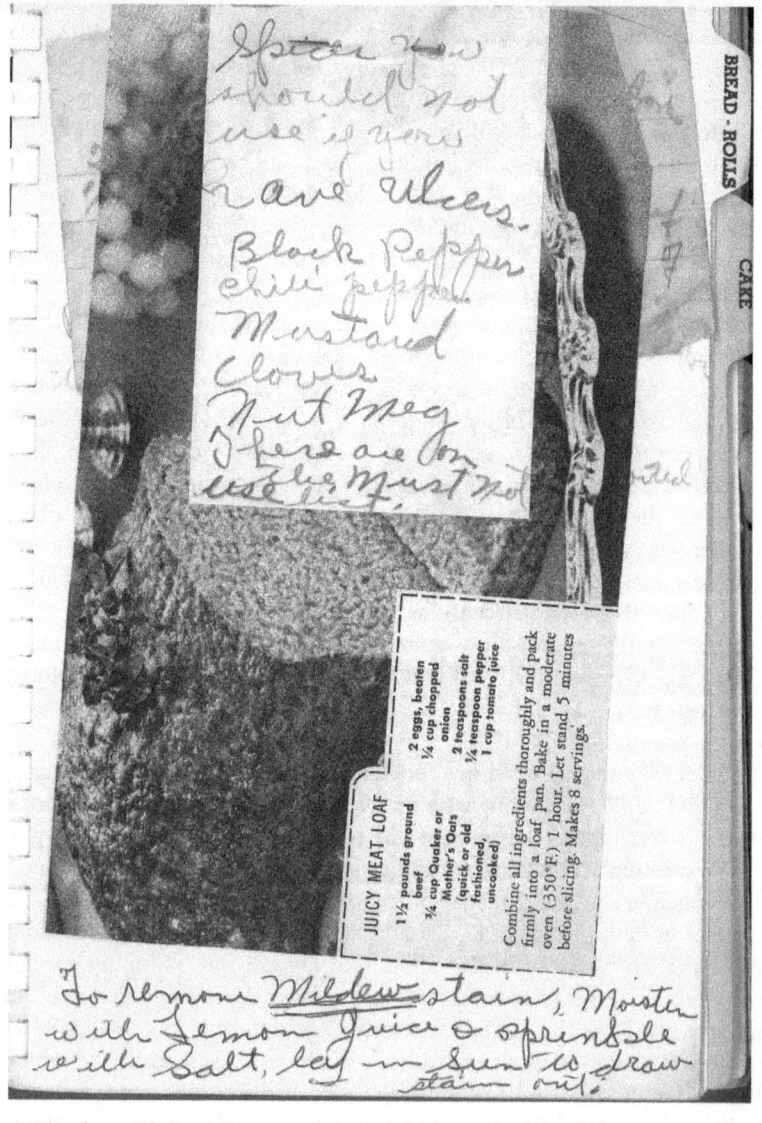

Figure 5. The front of the BREAD - ROLLS divider with pinned ephemera and handwritten notes

Stedman also observes that a remix literate composer "Accommodates various purposes/exigencies in her remixed composition, often using multiple layers of meaning that exist simultaneously" (119). She doesn't just focus on food in her remix; she attends to all relevant aspects of domestic life that she'd like to improve upon or use as a memory aid. For example, sometimes literary texts will be included. On the "CAKE" section divider, a poem clipped from a magazine, titled "Inevitable," is about children sampling a cook's baked goods, and the joy of having people enjoy one's cooking. A curious edit by the user is the change of the children's gender in the poem, writing in "Girls" below the line "Two boys hustle in for a lick" (30-31). While it may have been more accurate to this woman's own personal experience, we can't be certain. Whatever the reasoning is, this woman was comfortable enough with this cookbook genre to insert the poem, and edit it as well, to fit her own experience in the kitchen, remixing this community cookbook and localizing her experience further.

Domestic tips are also added to the cookbook. On the reverse of the "PIE" divider, the entire page is filled with handwriting in pencil, titled "Care of Azalea Plants" (108-109). Other times, she writes notes to herself, without further context: on the back of the "MISC. Canning - Preserves" section divider, above a handwritten recipe for ham salad, are the words "Pertussin Cough Medicine," circled in pencil. Underneath is the handwritten line "Course with Cold Meats" (212-213). While these phrases mean little to an outside reader, the user of this cookbook was comfortable enough with her remix skills to use this text for notetaking.

The user of this cookbook is remix literate. She meets the three dimensions of remix literacy, as described by Lankshear and Knobel: First, technical—knowing the processes and tools for remixing (14). She is competent in how and where to search to find relevant texts to add, and has the skills to do so, using the text as a commonplace book. Second, discourse—using cultural knowledge in remixing (15). Her remix choices reflect the cultural expectations of the time period, with her focus on food, health, and a clean household, helping her fit into her gender role. Finally, third: evaluative—knowing how to enhance or improve the practice/remix (15). She is able to evaluate the text as originally printed in the cookbook and make necessary edits or mark which recipes are the best, as well as know what texts need to be added to enhance the text and improve the usability of the cookbook.

Naming the user as remix literate is important here to establish the level of skill she employs in this practice. Her competency in manipulating and combining these texts to serve her kitchen in an improved way is important to observe, to define her process as skillful and rhetorically powerful. She remixes in pursuit of a better domestic life. Lankshear and Knobel cite Gee in their work, who explains that humans feel empowered when they can use tools that expand their effectiveness (15). Thus, this user remixes to gain literacy and improve her life; she also remixes to empower herself and her situation.

Conclusion: Cookbook Remix as Empowering Practice

This copy of OUR FAVORITE RECIPES has multiple discourses embedded within it—first, the rhetorical moves afforded by the collection of women's recipes printed in the book, which was used to political and economic advantage by these women, raising money and awareness for their local church. The text also implicitly constructs these women as part of a community of women cooks, sharing advice and recipes for foodways practices that best fit their likes, needs, economic access, and ingredient availability. The recipes shared are ones popular at this time among these women and are most familiar to them and the surrounding community. These recipes are practical, not aspirational—these recipes are written to be used and include ingredients both available in the area and affordable for the community. This is a text that is meant to be engaged with.

Indeed, this copy has been used quite frequently. Not only has the book been used to make the recipes from, it has also been manipulated to compile the user's own foodways practices and construct a more useable document. In this embedded discourse, she has worked outside the capitalist system, creating her own text for free by assembling a series of found ephemera into a framework suitable for her own use, avoiding the formalities of publishing or editing, and working outside of copyright rules. Like a Duchamp Ready-Made, these *objets-trouvés* of newspaper clippings and handwritten notes are arranged rhetorically to form a new meaning—this time, to aid in the improvement of one woman's domestic life. This new meaning is a material meaning, as the text's placement and physical appearance are rhetorical choices meant to form a useable text.

This new meaning is also transformative, as the process of composing often transforms the resources at hand, as well as transforms the composers themselves (Trimbur 263). Theophano explains the power of a community cookbook, saying that "women have written a place into being" (84). The unnamed user transforms this text by her literacy practice. Even though she does not use her name, her act of remixing this text helps her claim authority as a user, restyling the genre and reinventing the genre's rules as she remixes. Her collection of texts and handwritten notes, placement of such, and visual cues throughout the text function rhetorically to create a more useable text, making do with the resources available to her. Theophano describes the idiosyncratic nature of the compiled texts within a community cookbook: "Alive with the personal traces of its owner, a woman's cookbook became a talisman for those who followed" (89). This textual remix, rhetorically compiled by its owner, is more than just an assortment of ephemera: it functions as an act of resistance, allowing the user to speak her authority and expertise and craft an original text based on her own literacy practices. The text is transformed into a useable text for her own kitchen. The ephemera themselves are now not temporary, as their name implies, but instead are memory aids. Thus, these women of the cookbook and our unnamed user prove that, to paraphrase Cheryl Glenn, invisible and silent are not the same as absent (3). While they may have been silenced in the public sphere due to their gender, they were able to make do and express themselves within the space of the cookbook. Their literacy practices speak through their act of remix.

Works Cited

Bizzell, Patricia. "Opportunities for Feminist Research in the Histories of Rhetoric." *Rhetoric Review*, vol. 11, no. 1, Autumn 1992, pp. 50-58.

Block, Lauren G., et al. "From Nutrients to Nurturance: A Conceptual Introduction to Food Well-Being." *Journal of Public Policy & Marketing*, vol. 30, no. 1, Spring 2011, pp. 5-13.

Bower, Anne L. "*Our Sisters' Recipes*: Exploring 'Community' in a Community Cookbook." *Journal of Popular Culture*, vol. 31, no. 3, Winter 1997, pp. 137-151.

Brandt, Deborah. "Accumulating Literacy: Writing and Learning to Write in the Twentieth Century." *College English*, vol. 57, no. 6, October 1995, pp. 649-668.

Carr, Jean Ferguson. "Nineteenth-Century Girls and Literacy." *Girls and Literacy in America: Historical Perspectives to the Present*, edited by Jane Greer, ABC CLIO, 2003, pp. 51-78.

Carter, Sue. "Using the Needle as Sword: Needlework as Epideictic Rhetoric in the Woman's Christian Temperance Union." *Rhetorical Agendas: Political, Ethical, Spiritual*, edited by Patricia Bizzell, Lawrence Erlbaum, 2006, pp. 325-35.

De Certeau, Michel. *The Practice of Everyday Life*. Translated by Steven Randall. U of California P, 1988.

Ferguson, Kennan. "Intensifying Taste, Intensifying Identity: Collectivity through Community Cookbooks." *Signs: Journal of Women in Culture and Society*, vol. 37, no. 3, Spring 2012, pp. 695-717.

Floyd, Janet, and Laurel Forster. "The Recipe in its Cultural Contexts." *The Recipe Reader*, edited by Janet Floyd and Laurel Forster, Ashgate, 2003, pp. 1-11.

Gannett, Cinthia. *Gender and the Journal: Diaries and Academic Discourse*. SUNY P, 1992

Glenn, Cheryl. *Rhetoric Retold: Regendering the Tradition from Antiquity Through the Renaissance*. SIUP, 1997.

Goggin, Maureen D. "Visual Rhetoric in Pens of Steel and Inks of Silk: Challenging the Great Visual/Verbal Divide." *Defining Visual Rhetorics*, edited by Charles A. Hill and Marguerite Helmers, Lawrence Erlbaum, 2004, pp. 87-110.

Ladies Aid Society of Hope Lutheran Church. *OUR FAVORITE RECIPES*. 1950.

Lankshear, Colin, and Michele Knobel. "Digital Remix: The Art and Craft of Endless Hybridization." *International Reading Association Pre-Conference Institute*, Toronto, Canada, May 13, 2007. https://www.academia.edu/3011376/Digital_Remix_The_Art_and_Craft_of_Endless_Hybridization.

Lessig, Lawrence. *Remix: Making Art and Commerce Thrive in the Hybrid Economy*, Penguin, 2008.

Manovich, Lev. "Who is the Author? Sampling / Remixing / Open Source." http://manovich.net/content/04-projects/035-models-of-authorship-in-new-media/32_article_2002.pdf.

Mastrangelo, Lisa. "Community Cookbooks: Sponsors of Literacy and Community Identity." *Community Literacy Journal*, vol. 10, no. 1, Autumn 2015, pp. 73-86.

Mattingly, Carol. *Appropriate[ing] Dress: Women's Rhetorical Style in Nineteenth-Century America*. SIUP, 2002.

Meyers, Miriam. *A Bite Off Mama's Plate: Mothers' and Daughters' Connections through Food*, Bergin & Garvey, 2001.

Newlyn, Andrea K. "Challenging Contemporary Narrative Theory: The Alternative Textual Strategies of Nineteenth-Century Manuscript Cookbooks." *Journal of American Culture*, vol. 22, no. 3, Fall 1999, pp. 35-47.

Royster, Jacqueline Jones. *Traces of a Stream: Literacy and Social Change Among African American Women*. U of Pittsburgh P, 2000.

Shipka, Jody. *Toward a Composition Made Whole*. U of Pittsburgh P, 2011.

Sirc, Geoffrey. "Box-logic." *Writing New Media: Theory and Applications for Expanding the Teaching of Composition*, Utah State UP, 2004. 111-146.

Stedman, Kyle. "Remix Literacy and Fan Compositions." *Computers and Composition*, vol. 29, no. 2, 2012, pp. 107-123.

Sumner, Jennifer. "Food Literacy and Adult Education: Learning to Read the World by Eating." *The Canadian Journal for the Study of Adult Education*, vol. 25, no. 2, May 2013, pp. 79-92.

Theophano, Janet. *Eat My Words: Reading Women's Lives through the Cookbooks They Wrote*. Palgrave Macmillan, 2002.

Trimbur, John. "Delivering the Message: Typography and the Materiality of Writing." *Visual Rhetoric in a Digital World: A Sourcebook*, edited by Carolyn Handa, Bedford/St. Martin's, 2004, pp. 260-71.

Walden, Sarah. *Tasteful Domesticity: Women's Rhetoric & the American Cookbook, 1790-1940*. U of Pittsburgh P, 2018.

Author Bio

Elizabeth J. Fleitz is an associate professor of English at Lindenwood University in St. Charles, Missouri. She teaches writing pedagogy, digital humanities, technical writing, grammar, and first-year writing. Her research specializes in the rhetorical practices of cookbooks. She has been published most recently in *Peitho* on the cookbook author Amelia Simmons. She has also published previously in *Harlot*, *Present Tense*, the Sweetland Digital Rhetoric Collaborative's *Blog Carnival*, and the edited collection *Type Matters*, among others. She is also part of the editorial collective for the Praxis and Topoi sections of *Kairos: A Journal of Rhetoric, Technology and Pedagogy*.

Issues in Community Literacy

Writing Group in an Emergency: Temporary Shelter

Alison Turner

Abstract

> The author shares the challenges of facilitating a writing group in a temporary emergency shelter in the early months of the COVID-19 pandemic. She shows how within this constantly changing environment and its safety protocols, community literacy was as difficult to establish as it was vital to make available. Exploring some of the best practices in community literacy, including reciprocity (Miller et al.), fruitful forms of conflict (Westbrook), "meaningful acts of public rhetoric" (Mathieu and George), and flow (Feigenbaum), the author proposes that this challenging environment made possible new shapes for each of these concepts. This experience suggests that while best practices can guide creation of a writing group during an emergency, an emergency, in turn, can generate innovation with these best practices.

In June 2020, twelve writers and I pulled card tables away from their positions in front of a large TV showing a muted musical that no one was watching. We fit the tables into a choppy circle, between a stall that advertised *Nachos!* but whose garage door was rolled down, and a thick black curtain covering the entrance to stadium seating. We were in an event center, but we were not here to see a wrestling match or celebrate a high school graduation; instead, we wore masks and had to yell through them to hear each other. We were adapting to a global crisis that put us in strange settings with new purposes—and we were trying to write about, through, despite, or during that crisis.

In early April of 2020, the Denver Coliseum was transformed into a 24/7 emergency shelter for women and trans folx experiencing homelessness during the COVID-19 pandemic. The Coliseum served this purpose until early August 2020, when, for logistical reasons, current guests were offered shelter in a variety of other locations and men experiencing homelessness moved in. The Coliseum was a collaborative effort between the City of Denver, several agencies serving women and trans folx experiencing homelessness before the pandemic, and at least two volunteer organizations. People's "essential" needs were well taken care of in this shelter: three hot meals a day, showers, laundry, an indefatigable team of medical volunteers, and, against the odds, only rare cases of COVID-19. But what of a person's other essential needs?

As a part-time, non-essential city employee, I was offered a redeployment position to help at the Coliseum for ten hours each week, where, within commendable physical safety, I saw the human need for communion and creativity begin to sprout. I often passed by people writing in notebooks, their backs against one concrete wall or another, or arranging pages of handwritten text across card tables. Brightly colored pages torn out of coloring books grew over the concrete walls; a guest began a Bible study group on Wednesday evenings; another organized walks down to the river one night a week. And, after six weeks of deliberation, on Friday afternoons there was the Coliseum writing group.

In this essay, I share the story of the Coliseum writing group that began and ended during the COVID-19 pandemic. I celebrate this drop-in group as a space of community writing that created a form of shelter within an emergency shelter. I also explore the challenges that prevented this group from achieving the standards of reciprocity (Miller et al.), fruitful forms of conflict (Westbrook), "meaningful acts of public rhetoric" (Mathieu and George), and flow (Feigenbaum), that many practitioners of community literacy aim to create. I lead the following sections, with permission, with excerpts from a story written by one of the most prolific and passionate writers in the group, Gabriel.[1] An apocalyptic, impressionistic break-up story written from an "I" to a "you" about several forms of pandemics, Gabriel's work evokes the feeling of emergency and the search for shelter that I explore. I use these excerpts in the order in which they appear in his piece.

I. Grasping for Reciprocity: "The communication was staticky as we tried to regain the knowledge of each other's damage from the plague that rose across our lands."

As a writer and a student of community writing, I knew that the tougher the situation, the more urgent the need for writing in community—but how would people responsible for other definitions of "urgent" and "need" perceive a writing group? Seeking partnership between myself as facilitator, guests as participants, and staff as supporters, I asked guests I saw writing if they would like a group, and most said that they would; getting direct answers from staff was more complicated. I valued and wanted to create what Elisabeth Miller, Anne Wheeler, and Stephanie White call the "circular work of reciprocity" between institution and community partner (175), but how could I join a reciprocal relationship with an amorphous conglomerate of organizations and different branches of the city, everything patched together in emergency fashion to hold water as quickly and efficiently as possible? How could I communicate to the people responsible for the immediate physical safety of 300 shelter guests that we needed to add space and time into the daily schedule for a writing group? The question in an emergency setting was not how can I "give...back to the community through renewed understandings of writing" (Miller et al. 175) so much as it was *would a writing group do anything that would increase the odds of someone contracting a deadly virus?* Would these organizations value the role of writing in an emergency?

Even before navigating the possibility of reciprocity, however, I faced the more immediate challenge of identifying whom among the scattered flow chart of organizations would grant permission and provide support for a writing group. The collaborative staffing of the Coliseum meant that each organization brought their own status quo for how "shelter work" is most effective and what needed to be prioritized: I needed to determine not only who had the authority to grant permission, but also who would be open to the idea. While a colleague of mine already facilitating a group in the nearby men's emergency shelter offered generous mentorship as I tried to establish this writing group, different organizations staffed each shelter, so seeking support for a Coliseum writing group required starting from scratch. I first tried an email to several City of Denver employees responsible for the shelter's creation, an email that passed from person to person over weeks, no one believing themself to be the approving authority. None of these decision makers had ever operated an emergency shelter during a global pandemic before. None of them had thought about how a writing group might fit into an emergency shelter during a global pandemic.

After several weeks, the email chain wrapped around one particular supervisor who the handful of city and shelter employees agreed might be the one to say "yes." This staff member, a tireless woman responsible for large and small-scale operations in the Coliseum, in addition to her full time job at a day shelter, rarely answered emails and was the kind of person you couldn't catch during a break because she was never on a break—but sometimes she was in the break room. Each time I walked into the break room determined to pitch the idea of a writing group, she'd be discussing new protocols for hazardous materials with medical staff or how to maintain trauma-informed care when kicking someone out because they were found using meth. Could I really interrupt with, "Excuse me, I was wondering if we could start a writing group?"

I *did* do this, several times, and finally, six weeks after the Coliseum opened, I got the green light. I was not an academic institution, and I did not have a community partner. After approval from staff, no one checked in on the group, asked for updates, or offered feedback. I was an individual whose community partner was initially the *possibility* of a writing group, a space carved out in place and time, in which I wondered, every Friday, whether anyone would help me fill it. After approval from staff, the reciprocal relationship was between myself and the writers, a group that was ever changing.

Facilitating a writing group that was not beholden to an institutional goal offered great freedom, but with this freedom came scattered focus. I printed flyers and taped them around the arena, sometimes next to "Masks Required" posters, sometimes under extinguished "Cocktail and Taco Special!" signs, vestiges of another time. I could see that the signs would be swallowed into the concrete walls and buried in the movement of security screenings at the entrance, the long, spreading and contracting lines for meals, laundry, and showers, and an art table full of haphazard materials and information. Instead of through flyers, the first meeting was rallied together by a writer I call Rhonda, who had spent all week tapping people for the group and reminding them to come. By the time we got the tables into their boxy circle, Rhonda waved a sign-up sheet and yelled, "Come on ladies, we need to show them with this writing class that we're not just sitting around!" I had not prepared a *class*, nor did I know who *they* were or why they needed to see what Rhonda thought they did. Did all twelve writers on that first day think the group was *for* something beyond the circles of a concrete arena during an emergency? If so, what?

Reciprocity between myself and writers, without an institution in the middle to anchor us to a particular goal, required more explicit communication about what a writing *group* was than I had at first expected. There would be no certificate or credit for participating, because it was not a *class* or *program*: this was about the act of writing and possibly nothing more. After the first group, I added a sprawling extra statement to the flyers that previously provided only basic information about time and place: "This group is open to all writers regardless of experience and materials are provided. This space is for all writers to use for writing, thinking about writing, and reading the writing of others." Reciprocity during an emergency was a relationship that had to change and bend every week, but whose overall aim was to provide time, space, and inspiration to write. It was not about developing a "circular work of reciprocity" (Miller et al. 175) with a community partner, but about becoming a part of the circle that functioned as shelter. Reciprocity in an emergency was not about a "renewed understanding of writing" (Miller et al. 175) but about the act of writing as a form of renewal.

II. Coliseum Contact Zone: "Swollen tendons, and erupting nerves from capture of an illusion that a plague can replace a spouse. I hereby declare war upon all in my path to the pursuit of happiness."

On the Friday of the second group, Rhonda was no longer in the shelter and no one knew where she'd gone. Her social capital was much greater than mine, and the group was never as large as it was that first meeting. As the weeks went on, we had a steady mix of new and returning writers (see Graph 1).

Graph 1: Number of total writers (blue) and repeat writers (red) at the Coliseum writing group over the summer of 2020.

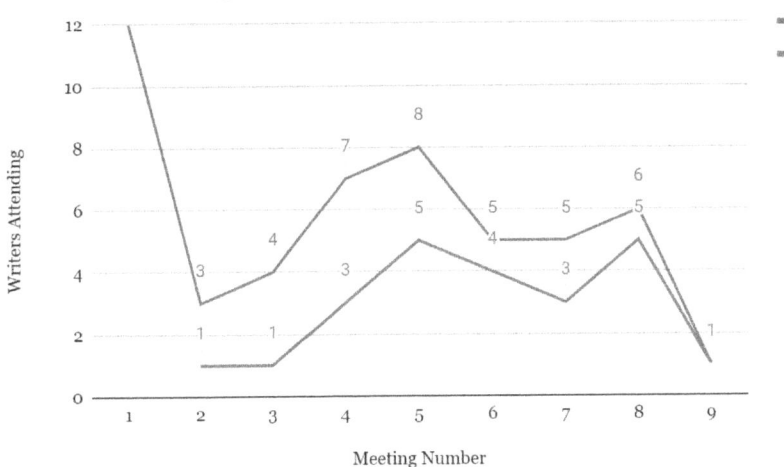

Coliseum Writing Group Attendance: Summer 2020

The challenges of facilitating a writing group whose members are constantly in motion meant that every Friday, anything could happen. Anjali Nerlekar and Jill Zasadny describe a similar experience facilitating a writing group in a transitional facility as one of "polyphonic" dialogue (42) that could become a "cacophony" spinning away from any agenda: "what about our schedule [?...]and they made us ask ourselves should anyone be in charge in quotation marks [sic]" (43). While polyphony and challenged agendas are wonderful in writing groups, this kind of motion makes it difficult to establish an identity based on what Nels Highberg, Beverly J. Moss, and Melissa Nicolas call "group rules" (2). How could an identity develop when the only constants were me and the space? Just as enacting reciprocity was compressed into an hour and between current writers, rather than spread over a semester with an institution, writing group identity was also created, enacted, and taken down in each meeting.

The "polyphony" of the Coliseum writing group came from writers ranging from those with notebooks full of poems and ideas, to a woman who produced a publishable rap about her father within three minutes then never came again, to people who, after a five-minute space of time to respond to a prompt, found one sentence and were not sure if it was the "right" one, to a woman I call Isa with long gray hair and a beanie resting on top of her head, who was legally blind and could not read words on the page. In addition to verbal invitations to people I saw throughout the week with a pen and paper, fifteen minutes before each group, a staff member announced via microphone to the 300-cot dormitory that "The writing group will begin in fifteen minutes!," a call that occasionally inspired a few people to join. Most new writers came from the lap I did around the upstairs arena directly before each class, orally tapping on shoulders: "Just so you know, we're having a writing group…." Some people came to escape and to reflect, to learn and to share; some came because they were too shy to say no to me or the friend who dragged them there; some came to pass the time between lunch and dinner.

Alongside this weekly new iteration of group norms and culture around the writing table, writers negotiated the more consistent, but also more complex, norms of the Coliseum that surrounded us. Evelyn Westbrook's celebration of writing groups as an example of Mary Louise Pratt's contact zone that "legitimizes the role of conflict and difference in literacy communities" (232) was unlikely to occur in our scattered hours together. Conflict, productive or otherwise, was more likely brought to the table than started around it. For example, once a writer began to cry while writing a fictional story inspired by a print of an R.C. Gorman painting. I was about to approach her to check in when she stood up, handed me a note, looked at the ground, and walked away. The note said the following:

> "I am unable to concentrate because [another writer present] got in my face drunk yesterday. This is why I'm so upset. I came to try not to think about my abuse. And I tried...I'm sorry."

This note tore me in two directions: I wanted the space to be for everyone, both the writer who allegedly got drunk and rowdy the night before, and the writer who is vulnerable with her own addictions and is sensitive to triggers. For the next meeting, I designed activities to allow both of these writers to continue participation, but I never saw either of them again. How could we build our own group norms when we were one of so many circles, one site of collision from so many lifeboats looking for space to dock?

There may have been other moments of interpersonal triggering around our table that were blocked by my blind spots, but the table also made possible a unique form of togetherness. Writers whom I'd only seen alone in the hallways, alone at the meal tables, alone in a sea of 300 cots, laughed and joked with other writers around our boxy circle. And though these connections dissolved into the crowded and moving daily schedules directly after the group, and I continued to see those same writers alone throughout the days and weeks, different combinations of communion returned during the next group. Some guests carried a loneliness that appeared to run deep, a developed resilience to the constriction that occurs at the center of circles within circles; the people who returned to the writing group the most often seemed to be the hungriest for community. The group seemed to give permission for a temporary camaraderie that had nowhere else to grow when living in temporary, living in emergency.

III. "Meaningful Acts of Public Rhetoric": "Stay indoors as one disease spreads from skin to organs, to blood, to mind, to protect us from another that seeks to put us in a snow white sleep."

Halfway through the summer, I learned of a local newspaper collecting Denver pandemic experiences and perspectives. The call was for essays of 1,000 words or less, with an author's photo, considered on an ongoing basis, and I wondered if some of the writers in the Coliseum might be interested. When I contacted the editor, he seemed excited about publishing work from the Coliseum, though he would not budge on the photo requirement, even after I explained that some people staying in shelters don't want to be identified.

When I pitched the publication opportunity to the writing group, only Gabriel brought back a submission. She handed me seven hand-written pages, front and back, which I typed and excerpt in this essay: the piece was over 1,600 words, muscular with pungent metaphors, and did not mention Denver. There were rats and wounds and puss, and I knew right away that it would be too gritty for a section in a local newspaper for which an author's photo was required. Gabriel's bird's-eye view soared above Denver, up high enough to see that any of us could get the virus at any minute, but only because before COVID, any of us could have gotten something else: hit by a bus, the jackpot, a section 8 voucher, an eviction notice, a first line for a new poem. Gabriel did not want to edit down to 1,000 words, anyway. And he definitely did not want to submit a photo.

When the writing group began, I dreamed of producing the kind of "meaningful acts of public rhetoric" that Paula Mathieu and Diana George discuss when sharing examples of "delivery systems" that serve as "advocacy for and by homeless people" (132). After each writing group, the way I viewed the world shifted, sometimes subtly and sometimes significantly. I wanted others living outside of the shelter to hear these writers, and, more than anything, I wanted these writers to feel heard. Mathieu and George write that the "aim" of advocacy for people experiencing homelessness "is simply to be heard, to let the public know that oppositional voices do exist" (138). But writers in the group had little interest in publishing their work, reaching wider audiences, or, for some, having any audience at all.

As with reciprocity and group norms, a form of "public rhetoric" developed that was not in the form I had expected, but that was particular to this emergency shelter. Rather than circulating to a public outside of the Coliseum, work created in the writing group found a "delivery system" within those circular walls. At the end of each session, I invited writers to make a more "finished" version of something they had written. While I had intended this to be a form of drafting, in which writers might consider word choice or organization, often it meant adding stickers or using colored pencils on the original piece. For those who agreed, I hung final pieces over closed vendor doors in two droops of clotheslines, attaching work with clothespins. The space started with one closed eye lid, then two, then a double layer on one side (see photo), and a double layer on the other. A few weeks in, writers were no longer peer pressured into hanging their work but eager to do so. One writer took a picture of her displayed rendition of Langston Hughes' "I, Too," in which writers wrote their own poem within Hughes' first and last lines, and showed it off to staff and guards.

Mathieu and George argue that the changes that can come from writing that advocates for people experiencing homelessness happen not only on the page, but also "in the writing's circulation, in how it works in the world, fostering conversation, creating pressure, and even creating unexpected allies" (144). This gallery, though limited to an internal audience of the Coliseum, nevertheless formed new alliances. By attracting not only guests, but also staff and guards, the gallery reversed the movement of circulation: writing did not go out to an audience, an audience came to the writing. Viewing this work offered a pause for people whose job it was to be on guard, to enforce the rules, and to prioritize physical safety. In this gallery, they could see the imaginations, dreams, and aspirations within the bodies they protected. These clotheslines of writing became something to grab onto, a form of lifeline to keep whoever stopped to read from floating too far adrift in this emergency, offering a moment of emergence from the sea.

IV. Grasping for Flow: "The ideas run through the vents, pumped out through water pipes of becoming someone else as they try to escape their flaws of being inhuman."

My vision for a writing group in the Coliseum before I got permission to facilitate one, and before I knew who would come or what they would write when they came, was to offer Coliseum guests a place that offered the possibility for flow. Paul Feigenbaum's challenge to community literacy practitioners that we do our "best work" by creating flow, "the condition of being so resolutely focused on an activity that one loses sense of external time and space" (33), was, I thought, all the more urgent in the Coliseum's emergency ecology. Feigenbaum suggests that practitioners encourage self determination, by which writers "feel a sense of purpose and connectedness to others" (34); enact wise mentorship, in which the facilitator might "maintain high expectations of all students..., and provide rigorous feedback" (34); and foster a listening stance, in which everyone "listens as robustly as they speak" (34). How could we enact what Feigenbaum calls the "principles" that help to create flow (34) when each Friday's group created its own norms and needs that were constantly in relationship with an emergency?

I followed Feigenbaum's principles like a North Star that only sometimes showed itself through the storm over the sea. Given the circumstances, any sense of "purpose" could be no greater than the length of each meeting, my ability to offer "rigorous feedback" was inhibited by the possibility that some writers wanted simply to write more so than to work on writing, and "robust" listening was constantly sabotaged by fans, masks, and distance. Perhaps most confounding, the safety rules that make possible shelter during a pandemic were designed against flow. There were consequences for removing a mask out of excitement, or for jumping up and hugging someone; and, as I knew from witnessing angry guests be asked to leave the Coliseum, sometimes for a few nights, sometimes for good, there were consequences for getting angry. We were set at sea without goals or requirements for the group, but we were also limited in how our bodies could express emotion. We had to keep one foot on shore while also, somehow, feel the pull of flow against the other foot.

Like the other components of community literacy, the Coliseum writing group found a form of flow that was particular to its own terrain. Flow in the Coliseum was possible only for brief moments, more so than entire meetings. Some writers were able to "los[e] sense of external time and space" (Feigenbaum 33) only for that resting moment between someone's angry yells at a guard at the entrance and when the cleaning crew came by with their packs of chemicals, spraying tables and chairs. These small, disconnected moments made possible flow that was not smooth like running water, but a form of paddling against stagnation. Flow in the Coliseum was not about losing sense of time and place but about finding a rhythm within it.

V. Conclusion: "I will bid my thanks as one plague becomes stories, myth, but the other remains to scorch our very being .... Both created diabolically to trap us in a box with a question mark stamped upon its open jaws. So you see my state of mind is to apocalyptically prepare from one plague to another."

Feigenbaum ends his thoughts on flow by challenging "engaged infrastructures," such as the Coalition for Community Writing, or, I propose, a community writing group, that they "should never be a given" (37). Practitioners, he argues, "need to be ready to tear down what they have built if the benefits no longer outweigh the costs and if the infrastructure has become an end in itself rather than a means to promoting social change, community building, and flow" (37). Once again, the writing group in the Coliseum required an adaptation to this advice: this was a temporary emergency shelter, so from the first, we knew that the Coliseum writing group would be torn down from the outside.

When women and trans folx moved out of the Coliseum, guests were notified a week in advance—staff did not find out much sooner than that. The last meeting of the writing group was three days before the move. The chaos of change and uncertainty began to crack open anew, and the arena was thick with anxiety. Only Isa came to our last meeting, this time before I could tap her shoulder. She seemed un-phased by the move. She seemed like she'd done this before.

The staff break rooms became cluttered with boxes holding the coffee urn, envelopes of masks, half-empty bottles of hand sanitizer, each box labelled with one of the three new locations across which guests would be divided. Men would move into the Coliseum one week after the women and trans folx moved out, and I considered leaving the gallery up to welcome them into their new home. But the Coliseum would be deep-cleaned, cleaning crews and security teams were being shuffled, and no one knew who would be working where: I pictured the gallery sucked into a shop vac. I had to rescue it.

I let down the lifelines of the gallery one clothing pin at a time. Some of the pieces were made by writers I hadn't seen in months, others had been put up the previous week. I didn't know where any of these writers would go next, or if I would see them again. I put the papers in an envelope and made a messy bundle of the line. I would keep all of it for later. We were still in an emergency and you never know what you might need, or when.

Note

1. This writer asked that I use the name Gabriel for this essay. Gabriel uses she/her, he/his, and they/their pronouns.

Works Cited

Feigenbaum, Paul. "Cultivating the Flow of Community Literacy." *Community Literacy Journal*, vol. 11, no. 1, 2016, pp. 33-40. *Project MUSE*, doi:10.1353/clj.2016.0012.

Highberg, Nels, et al. Introduction. *Writing Groups Inside and Outside the Classroom*, edited by Beverly J. Moss, Nels Pearson Highberg, and Melissa Nicolas, Lawrence Erlbaum, 2004, pp. 1-10.

Mathieu, Paula and Diana George. "Not Going It Alone: Public Writing, Independent Media, and the Circulation of Homeless Advocacy." *College Composition and Communication*, vol. 61, no. 1, 2009, pp. 130-149.

Miller, Elisabeth, et al. "Keywords: Reciprocity." *Community Literacy Journal*, vol. 5, no. 2, 2011, pp. 171-178. *Project MUSE* muse.jhu.edu/article/471039.

Nerlekar, Anjali, and Jill Zasadny. "A Dinosaur in My Pocket: Lessons for Teaching at a Women's Shelter." *Writing on the Edge*, vol. 14, no. 1, 2003, pp. 33-47.

Westbrook, Evelyn. "Community, Collaboration, and Conflict: The Community Writing Group as Contact Zone." *Writing Groups Inside and Outside the Classroom*, edited by Beverly J. Moss, Nels Pearson Highberg, and Melissa Nicolas, Lawrence Erlbaum, 2004, pp. 229-248.

Author Bio

Alison Turner is a recent PhD graduate in English and literary arts from the University of Denver. Her critical work appears in *Reconfigurations: A Journal for Poetics and Poetry / Literature and Culture, Reflections: A Journal of Community-Engaged Writing and Rhetoric*, and *American Archivist*. She is an emerging community-engaged scholar interested in archive-making as community literacy praxis and is a 2020–2021 Herstory/Coalition for Community Writing Fellow.

Rhetorical Curation of Patient Art: How Community Literacy Scholars Can Contribute to Healthcare Professions

Maria Novotny

Abstract:

> In the era of a global pandemic, this article claims that community literacy scholars are well poised to support challenges currently facing healthcare providers. To demonstrate this, I offer one example drawing on my work with The ART of Infertility and explain how I repurposed patient art and stories to curate emotional literacy amongst healthcare professionals. I argue that "rhetorical curation" is an innovative method that can support public engagement around stigmatized or underrepresented health experiences. I end with an invitation for community literacy scholars to build upon their expertise and design innovative public projects that contribute to improvements in healthcare.

Keywords

> rhetorical curation, emotional literacy, reflection, patient art, healthcare, infertility

The COVID-19 pandemic has evoked a pause and recalibration in our daily lives. Simultaneously, the pandemic has asked us, as community literacy scholars and practitioners, to reflect on our role as public intellectuals. In doing so, we have been asked to confront the question: *What can we, as community-engaged scholars, do to improve the health of our communities?* My response is: a lot and not just regarding the pandemic and public health. Right now, the entire country faces direct challenges in accessing not only reliable and accurate health information, critical to health literacy, but also broader challenges to having affordable healthcare. Given these threats, I find that community literacy scholars have an increasing obligation to work alongside healthcare communities that are encountering barriers to receiving care.

Such a claim, I realize, may seem rather obvious on its surface. For instance, the related sub-field rhetoric of health and medicine (RHM) has gained much scholarly interest and parallels some of community literacy's aims. RHM scholars are studying a range of literacy practices in health and medicine, such as the use of social media during in vitro fertilization (Johnson et al.) to how health information is shared between patients, medical interpreters, and providers (Gonzales and Bloom-Pojar). In their 2019 introduction to the *Rhetoric of Health & Medicine*, J. Blake Scott and Lisa

Melançon claim that rhetorical scholarship produced by RHM scholars has positively contributed to those practicing, communicating, and caring for others in health and medicine. As health and medical stakeholders begin to value the work of RHM, so too have scholars in rhetoric, composition, and communication who see potential for their research to extend beyond university walls and contribute to new locations, like that of health and medicine.

My point in overviewing the contributions of RHM in the context of this journal is that we, as scholars in rhetoric, composition, and community literacy, *also* offer much to health and medicine. Our disciplinary training in community literacies and public writing also has the potential to intervene in the inadequacies of health and medicine. While the work of RHM often offers specific methodological responses to rhetorical dilemmas occurring at health and medical sites, community literacy scholarship can expand the purview of health—to scenes and stakeholders beyond those working in the clinic or hospital. All communities, because they are created and sustained as relationships between and amongst bodies, are health communities. As such, community literacy scholars understand the need to listen and learn how specific communities are impacted by health and medicine.

Much of the reason for this is because of the methodological commitments we carry forward in our work. For instance, Dawn Opel and Donnie Sackey in their guest introduction theorize *reciprocity* as a guiding concept which informs: (1) "how we define and categorize oppression before we enter communities;" (2) "how we gain access to the lives of people outside of universities;" (3) "a commitment to community partners in the interpretation of data and in how we tell stories that are not our own;" and (4) "an emphasis on scholarly activisms, or commitment to effectuating change" (1). Their special issue aids in defining community literacy work as scholarship that not only contributes to disciplinary knowledge but also contributes to community knowledge.

Reciprocity then is a critical concept informing community work in healthcare for two reasons. One, it demands that we position ourselves and our relationships with communities in our work. In this way, it asks that we build an ethical backbone to our work by demanding transparency and critical reflection. For instance, reciprocity is built into my work because of my embodied positionality as an infertile woman. By being infertile and making that visible to all the communities I am a member of, I am embodying my own commitments to this community. When working with marginalized health communities, positionality is vital in building not just ethos but trust. Such is especially true considering how BIPOC communities have been unethically experimented on (i.e., Henrietta Lacks, the Tuskegee experiment, etc.) under the guise of advancing health research. In other words, reciprocity demands that our work cares for the very communities that make our work possible. Two, reciprocity invites a critical process to ensure that the outcomes of our work are not just shared with our communities (i.e., sharing our research article with the community), but have value and can be engaged by the very stakeholders our communities see as needing our research (i.e., developing a public engagement event for the community to be featured). In this way, reciprocity reshapes the outcomes of our work by repositioning where and for whom our work has value: no longer solely within a disciplinary realm but demanding innovation in reexamining how our work engages publics.

By situating reciprocity as a core concept guiding my infertility scholarship, I have found myself asking: *How does my work improve the day-to-day lives of the fertility patient?* To answer this question, I share with readers how I have repurposed much of my patient narrative research "data" into an exhibit educating the public and healthcare professionals about the everyday challenges of an infertility diagnosis. In this way, I see reciprocity as an undercurrent guiding the development of this project and suggesting reciprocity as a useful concept to inform future community literacy scholarship in health and medicine.

In what follows, this article articulates the need for emotional literacy in fertility healthcare and, more broadly, how community literacy scholars can incorporate literacy work in the healthcare professions. To do this, I share how I designed a patient art exhibit using rhetorical curation to facilitate moments fostering attendees' emotional literacies. I conclude with broader discussions about the role of the community-engaged scholar, the use of curation as a tool, and how emotional literacies impact experiences of health.

The Fertility Industry, Communicative Breakdowns, and the Need for Emotional Literacy

The fertility industry is booming with more people reportedly building their families using assisted reproductive technology (ART). On average, in the U.S. 1 in 8 couples are diagnosed with infertility, with 7.4 million women reporting they have used some form of assisted reproductive technology to build their family ("Fast Facts"). In fact, the Centers for Disease Control and Prevention (CDC) reports that about four million births per year in the U.S. are the result of in vitro fertilization (IVF) ("IVF By the Numbers"). Despite this large number of births, the American Society of Reproductive Medicine (ASRM) cites that on average it takes about five to six rounds of IVF before a patient becomes and maintains their pregnancy, resulting in a "take home baby." These statistics, coupled with the reality that the out-of-pocket costs for one round of IVF on average cost $12,000, perpetuate a real sense of patient anxiety and stress when undergoing treatment (Cousineau and Domar).

As such, when the patient comes to the fertility clinic, fertility healthcare providers often meet with anxious, stressed, perhaps even depressed patients hoping that ART will help them build their families. A 2018 study examining the communicative exchanges between the fertility patients and fertility providers, conducted by Robert Klitzman, found significant barriers to adequately addressing patients' needs. One reason for these communicative breakdowns relates to the emotional extremes experienced by both the patient and the provider.

Klitzman's study found significant communicative differences in how patients and providers emotionally responded to fertility treatments. While infertility patients reported feeling extremely anxious while talking with their fertility doctor, nurse, or receptionist about a fertility treatment to even the statistics of them being able to carry a pregnancy term, Klitzman reported that providers in these moments desired to maintain a sense of medical objectivity when addressing patients' concerns. Talking with fertility providers about their communicative decisions, Klitzman found that these providers relied on communicating medical facts, as they reportedly felt remarkably underprepared to address the emotional complexities of patients. As a result of these communicative tensions, many infertility patients reported feeling angry and frustrated about the lack of emotional care they received while providers felt underprepared to offer emotional support in order to resolve the patients' anxiety.

One solution to resolve these emotional tensions, proposed by the study, centers around increasing the provider and their staff's emotional literacy by providing training events. Klitzman writes that "providers are insufficiently sensitive to these [emotional needs], reflecting in part lack of training and competing perspectives and promises" (6). Fertility clinics could improve patient care by offering more opportunities to develop not just clinical skills but emotional skills as well. Healthcare professional development events centered on emotional intelligence may improve the emotional literacies of fertility providers and staff and, thereby, improve the fertility patients' experience of care. An example of an emotionally literate curriculum includes reflective learning experiences and opportunities for working creatively with the arts and humanities (Freshwater and Stickley). In what follows, I recount how I designed an emotionally literate curriculum for a pharmaceutical company using rhetorical curation as a method. Doing so, I illustrate how disciplinary training in rhetoric and composition, broadly, and how methodological commitments guided by reciprocity can offer tools for community literacy scholars to contribute to the healthcare professions.

Applying Rhetorical Curation to a Professional Development Event

In 2017, a large, U.S.-based pharmaceutical company, manufacturing fertility drugs and products, invited The ART of Infertility to curate a 1-day pop-up patient art exhibit and educational talk during National Infertility Awareness Week. The objective of the event was to emphasize patient perspectives when undergoing fertility treatment. The rationale behind this objective was two-fold. First, those working at the pharmaceutical company often have limited knowledge of the complexities of an infertility diagnosis. For instance, while employees may understand or identify as supporting the infertile patient by developing effective treatments and products for the fertility doctor, they may have difficulty understanding the embodied experiences a patient undergoes when using the treatment or product. Second, some employed at the pharmaceutical company are tasked with developing effective marketing and branding of the treatment and drug. This task relies upon an informed understanding of the user of the drug or product. Yet, those working in the marketing department may have little knowledge of the lived experiences of the fertility patient. By inviting The ART of Infertility to curate an exhibit of patient art, the pharmaceutical company hoped that the exhibit would remind employees of the complex, embodied, and often rollercoaster of emotions that fertility patients encounter. To meet these aims, The ART of Infertility drew from the organization's archives of patient art and narratives to create an event that modeled emotional literacy curriculums by using art, story, and reflection to build emotional awareness around infertility.

As The ART of Infertility began to discuss the design of the event, we decided to engage in the practice of what we call "rhetorical curation." Rhetorical curation is a practice that applies the rhetorical situation, i.e. the texts, audience, purpose, and setting, to inform the creation of the exhibit. Such a practice is locally responsive to the specific settings, audiences, and purpose of the exhibit. We saw rhetorical curation as helpful to informing the design of this project as it allowed us to account for both the complexities and nuances when representing "infertility" as well as useful to accounting for the variety of perspectives, knowledges, and experiences viewers at this employee event would have about the topic.

The Texts

The primary texts for the event would consist of patient art and stories selected from The ART of Infertility's permanent collection. Artwork was selected based upon a variety of mediums to visually engage the viewer while also considering the corresponding story with the art. Meaning, each piece of patient art is displayed with a brief artist narrative that provides context around the significance of the piece of art in relationship to their infertility experience. For instance, while the artist may choose to depict their experience via a sunflower, the narrative may explain the symbolism behind the sunflower and the artist's infertility. Given the location of the pop-up exhibit and use of tables to display art and stories, around forty pieces of art and their corresponding narratives were displayed.

Secondary texts included infertility statistics and recordings of patient oral histories, which would be presented during the educational talk. These texts were selected in order to provide context on the number of people facing an infertility diagnosis, the challenges infertility patients face, and hearing patients recount these challenges in their own words.

The Audience

As an event hosted at a pharmaceutical company, the audience included a range of employees including pharmaceutical representatives, product managers, engineers, product designers, and marketing/sales teams. Given the range of employees, it was expected that there would be various levels of comfort in understanding an infertility diagnosis.

The Setting

The event was hosted on-site at the pharmaceutical company's U.S headquarters. The talk and the exhibit space would occur in separate rooms, with the talk allowing for a more formal presentation and the exhibit space hosted in a frequented hallway to encourage employees to peruse the pieces between meetings and appointments.

The Purpose

Broadly, the purpose of this event was to offer patient-centered education in coordination with National Infertility Awareness Week. As a company that develops, manufactures, and markets several fertility drugs and products, the purpose of the event was to foster employees' emotional literacies around infertility. The idea resonated with the pharmaceutical company's mission to offer compassionate care.

Focusing on these four areas allowed us to construct a professional development embracing elements of emotional intelligence and inviting employees to emotionally engage with infertility. In what follows, I share what occurred the day of the event.

The Pharmaceutical Event

The day of the event began by setting up the exhibit. By rhetorically curating the event and selecting the pieces of art to be displayed prior to the event, we were able to quickly install a 40-piece pop-up exhibit. With the exhibit set up, we moved to the educational talk portion of the event. The structure of the talk incorporated statistics about infertility, our personal history as prior fertility patients, slides containing patient artwork and their art label, patient portraits and their fertility narratives, and even poetry recited by former patients. To be clear, the patient stories that were represented were not all success stories. Meaning, not all the stories shared demonstrated a sense of empowerment over their fertility after using one of the pharmaceutical drugs or products. This was intentional, as we wanted to emphasize statistics that contradict public assumptions that assisted reproductive technologies are often successful. A question and answer session followed the talk.

Employees were then invited to stop by the pop-up exhibit throughout the day to view patient artwork and read narrative labels that described the meaning behind such art. To encourage viewing, the company hired a barista to set up near the exhibit and offer coffee and snacks free of charge to employees. Two examples of artwork shown appear below in images 1 and 2.

Image 1.

Image 2.

One critical component of the event was to include the opportunity for employees to reflect and share their insights with each other. Wanting to gather data and measure how employees were developing emotional literacies about infertility, we set up a table alongside the exhibit with a series of notecards with the phrases "Infertility is…" and "Life without my children would be…" Instructions were placed on the table and invited employees to fill out a card and then post on a corkboard as part of an interactive component of the event. While not mandatory, the intention was to encourage employees to engage in reflective learning offered by the exhibit. This strategic use of reflection follows what Sara Horton-Deutsch and Gwen Sherwood have found as essential to developing emotionally-competent healthcare workers: reflection as key to fostering emotional intelligence and thereby enhancing emotional literacy. As such, the reflective cards were designed to help us measure the emotional impact of the exhibit. Image 3 below offers a snapshot of the feedback.

Image 3.

Using Reflection to Assess Emotional Literacy

Following the event, I gathered the reflective cards created and posted during the exhibit and later transcribed the reflective feedback provided by employees at the event. In total, there were seven responses posted under "Infertility is..." with one additional response that crossed out "Living without my child would be" to read "Living without children..." Because this response appeared purposefully hacked and placed under the "Infertility is..." section, I counted this response there. As such, I tallied a total of eight responses for the prompt "Infertility is... write on the cards telling us what infertility is to you."

A total of nine responses were received under the prompt "Living without my children would be..." The card was further explained with a prompt "Those diagnosed with infertility are faced with the possibility that they may never have children. If you have a child, or children, what would life without them be like for you? Give it some thought for a better perspective on what receiving an infertility diagnosis might feel like. Then, write it on the cards to let us know."

After transcribing each response, I used discourse analysis (Gee) to analyze each response, coding each by applying Daniel Goleman's model for emotional intelligence domains. Goleman's emotional intelligence framework was developed in the mid 1990s using the Emotional Intelligence Competency Inventory. From that, Goleman initially found five domains of emotional intelligence, which were then collapsed into four. These four domains include: (1) self-awareness, (2) self-management, (3) social awareness, and (4) social/relationship management. Within each domain are multiple competencies. Table 1, attributed from Barbara Kooker, Jan Shoultz, and Estelle Codier's emotional intelligence nursing study, illustrates the four domains and competencies.

Table 1.

Domain	Self-Awareness	Social Awareness	Self-Management	Relationship Management
Competencies	Emotional self-awareness Accurate Self-assessment Self-confidence	Empathy Service orientation Organizational Awareness	Emotional self-control Trustworthiness Conscientiousness Adaptability Achievement orientation Optimism	Developing others Inspirational leadership Influence Teamwork Change catalyst Conflict management

In the example below, I walk readers through how I coded each reflective response using Goleman's model by first reading a transcribed response and then identifying any visible competencies within each response. Take the card below in image 4:

Image 4.

This card was placed under the prompt "Infertility is…" I transcribed it to read: "Infertility is… sad & unfair." Using discourse analysis, I coded this card as falling under three of Goleman's domains: (1) self-awareness, as it alludes to a personal emotion with the word "sad," (2) social awareness, as it alludes to an orientation beyond oneself with the word "unfair," and (3) relationship management as it indicates a need to enact change. This process was then replicated for the seventeen other reflective postings found on image 3.

The appearance of the four domains seems to suggest that attendees at this event were able to develop some additional emotional awareness and literacy about their relationship to infertility. To be clear, we did not assess attendees' emotional literacy prior to the event. In hindsight, we would have liked to incorporate an activity at the beginning of the event to capture the emotional literacies of each attendee so to assess how emotional literacy was further cultivated. Nonetheless, we do believe that the willingness to share a reflection after viewing the exhibit and attending the talk demonstrates how emotionally moved individuals were. No incentive was offered to compose emotional reflections by the pharmaceutical company and thus, we believe, signals a heightened sense of emotional literacy.

Emotional literacy is defined by Claude Steiner as the ability "to handle emotions in a way that improves your personal power and the quality of your life and—equally important—the quality of life of the people around you" (1). When emotional literacy is practiced, outcomes include (1) the improvement of relationships, (2) increasing cooperation, and (3) facilitating and addressing community needs (Steiner). While all three outcomes can positively benefit the individual person, the third outcome underscores the potential ripple effects and greater impact such programs and events fostering emotional literacy may have on communities and not just individuals.

By recounting how reflection was used to capture the emotional learning occurring at this event, I find that emotional literacy is particularly important not just in fertility care but in other healthcare professions as well. All too often there is an implicit understanding that valuable humanities-based healthcare work needs to happen with the very providers who will be working with patients. Yet, this case study invites us to expand that purview and to consider the range of healthcare professions that could also benefit from our work, beyond doctors and nurses. Despite the fact that many pharmaceutical company employees do not work directly with fertility patients, many are in positions where they make decisions about how fertility patients experience treatment. For instance, while pharmaceutical employees may have less of a direct relationship with patients, their work, the design of the product, and the communication about the product has a direct impact on how patients embody their infertility. In this way, this example illustrates how community literacy scholars can critically imagine (Royster and Kirsch) new scenes and stakeholders their scholarship can reach. In the context of this article, community literacy can serve as a bridge to addressing needs in health and medicine.

A Call to Incorporate Community Literacy Work in the Health Professions

My intention in writing this article is to invite community literacy scholars to reimagine the product/s and purpose of our scholarship. Other community literacy scholars, and this journal in particular, have contributed to connecting writing and literacy to non-academic spaces including prisons (Barrett et al.; Cavallaro; Jacobi), disability advocacy centers (Konrad), and after-school health literacy programs (Del Hierro et al.). This article, however, calls upon community literacy scholars to consider their work in relationship to health and medicine. As scholars with bodies and connected to communities of bodies, the opportunities and breadth of how we may apply our disciplinary knowledge is vast. Furthermore, the daily managing of COVID-19 in our lives creates a particular exigence to apply our work to healthcare communities.

Additionally, many readers of this journal are working with community projects that result in the creation of some deliverable—whether that is creative writing, art, blogs, or performances. As writing and literacy scholars, we understand the value and insights those deliverables offer about those communities. For instance, visual artist and Conference on Community Writing Keynote Michelle Angele Ortiz explains that the public circulation of art through public art exhibits can act as "platforms for social change" (25). Ortiz's work pushes the community-engaged scholar to consider how the deliverables our communities produce, when shared with others, can be "a way to record, reclaim, and elevate these stories that connect us to our humanity" (37).

Repurposing our scholarship into more visible public arenas, though, requires a particular type of care to ensure that the very communities we seek to empower are not further exploited when we move their community work into public spaces. To help ensure that care is core to the practices moving us towards more public scholarship, Ortiz offers a series of questions to help guide community-engaged scholars seeking to repurpose and share community work with others. She asks (1) "How do I begin to shift power structures?" (2) "How do I utilize my privilege, skills, and resources as a way of providing opportunities to others?" (3) "How can I support others to have courage to share their stories, especially in spaces where they are not represented?" (37). These questions can be addressed by embracing the concept of reciprocity in our work.

And by returning to reciprocity, we must reimagine what we as a discipline come to value with our work. No longer can we remain siloed in our approach to community work: publishing about a community rather than co-creating public research-informed experience with a community. There is a difference in these approaches. My point in raising these two orientations to community work is to be more cognizant of the impact and outcomes of our work. If we truly want to improve the lives of bodies in need of care, if we see community literacy scholarship as valuable to the health professions, then we need to rethink the products our scholarship produces. In short, we—community literacy scholars—need to begin discussing how we effectively and ethically do public work, especially as we identify more non-academic spaces that could benefit from our expertise. Rhetorical curation is just one out of many methods we can draw on to improve care in communities. Believing this, I end this article with an invitation for you: *How may you practice care?*

Works Cited

Barrett, Larry, et al. "More Than Transformative: A New View of Prison Writing Narratives." *Reflections: A Journal of Community-Engaged Writing and Rhetoric*, vol. 19, no. 1, 2019, pp. 13-32.

Cavallaro, Alexandra. "Making Citizens Behind Bars (And The Stories We Tell About It): Queering Approaches to Prison Literacy Programs." *Literacy In Composition Studies*, vol. 7, no.1, 2019, pp. 1-21.

Cousineau, Tara M. and Alice D. Domar. "Psychological Impact of Infertility." *Best Practice & Research Clinical Obstetrics & Gynecology*, vol. 21, no. 2, 2007, pp. 293-308.

Del Hierro, Victor, et al. "Nutrition, Health, And Wellness at La Escuelita: A Community-Driven Effort Toward Food and Environmental Justice." *Community Literacy Journal*, vol. 14, no. 1, 2019, pp. 26-43.

Freshwater, Dawn, and Theodore Stickley. "The Heart of The Art: Emotional Intelligence in Nurse Education." *Nursing Inquiry*, vol. 11, no. 2, 2004, pp. 91-98.

Gee, James Paul. "Discourse Analysis: What Makes It Critical?" *An Introduction To Critical Discourse Analysis In Education*, edited by Rebecca Rogers, Routledge, 2004, pp. 19-50.

Goleman, Daniel. *Working With Emotional Intelligence*. Bantam, 1998.

Gonzales, Laura and Rachel Bloom-Pojar. "A Dialogue with Medical Interpreters about Rhetoric, Culture, And Language." *Rhetoric of Health & Medicine*, vol 1, no. 1, 2018, pp. 193-212.

Horton-Deutsch, Sara and Gwen Sherwood. "Reflection: An Educational Strategy to Develop Emotionally Competent Nurse Leaders." *Journal Of Nursing Management*, vol. 16, no. 8, 2008, pp. 946-954.

"Infertility FAQs." *Centers For Disease Control and Prevention*, 16 Jan. 2019, https://www.cdc.gov/reproductivehealth/infertility/index.Htm. Accessed 25 April 2020.

"IVF By The Numbers." *Penn Medicine*, 14 March 2018, https://www.pennmedicine.org/updates/blogs/fertility-blog/2018/march/ivf-by-the-numbers. Accessed 14 November 2020.

Jacobi, Tobi. "Against Infrastructure: Curating Community Literacy in a Jail Writing Program." *Community Literacy Journal*, vol. 11, no. 1, 2016, pp. 64-75.

Johnson, Bethany L., et al. "'Sticky Baby Dust' And Emoji: Social Support on Instagram during In Vitro Fertilization." *Rhetoric Of Health & Medicine*, vol. 3, no. 3, 2020, pp. 320-349.

Klitzman, Robert. "Impediments to Communication and Relationships Between Infertility Care Providers and Patients." *BMC Women's Health*, vol. 18, no. 1, 2018, pp. 1-12.

Konrad, Annika. "Reimagining Work: Normative Commonplaces and their Effects on Accessibility in Workplaces." *Business And Professional Communication Quarterly*, vol. 81, no.1, 2018, pp.123-141.

Kooker, Barbara Molina, et al. "Identifying Emotional Intelligence in Professional Nursing Practice." *Journal Of Professional Nursing*, vol. 23, no. 1, 2007, pp. 30-36.

Opel, Dawn and Donnie Johnson Sackey. "Reciprocity in Community-Engaged Food and Environmental Justice Scholarship." *Community Literacy Journal*, vol. 14, no. 1, 2019, pp. 1-6.

Ortiz, Michelle Angela. "Amplifying Community Voices through Public Art." *Community Literacy Journal*, vol. 14, no. 2, 2020, pp. 25-37.

Royster, Jacqueline and Gesa Kirsch. *Feminist Rhetorical Practices: New Horizons for Rhetoric, Composition, and Literacy Studies.* Southern Illinois Press, 2012.

Scott, J. Blake and Lisa Melonçon. "RHM's Relations And Relationships." *Rhetoric of Health & Medicine*, vol. 2, no. 4, 2019, pp. iii-x.

Steiner, Claude. *Emotional Literacy: Intelligence with a Heart.* Personhood Press, 2003.

Author Bio

Maria Novotny is an assistant professor of English at the University of Wisconsin-Milwaukee. As a community-engaged scholar, she co-directs The ART of Infertility which curates exhibits featuring patient perspectives of reproductive loss. Her research has been published in *Computers & Composition, Communication Design Quarterly, Peitho, Present Tense, Reflections, Rhetoric Review,* and *Technical Communication Quarterly.*

'I knew this was gonna be chaos': Voices Collide While Decolonizing Intersectional Injustice

Danielle Kubasko Sullivan and Mary L. Fahrenbruck

Abstract

> Events following a display of archival photographs depicting a Navajo Civil Rights march that was sponsored by One Book/One Community of San Juan College illuminated racial tensions and competing injustices in the community of Farmington, New Mexico. These events are analyzed through a paradigm, indigenous-sustaining literacy, which could benefit common reading programs that conduct literacy work in communities with populations of indigenous people or border Native American reservations and are seeking to decolonize community literacy practices

One late November afternoon, five members of the One Book/One Community (OBOC) committee hung archival photos of the 1974 Civil Rights Protests in Farmington, New Mexico, in a gallery space on the campus of San Juan College, located in Farmington. Several students stopped to look the 26 poster-sized photos selected by the committee from the Bob Fitch Photography Archive Movements of Change. The display was part of the OBOC programming associated with the committee's selection of the graphic memoir *March* (Lewis et al.), a retelling of Congressman John Lewis's civil rights activism. The committee recognized that *March* could provide an interesting connection to the 1974 Civil Rights protests in Farmington that resulted from the minimal sentencing of three white teenagers who had murdered three Navajo men and provide an opportunity for students and community members to explore this legacy and their situatedness in the community.

The photos were compelling. One photo showed protestors marching down Farmington's main street. Another depicted a Navajo man holding a cardboard sign that read "veteran WWII. Holder Purple Heart. My son was kill [sic] by a white boy on the reservation." Three of the photos depicted protestors holding upside down American flags. Other photos showed groups of Native Americans facing off with law enforcement. Onlookers identified relatives in the photos and expressed their gratitude for showcasing an important moment in local history. Others stated they had no idea that there had been civil rights protests in Farmington and were glad to learn about them through the display. One onlooker, though, was not supportive. He said that the committee should not hang any photos near the glass display located in the gallery that is dedicated to veterans. Committee members agreed with the man, citing the need to be respectful. Still, displeased, he asked why the committee was displaying the photos. (Danielle), the director of the OBOC committee, explained the historical nature of the photos and the connection to the OBOC selection. She also explained that she had obtained permission to display the photos in the gallery. The onlooker seemed satisfied and left.

The committee completed the display and many members went out for dinner to celebrate the implementation of an important event in the OBOC programming. During dinner, (Danielle) received notification that someone had removed three of the posters and two other posters had been defaced. All committee members were stunned with the exception of one who grew up in the area, and said, "I knew this was gonna be chaos."

Word of the photo removal and defacement travelled quickly, and by the following morning, campus was abuzz with the event. A campus investigation revealed that the event was two separate incidents. In one incident, the photo of the WWII Navajo man holding the sign about his son's murder by a white man had been defaced by a student who had taped a sign to it that said, "who cares if your son was killed by a white man. If he's dead, he's dead." The same student had glued a piece of paper that said, "this is racist" to another poster that depicted a group of children holding a sign that said, "whites blow away with the wind."

The second incident was committed by the onlooker who had questioned the committee as they were hanging up the photos. The man, a white veteran and college employee, was offended by the depiction of the upside-down flags in the photos. The man had removed the photos and taken them to the college dean, urging him to take action to prevent the committee from displaying the photos as they were "offensive to veterans." Citing the first amendment, the president supported the committee in reprinting and displaying the posters again.

College administrators decided to host a forum the following week to address the event because it was creating tension on campus and in the community. The OBOC committee had no input in the forum. The forum was comprised of an equal number of Native Americans and veterans and was moderated by one of the deans. Each speaker had the opportunity to state two to three minutes of prepared statements followed by a formal commenting period whereby a moderator read aloud comments or questions submitted by attendees. Approximately two hundred people attended the forum, the majority of whom were Native American.

In the forum, two white veterans spoke about the importance of having their service honored and how a depiction of an upside-down flag dishonored that service. One of the veterans said that she never felt dishonored by an upside down flag and stated that one of the reasons she enlisted in the military was because she wanted to live overseas, not necessarily out of a sense of honor and duty. One of the Native American speakers with ties to the military said she had trouble dichotomizing the issue since both identities were important to her and her family. The librarian who originally selected the photos was also representing the "Native American voice" in the forum and expressed feeling scared since she knew the student who defaced the photos because he was a frequent patron of the library. Another spoke of her family being depicted in the photos and explained that it was offensive to her that her history was not valued. The commenting time following the forum was fairly stilted and many Native Americans left feeling as though they didn't have an opportunity to express their opinions or share their stories. Several Native American campus and community members stated that they felt that the white veterans' voices were privileged in the forum, in part because of the format that gave equal weight to these voices although in the community, there were far more Native Americans who were upset about the acts of vandalism than there were veterans who were upset about the photos depicting an upside down flag. Many left feeling disillusioned and devalued and that acts of racism and violence were being minimized. There were no additional steps taken to address the act, such as an all-campus email denouncing the act of vandalism and reassurance of community members that the campus was inclusive and safe. The posters remained on display throughout November, with a security presence for much of the time to prevent future acts of vandalism.

In this vignette readers witness the value and challenges of community work around sensitive issues and events. They see efforts of the OBOC committee to provide experiences like displays around *March* that provided a forum for community voice and activism. Readers will also see the missteps and missed opportunities that occurred during the programming.

OBOC And Farmington: Intersectional and Competing Interests

Farmington, the home of San Juan College and the community OBOC program, is a conservative community located adjacent to the Navajo Nation in northwestern New Mexico. In 1974, Farmington was the site of civil rights protests following the murders of three Navajo men by three white high school students who received minimal sentences. The New Mexico Advisory Committee to the United States on Civil Rights Commission launched an investigation and released *The Farmington Report: A Conflict of Cultures* in 1975, which included findings and recommendations to address the treatment of Navajo people (*New Mexico Advisory Committee to the U.S. Commion on Civil Rights*). In 2004, the follow-up report found that substantial improvements in areas of "equal protection" had been made, but that "problems continue to persist" (*New Mexico Advisory Committee to the U.S. Commion on Civil Rights,* ii).

Community literacy leaders have discussed the value and challenges of community work and the importance of attending to difficulty in negotiating community relationships, as this difficulty is what gives the collaborative work meaning (Rosenberg). The committee realized by selecting *March* that engaging in projects and collaborations around civil rights events in a community that had been the subject of a civil rights investigation could be difficult but deeply meaningful. However, the committee underestimated the degree to which the archival poster display would illuminate racial tensions that still exist in Farmington.

When planning literacy programming, the OBOC committee attempts to host events that reflect and address different community issues, but often they have to make decisions about whose needs to privilege in the programming. These decisions are further exacerbated by the fact that OBOC committee members are overwhelmingly liberal and educated, which does not reflect the greater community of Farmington. Additionally, while the OBOC committee includes members of the Navajo tribe,

Latinx members, and whites, the committee's diversity does not match the cultural diversity of Farmington, as it is more heavily white than the community of Farmington, a fact that the committee was aware of when planning community events. The committee knew that they had to navigate competing community voices and chose to privilege Native American voices in much of this year's programming, largely because of the connections between *March* and the civil rights investigations that occurred in Farmington and because the committee recognized that many civil rights issues were still unaddressed in the community.

For this article, the authors analyze the events presented in the opening vignette. This analysis is conducted through the lens of critical constructivism coupled with tenets of racial literacy and oral literacy, a paradigm that we call indigenous-sustaining literacy, which may be useful in analyzing community book selections and associated literacy work in communities that struggle with systemic oppression and seek to decolonize community literacy practices, particularly with indigenous cultures. The analysis is also informed by both authors' power and privilege of being white and by Danielle's position as the director the OBOC program.

Avoiding the "White Gaze"

Jackson and DeLaune discuss the difficulty of imposing a conceptual framework on discussions of indigenous literacy, arguing that these frameworks for "western minds" belie decolonization, arguing that the collaborative nature of community storytelling and listening decolonizes rhetorical listening that is ubiquitous in western institutions. This approach sustains cultural knowledge of indigenous people. Ideally, Jackson and DeLaune's approach would be the default in work with indigenous communities; however, in many institutional settings that border Native American land such as Farmington, competing philosophical orientations must be navigated. For example, Danielle is white and administering a program in higher education that values theoretical frameworks. Rather than avoid frameworks altogether, we find it more useful to analyze work with indigenous communities and attempt to define a paradigm that may be useful for others in similar situations. Notably, we present a paradigm rather than a framework. A paradigm serves as a model and does not carry with it the authority nor the confines of a theoretical framework. This paradigm is potentially useful as a form of guidance for whites working to foreground indigenous voices and acknowledges the problem of the "white gaze" (Paris and Alim) and the need to hold both traditional and evolving cultures in pedagogy.

Indigenous-sustaining literacy acknowledges the critical role of co-construction in oral/aural storytelling that Jackson and DeLaune discuss. It is also rooted on the premise that colonization is endemic to western societies, the primary tenet of Tribal Critical Race Theory (TribalCrit) posed by Brayboy. Indigenous-sustaining literacy is based on the theoretical frameworks critical constructivism, racial literacy, and oral literacy, but rather than viewing it as a framework, we suggest that the paradigm can be a model to hold whites, who are often in positions of authority in communities that border Native American land, accountable for foregrounding indigenous knowledge.

Critical constructivism uses critical pedagogy as an orientation while recognizing that all knowledge is context-bound and co-constructed (Kincheloe). The focus of critical pedagogy is to awaken the critical consciousness to achieve a state of *conscientizacão* (Freire). This pedagogical focus mandates that educators like the OBOC committee have a role to guide learners not as consumers of knowledge but as people with agency who can play an active role in society, a role that has often been systemically subverted for many, including Native American communities.

Critical constructivism necessitates framing pedagogy in socio-political contexts (Freire). In alignment with critical constructivism, the OBOC committee schedules programming that we hope facilitates sharing of experiences. Using this approach required each committee member to become a critical analyst, "learning to be an emancipatory teacher, and assuming the role of a producer of dangerous, world-changing knowledge" (Kincheloe 11). When working with marginalized cultures and seeking to decolonize literacy practices, "dangerous, world-changing knowledge" necessitates creating opportunities for agency. In literacy practices, agency can come from creating opportunities to share experiences that foster voice and mutual understanding in marginalized cultures.

Critical constructivism alone is not enough to counter the hegemonic practice of erasure that Native Americans and other marginalized groups have experienced, which is why an overlay of racial literacy is necessary. Racial literacy draws on critical pedagogy and critical constructivism through the emphasis on systems of power and on social justice and agency; however, racial literacy makes the role of race specific, central, and dominant over other issues of marginalization. Vetter and Hungerford-Kressor explain that "racial literacy helps students think about the social cultural and political aspects of their experiences with a focus on race" (83). Racial literacy forces all participants of literacy transactions to consider how race shapes their identities. Racial literacy informed the committee's decision to defer to committee members who are Navajo when planning events associated with Native American civil rights, such as selection of the archival photographs; however, that put the indigenous committee members in the role of what Cote-Meke calls the "native informant," whereby a member of a racially minoritized group is asked to speak for all members of that group and dominant members of the group are absolved from examining their own values and beliefs because they referenced the "native" speaker. Aside from asking Navajo community members to select the photos, the committee did not involve Navajo community members in other aspects of the archival display and did not include additional programming associated with the display, the result of which was a failure to privilege rather than defer to Native American voice. Dialogue, even with a critical constructivist approach, was not enough to counter a legacy of entrenched racism in the community. The forum that followed the defacement was so regulated and allowed for only two Navajos to share their experiences in a two-minute time frame despite the fact that over 150 Navajos attended the forum in hopes that they could share their experiences. Cote-Meke explains that acknowledging and validating the collective history of oppression and colonization is a critical aspect of decolonization and healing: "it is important to contextualize any discussion on colonizations within an understanding of violence and how violence has permeated the daily life experience of Aboriginal peoples" (25). Racial literacy provides an avenue to combat the contradictory cultural values inculcated by a country that espouses justice and equality while systematically committing racial atrocities and should have been a primary consideration in the initial roll out of the archival poster display and more importantly, in the forum that followed the defacement.

The final component of the indigenous-sustaining literacy paradigm is oral literacy. Many Native American cultures are centered around the oral tradition; however, Piquemal explains that oral cultures are often characterized as being illiterate according to the Eurocentric notion of literacy which is focused on reading and writing. This view delegitimizes orality and according to Battiste creates a system of cognitive imperialism that "maintains legitimacy of only one language, one culture, and one frame of reference" (20). This frame of reference is especially important to consider since Eurocentric forms of literacy were frequently used to manipulate Native Americans out of rights and lands and force them into mission schools designed to obliterate their culture. While oral literacy is an effective aspect of the paradigm in that it legitimizes Native American positionality, beyond that, it has attributes relevant to all literacy workers who operate in culturally plural environments because this tradition values the narrative form and listening, which are imperative when operating in communities with competing and intersectional injustices when seeking to create generative spaces for pluralistic literacies. Paris and Alim advocate for a culturally sustaining pedagogy that sustains "linguistic, literate, and cultural pluralism" (88), and storytelling and listening are essential practices for this type of pedagogy. In hindsight, the committee should have hosted an opening event associated with the display so that Navajo community members could share their stories of the historic march in Farmington and of the racism that they experienced then and now. Not only would this have provided the opportunity for story sharing, a key aspect of indigenous-sustaining literacy, it could have offered important context to the display and potentially mitigated some of the tensions that ensued.

When Voices Collide: The Event and Intersections

The civil rights display of photographs ended up revealing competing and intersectional injustices, which the committee did not foresee. Had the committee used a paradigm such as indigenous-sustaining literacy to consider the implications of the display, they may have been able to anticipate and then mitigate issues prior to the event.

The display was planned after selecting *March*. Honoring the 1974 New Mexico Navajo protest and subsequent civil rights investigation was a primary reason *March* was selected. One OBOC committee member noted that many community members were unaware that this event had even taken place or that Farmington was under a civil rights investigation through 2004. The committee was acutely aware of the potential erasure of the event and the need to not only show the violence, a potential deficit approach, but to showcase the effectiveness of the protests that resulted in a civil rights investigation that addressed longstanding, rampant racial injustices in the community. The committee wanted to avoid the perception that Native American community members' "poverty and powerlessness are the result of their cultural and racial status and origins" (Battiste 21). Another committee member who is Navajo was a child during the events and added important historical context about the marches. She explained that although the marches began in protest to the murders and subsequent light sentencing of the white teenagers, the American Indian Movement (AIM) was active at the time and used the protests as a catalyst for advancing some of their economic agenda, to the dismay of many Navajos who felt that the presence of AIM detracted from the injustices that initially spurred the protests. Because of her knowledge, our committee asked her to play a critical primary role in the photograph selection to ensure that the photos selected were of Navajos protesting the murders, rather than members of AIM. Other Native members of the OBOC committee shared their different Native perspectives about the events, which largely stemmed from generational perspective differences, thus avoiding putting anyone in the role of "native informant." These committee members also ensured that the photos selected were culturally sensitive and appropriate for display.

The way that the forum was set up falsely dichotomized the events as pro-veteran or pro-Native American and failed to account for the possibility of multiple viewpoints or intersectionality of identities. Approximately nineteen percent of Native Americans serve in the military, a rate that is higher than any other ethnicity, and many have long familial identities that tie to military service. This fact was not acknowledged in the forum and left attendees with the impression that one was either a Native American or a veteran, failing to present Native American culture as evolving. In their presentation of a culturally sustaining pedagogy, Paris and Alim state the importance of cultivating "contemporary understandings of culture as dynamic, shifting, and encompassing both past-oriented heritage dimensions and present-oriented community dimensions" (90). This forum did not account for a present-oriented Native American culture, nor did it foreground the role that racism and racial violence play in the present experience of Native Americans. Instead of offering opportunities for meaningful dialogue and sharing of stories, voices were highly regulated by the format of the forum. Although the OBOC committee was not invited to speak at the forum and was not involved in planning it, the committee was criticized for the forum because the events surrounding the archival display were initiator of the forum. Danielle, the director of the OBOC, was put in the position of having to answer questions about the format of the forum.

The choices that the committee made to display the photos stemmed from a recognition that Native American voices needed to be privileged in the decision making around the event. In this manner, the dialogue around the photograph selection was effective in that it put race and racial violence at the center of the committees' decision-making. Recognizing that this display might make people uncomfortable, the committee was aligned that the discomfort was one of the reasons the display was needed. The committee's intentions were short-sighted, though, and perhaps had they considered the possibility that the community had not fully healed from this legacy, committee members could have anticipated chaos from the photo display.

The committee could have done much more to effectively set up the display by emailing the community and campus to explain its nature and intent. Including an open mic so that community members could discuss their ties to the historical event and connections to their present identities could have helped as well, although the people who had defaced and removed the posters might not have attended these events. Regardless, these actions would have provided an opportunity for many people to hear and learn from this history, which could have created a sense of *esprit de corps* in the community that would have fostered understanding rather than divisiveness. Jackson and DeLaune argue that story "creates resistant spaces for cultural regeneration and community building both within Native communities and beyond them" (41). Informing the community and including an opportunity for story sharing could have disabused community members, including OBOC committee members, of naivete that racial violence is in the past and forced whites to confront the reality that they are still benefitting from a colonial legacy, a fact that is uncomfortable, but necessary for community healing.

Adding a preemptive informative email and opportunity for story sharing also would have mitigated potential retraumatization of Native Americans. Cote-Meke discusses the need to accurately report and reflect historical colonial violence but asserts that it must be done with consideration for how revisiting the past can affect people who cope with racial violence regularly. The committee did consult with the Native American center, and members were enthusiastic about the display, but the onus was on the committee to consider the ramifications of the display more carefully

Marching On

This series of events taught the OBOC committee that they need to proceed with intention in situations where values collide. Although it is important from a community understanding perspective to listen to these competing injustices, it is easy for more privileged voices to subvert less privileged community voices. The paradigm of indigenous-sustaining literacy, which foregrounds racial literacy and orality, can be useful in these situations to counter hegemony in community literacy projects and has become instrumental in planning for future OBOC committee work.

Works Cited

Battiste, Marie. "Enabling the Autumn Seed: Toward a Decolonized Approach to Aboriginal Knowledge, Language, and Education." *Canadian Journal of Native Education*, vol. 22, no. 1, 1998, pp. 16–27.

Brayboy, Bryan McKinley Jones. "Toward a Tribal Critical Race Theory in Education." *Urban Review*, vol. 37, no. 5, 2005, pp. 425–446, doi:10.1007/s11256-005-0018-y.

Cote-Meke, Sheila. *Colonized Classrooms: Racism, Trauma, and Resistance in Post-Secondary Education*. Fernwood Publishing, 2014.

Freire, Paulo. *Pedagogy of the Oppressed*. Herder and Herder, 1972.

Jackson, Rachel C., and Dorothy Whitehorse DeLaune. "Decolonizing Community Writing With Community Listening: Story, Transrhetorical Resistance, and Indigenous Cultural Literacy Activism." *Community Literacy Journal*, vol. 13, no. 1, Project Muse, 2018, pp. 37–54, doi:10.1353/clj.2018.0020.

Kincheloe, Joe L. *Critical Constructivism*. Peter Lang, Inc., 2005.

Lewis, John, et al. *March: Book One*. Top Shelf Publications, 2013.

New Mexico Advisory Committee to the U.S. Commission on Civil Rights. *The Farmington Report: Civil Rights for Native Americans 30 Years Later*. 2005, www.usccr.gov.

Paris, Django, and H. Samy Alim. "What Are We Seeking to Sustain Through Culturally Sustaining Pedagogy? A Loving Critique Forward." *Harvard Educational Review*, vol. 84, no. 1, 2014. pp. 85-100.

Piquemal, Nathalie. "From Native North American Oral Traditions to Western Literacy: Storytelling in Education." *Alberta Journal of Educational Research*, vol. 49, no. 2, 2003, pp. 113–22.

Vetter, Amy, and Holly Hungerford-Kressor. "' We Gotta Change First ': Racial Literacy in a High School English Classroom." *Journal of Language & Literacy Education*, vol. 10, no. 1, 2014, pp. 82–99, http://jolle.coe.uga.eduhttp//jolle.coe.uga.edu.http://jolle.coe.uga.edu.

Author Bios

Danielle Kubasko Sullivan is the high-impact practices coordinator and associate professor of English at San Juan College in Farmington, New Mexico. She can be reached at sullivand@sanjuancollege.edu.

Mary L. Fahrenbruck is an associate professor in the College of Education at New Mexico State University in Las Cruces, New Mexico. She can be reached at mfahren@nmsu.edu.

Book and New Media Reviews

From the Book and New Media Review Editor's Desk

Jessica Shumake, Editor
University of Notre Dame

In Roxane Gay's CCCC 2021 keynote address she praised academic writing that people actually want to read, which she described as writing that "sings." As I viewed Gay's keynote with an eleven-week-old infant on my lap, I was reminded of Katherine May's spirited book *Wintering* because not only is her prose delightful to read but also because she inexplicably loses her speaking voice and slowly works to regain it through taking singing lessons. May also explores the loss of her writing voice following the birth of her son and how a "ball of ideas" would get stuck and refuse to emerge unless she went on long walks (152). Methods to work through blocks to written and vocal production have long preoccupied teachers of both writing and public speaking (Warren 179). Though May offers only provisional answers to the question of why in some seasons of life we find ourselves voiceless and in others full-throated, she does celebrate her voice's return and opines that in learning to sing again with her young son that she teaches herself and him "not just words and lyrics, but how to survive" (228). Becoming a mother in January 2021 occasioned my own metaphorical wintering or period of transition between two worlds. My wintering required preparation ranging from stocking my freezer with meals to preparing myself to give patient hospitality to the new little person who has taken up residence in my home and heart.

Now on the other side of winter, it is my hope that readers of the Spring 2021 issue will assess the reviews from Sherita Roundtree, Catherine Compton-Lilly, Cassie Wright, and Jamie D. I. Duncan as instructive guides to recent manuscripts they read and found illuminating. I further hope readers will appreciate the broad constellation of ideas these four authors explore: from racial trauma, Black freedom, and activist work to birth narratives, body literacy, and practices of reading out loud—there is much to recommend and appreciate herein. There is writing that sings.

Works Cited

Gay, Roxane. "Keynote with Roxane Gay." Conference on College Composition and Communication Virtual Convention. 9 April 2021. Keynote.

May, Katherine. *Wintering: The Power of Rest and Retreat in Difficult Times*. Penguin Random House, 2020.

Warren, Lee. "Singing and the Art of Writing." *Improving College and University Teaching*, vol. 29, no. 4, 1981, pp. 179–83.

My Life with Charles Billups & Martin Luther King: Trauma and the Civil Rights Movement

Rene Billups Baker
Peacock Proud Press, 2019, pp. 150

Reviewed by Sherita Roundtree
Towson University

Rene Billups Baker's book offers a personal and historical account of often overlooked details in the narratives of the civil rights movement: the legacies of fear and trauma faced by family members of civil rights leaders (4). The daughter of civil rights leader Charles Billups, Baker walks her reader through the untold stories of the civil rights movement in Birmingham, Alabama and her and her father's relationship with Dr. Martin Luther King Jr. as a close family friend. The genesis of *My Life with Charles Billups and Martin Luther King* derives from the disequilibrium Baker noticed between how the civil rights movement in Birmingham accounted for key figures in its success and what she knew to be true from her lived experience. She explains that Andrew Young's televised acknowledgement of her father's contributions to the civil rights movement tapped her on the shoulder and moved her to do the same, but that move to share came with its own set of obstacles. With the support of Keith Miller as well as Andrew Miller and Winston Baker (her husband), Baker began to share her story. She posits that "for years and years, [she] wasn't ready to do that because the whole experience was so painful," but she eventually started sharing her experience because "no books talk about Charles Billups' family" (1). Baker's family's and community's journey to healing and forgiveness serve as guiding principles for the events discussed in each chapter of *My Life with Charles Billups and Martin Luther King*.

Baker's book moves beyond some of the overlapping themes and tensions that members of the field might deem as inherit to civil rights scholarship to account for the narratives that have not been shared. She urges readers to disregard notions of literacy as historically tethered to aspects of reading and writing only and to see literacy as embodied and performed through protesting, demonstrating, and surviving. Baker explores how communities refigure local oppression—mediated by geographical scope—as a type of reclamation. Additionally, Baker challenges her reader to reconfigure timelines that mark Birmingham, Alabama as a catalyst for nonviolent, political unrest. She uses her own memories and conversations with family and friends to remap the narratives of the civil rights experience in 1950s and 1960s Birmingham, and includes newspaper clippings (alongside accessible reprints) and images as both evidence and affirmation of the stories being more than her own.

Chapter one introduces Charles Billups—civil rights leader, veteran, husband, friend, and father. Born in Jefferson County, Alabama in 1927, Baker explains that her father did not have a picturesque upbringing, but he was a devoted to being the change he wanted to see. However, Baker notes the dissonance between the recognition Billups received for his sacrifices to serve in the U.S. military and the fear, racism, and violence he faced when he returned home. For example, Billups became a minister of his own church, which the Ku Klux Klan burned down and, out of fear, the community never rebuilt. This led Billups to join as an associate minister of New Pilgrim Baptist Church of Birmingham. As Baker continues, she not only discusses Billups's belief in the power of African Americans being registered to vote as a countermeasure toward racism, she also describes how she wrestled with her embodiment of and fight for her father. Baker acknowledges, "sometimes I would be my daddy's mouthpiece" (9). Her book maps her journey in reconciling what it meant to serve as "daddy's mouth piece" at various stages of her life (Baker 9).

Chapter two, "We Must March to Complete Freedom" proposes a new timeline for the civil rights movement in Birmingham as starting in 1956 instead of 1963, which has traditionally been designated as the year of origin due the children's march. According to Baker, June 6, 1956 marks the "first official meeting" of the Alabama Christian Movement for Human Rights (ACMHR), a coalition of local church leaders and community members advocating for civil rights (11). Baker names key leaders in the movement as her father (Charles Billups), Reverend N.H. Smith, Reverend Ed Gardner, Reverend Fred Shuttlesworth, Lucinda Robey, Georgia Price, and Lola Hendricks. Here, Baker offers insight into some of the experiences of women in the movement both through their contributions and their traumas. She goes on to emphasize the excitement that energized the members and their organizing work, but that excitement was often counterbalanced by acts of violence enacted against the African American community in Birmingham. Reframing the narratives, nicknames often became a way of naming the violence that happened while turning it on its head as an act of survival. For example, nicknames like "Bombingham" and "Dynamite Hill" highlighted not only the frequency with which leaders such as Reverend Shuttlesworth faced bombing at home but also how fear of bombings created distrust among neighbors, through which civil rights advocates became a symbol of the threat to peace (Baker 14).

"Escaping a Lynching," the third chapter discusses the legacies of race-based trauma and the impact it had on Billups and his family's outlook on forgiveness. Baker explains that there were many close calls through which her proximity to her father put her life at risk (17). Due to the lack of media coverage in Birmingham from 1956–1960, Baker admits that it was difficult to track the progress and success of the civil rights work happening in the community. It required the ACMHR to lean on the community's hope and faith, but not necessarily their understanding. Despite the countless bombings and violent attacks against African American in all contexts, Baker noticed that no one was being held accountable for the fear that was being instilled in her or the backlash her family faced because of their African American neighbors' fear of the potential for retaliation. However, the police arrested Billups several times. Baker describes how helpless she felt when she had to bear witness to her father being arrested from their family home. She states, "I couldn't help him against the police. But he also knew I would try to help him" (Baker 18). It was through knowing—the oppressive environment they were fighting against, the goals and personalities of one another, and the risk at hand—that Baker and her father protected one another. Unfortunately, even in the moments of helplessness, like the night the Ku Klux Klan kidnapped and left scars of the harm done all over his body, Billups demonstrated a tool of resistance and healing that he always had at hand was forgiveness. Through prayer and forgiveness, Billups not only saved his life, but he planted the seed for what Baker's path to healing would require later down the road.

Social justice work takes a toll on each member of a family, not just those who actively participate or are in leadership positions; it uncovers the cost of justice. In chapters four and five, Baker explains how she and her mother battled with feelings of hate toward white people and the strain the civil rights movement put on her family's emotions and finances. However, Baker showcases how, in many ways, fear and tears had to be put on hold in order to not be left behind (36). In the case of Baker, Dr. King recognized early on that her path toward forgiveness would vary from that of her father's, to which Dr. King stated: 'I would hate to see her grow up with hate in her heart' (35). Nicknames also make another appearance in the form of both adults and children taunting Baker and her family with the label of "Jailbird," a criminalization of their fight for justice. As Baker notes, "They truly didn't understand what the civil rights movement was and why it was so important" (38). Chapter five continues on the conversation about how the often unforeseeable and intangible state of social justice can make quitting the fight appear as the best option. But as Baker emphasizes, quitting was never an option for Billups.

Chapter six accounts for the role of children in the Birmingham civil rights movement that countered the lack of adult participation due to fears of retaliation. With a significant increase of children participating in the demonstrations, a two-day demonstration in 1963 led to overpacked prisons and alternative actions for holding demonstrators under arrest. "Creating a Miracle," the seventh chapter of the book, builds on the demonstrations discussed in chapter six and documents one of the peak moments in Birmingham's nonviolent civil rights history. The chapter provides a detailed account of the 1963 Birmingham Children's March and the refusal of firefighters to use the firehoses as a weapon against the demonstrators, primarily because of the overwhelming presence of children (Baker 58). As Baker notes, "When the firefighters dropped their hoses, that decision strengthen people's resolve and their faith in nonviolence" (59). Baker highlights a type of awakening among African American adults in Birmingham to see that the movement was not an affront to their peace. Instead, the movement used peace as an actionable tool toward civil liberties. Baker emphasizes fear had little space for demonstrators at the march, but song acted as a balm for that fear. Quoting Myrna Carter, one of the women who attend the march, Baker reports, "'We were afraid of the dogs, but we were not to show fear. We were to keep walking and singing as if they were not there'" (55). The march gained national attention and forced the city to take measures to salvage its reputation in the face of the country, which led to negotiations and the organizers requests being honored. Although the agreement ended demonstrations on Birmingham, it served as the catalyst for demonstrations across the country and compelled President John Kennedy to draft a civil rights bill that President Lyndon B. Johnson got passed into law—the Civil Rights Act of 1964.

As civil rights progress became more visible in Birmingham, Baker shares how attacks against those civil rights also increased. The second bombing of NAACP lawyer Arthur Shores' family home and the bombing of the Sixteenth Street Baptist Church, which killed Addie Mae Collins, Denise McNair, Carole Robertson, and Cynthia Wesley set the precedent that African Americans in Birmingham were not free from violence in any space or at any time, including home and church. Baker recalls how her and her father were only minutes away from being at Sixteenth Street Baptist Church because they received an invitation to attend Youth Day. Even in its tragedy, these two bombings foreshadow the critical role the children played in civil rights actions in Birmingham and the vulnerabilities they had to confront. Baker expresses, "I cried because I wanted to see it myself and to learn what was happening. I wanted to help, too. Even though I was only nine or ten years old, I thought I could do anything" (73). As a young person, Baker describes feeling invincible while also having to come to terms with the reality of her constraints and vulnerability.

In chapters nine and ten, "Trading Birmingham for Chicago" and "The Worst Day," Baker calls attention to the brevity of human life and the murder of her father, alongside prolonged grief and healing. In 1966 Dr. King moved to Chicago and asked Billups to join him. Baker describes her excitement about the next chapter in her life in a new city, distanced from the one that had caused her such harm. This excitement somewhat mirrored the energy of the early days of ACMHR, but it was a new start. However, Baker reveals how her father and family's documented reputation as trouble makers—due to arrests from protests and activism—followed them to the upper Midwest and made seeking employment difficult. With time, Billups landed a supportive job and it served as a site of one of Baker's literacy experiences—learning to type and acting as her father's secretary. But with joy also came the reality of danger, the type of fear and danger through which Baker understood her growing desire to protect her father. Only a couple years after moving to Chicago at the request of Dr. King, Baker learned of Dr. King's murder in April 1968 and her father's murder in October 1968. Billups murder remains unsolved and the motive uncertain. She recalls the fear that she had in Birmingham but now it accompanied numbness and, again, she and her family feared for their safety. Baker states "Over and over my mother kept telling me that I could never talk about my father's murderer to anyone. So I didn't" (86). She became silenced by the reality of what she knew and by the fear of what she did not.

Chapters eleven, twelve, and thirteen document the puzzle pieces in Baker's life journey that allowed her to begin healing, understand her complex feelings about her father and his roles in the civil rights movement, and explore the narrative contributions that she would soon take on. Chapter eleven narrates the hurt and abandonment Baker felt after her father's murder. As Baker notes, "Back then, I wouldn't talk to people about my background and my life. When someone would ask, I would say, "Get out of my face!" For fifteen years, I hated God for taking my daddy away, so I refused to talk to God" (Baker 91). However, after meeting her husband Winston during a visit to see her sister, Baker opened up a bit more to what life had in store for her. Winston was able to see Baker as "a nice person" but "also realized that [she] didn't like white people" due to the trauma she and her family had experienced because of racism (92). Like her father, Winston was in the military, and so Baker got to travel and live in various part of the world that challenged what she considered the norm but there were also triggering familiarities. Chapter twelve revisits Baker's identity as "little Billups" and her path to understanding what forgiveness would look like within her life, which did not necessarily model her father's approaches to forgiveness. Therefore, birds, as described in chapter thirteen "A Tale of Two Parakeets" serve as a metaphor for Baker and demonstrate that recovering and healing take time.

In the final chapter, Baker describes reckoning with the belief that "God left [her] here for a reason" and her experiences growing up at the height of the civil rights movement (105). The disappointment and anger Baker felt after learning that Barnett Wright, a local news reporter, used an image of Billups and Dr. King for the cover of his book while omitting Billups from the book itself, propelled Baker to break her silence. The narratives that had been made accessible were failing to acknowledge the pivotal role that Billups played in racial protests of the 1950s and 1960s in Birmingham, and Baker identifies this moment as a shift in her outlook. Even in his passing, Baker found herself still fighting for her father again. Baker acknowledges the ways that traumatic experiences can silence voices, but they can also create bonds shared beyond conversations with her husband to a public audience. She also goes on to discuss the role of the media in the civil rights movement and how it acted as a signal of protest progress to non-local observers. Shared knowledge acted as the means for keeping the common goal at the forefront of demonstrators' minds—even though Birmingham was often overlooked for the multifaceted role it played in developing national buy-in regarding nonviolence as a tool of power and resistance.

My Life with Charles Billups and Martin Luther King is a reflection of the personal as political not only because of its inherent revisionary approach, but also because Baker was able to write herself into accounts in ways that other accounts rarely included. Baker provides storytelling that directly confronts traditional conventions concerning historical content, personal examples, and critical points of inquiry. Through personal and shared memories, Baker is able to add a significant context and tangibility to her lived experience. She calls attention to the lessons that she learned from her father about forgiveness, but her experiences with trauma required forgiveness to happen on her own terms. Baker calls for a historical weaving that allows for corresponding modes of seeing and knowing in reflections on the civil rights movement. Baker understands literacy histories as inherently intersectional and, therefore, creates an almost seamless, curricular transferability to the fields of Black studies, place studies, history, and education. Baker argues effectively for the necessity of reexamining how research on civil rights, community organizing, and political protests account for our ability to hear the voices of the civil rights movement as well as to listen for the silences.

Researching Protest Literacies: Literacy as Protest in the Favelas of Rio de Janeiro

Jamie D. I. Duncan
Routledge, 2021, pp. 251

Reviewed by Catherine Compton-Lilly
University of South Carolina

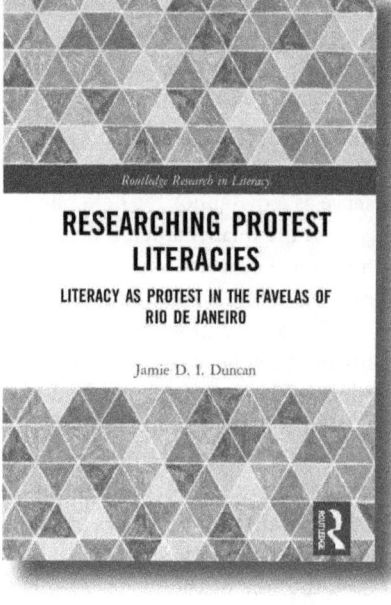

The propensity to protest is a global phenomenon. The Arab Spring, the international Occupy movement, the Women's March following Trump's election, the Me Too movement, protests in Hong Kong, rallies challenging Brexit, and Black Lives Matter share a commitment to social change that is grounded in the experiences of people. The most obvious literacy practices of protest are the signs carried by protesters; however, Jamie Duncan's book moves beyond what is readily apparent to explore literacy's layered roles in "mobilizing, performing, and disseminating of demonstrations and interrelated activities" (3).

As Duncan argues across the book, protest is a temporal process that involves trajectories of actions, texts, and people who mobilize to enact and simultaneously construct trajectories. In the book, protest literacies and associated texts are both parts of processes and moments—semiotic events that contribute to meaning construction. Through locating his research within the Maré *favela* or neighborhood in Rio de Janeiro, Duncan explores how space affects people's experiences and the mechanisms that define equity and inequity in people's lives. In America, there's the slum, the ghetto, and the other side of the tracks; in Brazil there is the *favela*. Using the *favela* as a place frame, Duncan demonstrates how time, space, and people come together to create a context for making meaning.

It is this longitudinal construction of meaning that fascinates me about Duncan's book. Literacy scholars, for example Louise M. Rosenblatt, tend to agree that meanings are constructed in transaction with texts. While Duncan's volume may seem to be about protest in one community, within a city, in a country, on the other side of the world, it examines universal flows that entail emergence, construction, and circulation of meanings through trajectories involving entwined literacy practices. Trajectories of meaning making are continual and ubiquitous; they are always happening around us. What is unique about this analysis of protest literacies is that Duncan has made the emergence of meaning visible and visceral. By attending to observable events—in this case a series of protests that can be conceived of as having a discernable beginning and ending—we witness the emergence of making meaning; observe how meanings loop in, through and across texts; and consider how sense-making translates into personal and collective action.

Through the example of protests in Maré, Duncan makes the theoretical concrete as local residents protest police violence and the gentrification of their community to accommodate the hosting of the FIFA World Cup. Duncan further explores the following five examples of protest literacies in the book: "campaigning literacies, memorial literacies, media-activist literacies, arts-activist literacies, and demonstration literacies" (11). Each chapter focuses on one of these literacies, while making connections and noting intersections across these forms. In each chapter, readers learn about a distinct but embedded layer of literacy practices that contributes to meaning making and its evolution. In chapter one, readers are introduced to Duncan's personal trajectory as they accompany him into the *favelas* of Rio de Janeiro. Chapter two provides a historical review of the Maré community and the Brazilian context. Duncan's historical ethnography is discussed and described in chapter three. Herein, readers learn about Duncan's role as a participant observer, his phases of data collection, and his "guided gaze" as residents discuss, display, reveal, and protect their worlds (55).

The next section of the book explores the literacy practices that Duncan tracked over time. Chapter four focuses on trajectories of symbols and how they are operationalized by protestors to become and serve as symbols of protest. Duncan focuses on the "Skull," which is a type of armored car that is routinely used by military police to control protests in Brazil. As Duncan aptly illustrates, this vehicle and images invoked by its name become a representation of excessive force, death, and a symbol of protest. Not only so does the word 'Skull' and associated symbols appear in political texts and news reports, but it is taken up and deployed in human rights campaigns, protest signs, and community documents. Thus, Duncan tracks the symbol and its associated meanings across time and within and beyond the community as the "Skull" assumes meanings, becoming a tool for collective resistance.

As described in chapter five, memorial literacies and their trajectories are deeply grounded in the community. As Duncan argues, memorialization of people who have been lost to the struggle serve as powerful symbols. In Maré, remembrances of an eight-year-old boy named Matheus—who was killed by military police—serves as a reminder of injustice. Agency is clearly local with commemorative protests occurring outside of the family's home and involving his mother, grandmother, and siblings. The associated texts are unpretentious and often handmade; articles cut from newspapers, photos, notes, placards, and print-outs are displayed and carried. A testament to this memorialization of individuals is the repetition and recurrence of symbols—Matheus' name and image—and the repetition and recurrence of similar atrocities. Acts of memorialization and their associated literacy practices and texts operate in chains of events and through literacy practices that are accompanied by speeches, song, and testimonials that further contribute to assemblages of protest. While located in the present, these assemblages, reference past acts and indexically reference collective and cultural memories that define communities. Thus, remembrance and protest come together through the memorialization of individuals whose stories represent collective loss and struggle.

Chapter six explores a third form of literacy involved in protest: media-activist literacy. In this instantiation of protest, residents of Maré collaborate with media agencies and journalists to raise awareness and mobilize action in response to local issues. These efforts involve the "production and publication of written 'articles', often accompanied with illustrational or photographic accompaniments" that include the accounts of local residents and increasingly involve social and online media (Duncan 107). The texts not only reach beyond local communities—sometimes involving international human rights issues—but also explicitly connect particular incidents (e.g., the death of an eight-year-old child) to contemporaneous policies (e.g., changes on community policing policies) and historical events (e.g., earlier protests, prior deaths). This linking of past and present presents a trajectory of textuality and protest that not only references retrospective patterns, but also references future dangers and possibilities, highlighting the need for social change. Thus, media-activist literacy plays a significant role in expanding the relevance of events through connections with the past, the present moment and possibilities for the future, while connecting events in Maré to global protests.

In chapter seven, resistance to the World Cup and policing practices come together and their emergence becomes a movement. This movement's consolidation and crystallization emerges through graffiti and street art, protest signs, and symbols that contribute to a "creative and transgressive political and semiotic landscape" (Duncan 141). The circulation of symbols of resistance extend beyond the *favela* through online spaces and begin to appear in more affluent communities.

In chapter eight, we join the protest. Focusing on a particular event in June 2014, readers witness the generation of texts with the protest spaces. People gather and are provided with resources—stencils, cardboard, markers, and spray paint—that they use to create physical texts of protest. Documented by local media, mass media, and participants' cell phones, the group moves along the parade route. Along the way, texts are created, negotiated, and confiscated. Following the event, images of this protest become symbolically useful for publicizing future civil actions.

In chapter nine, Duncan invites us to witness the cooling off of protest activities. In this final chapter, the people of Maré successfully prevent the eviction of a popular community museum and community center as protestors take up, operationalize, and invoke texts and practices from past protests. In the wake of this eviction victory, military police occupation ends in Maré, which diminishes a central concern of the protesters. In the months that follow, an economic recession, corruption scandals, a presidential impeachment, and an increase in far-right political influences diminish the energy surrounding local protest. As energy wanes, the movement is transformed "from a powerful anticipatory trajectory into the personal memories of people involved and the cultural memory of social movements of protest" (Duncan 215).

Given the abundance of protest movements around the world, documenting the emergence and trajectory of a sequence of protest—particularly one that resulted in discernable gains—is a valuable contribution to literacy educators. While scholars such as Norman Fairclough have discussed the circulation of texts for decades, there are few clear examples of textual tracking. Duncan, has brilliantly provided an exemplar in this book. With this in mind, I offer that a critical contribution of this book is that it extends beyond protest to the tracking of texts and meanings across time and space. Certainly understandings related to protest literacies are near and dear to the hearts of critical literacy educators, but there are many more textual flows and accompanying semiotic trajectories that could be explored by educators. What would it mean to track the emergence and use of texts that describe students (i.e., "struggling," "gifted," "traumatized"), literacy programs (i.e., "scripted," "multi-sensory," "scientifically-based"), or theoretical constructs (i.e., "anti-racist," "new materialist," "cosmopolitanism")? What might be questioned, revealed, recognized, and accomplished by applying ethnographic methods to track textual trajectories across literacy scholarship, within and across communities, and in relation to various educational institutions? These questions point to the significance of Duncan's book and its contribution to the field.

Works Cited

Fairclough, Norman. *Analysing Discourse: Textual Analysis for Social Research*. Psychology Press, 2003.

Rosenblatt, Louise M. "The Transactional Theory: Against Dualisms. *College English*, vol. 55, no. 4, 1993, pp. 377–86.

My Caesarean: 21 Mothers on the C-Section Experience and After

Eds. Amanda Fields and Rachel Moritz
The Experiment Press, 2019, pp. 256

Reviewed by Cassie A. Wright
Stanford University

Western lore often describes birth as miraculous. Upon some reflection, this makes sense. For thousands of years childbirth was the leading cause of death for women and still is for some women in certain parts of the world. Not surprisingly, maternal mortality is a key global health indicator. According to current global health data, annually 300,000 women die during childbirth, 95% of whom are from low-and middle-income countries (WHO). Seen in this context, birth really is a miracle. So too caesarean, which, thanks to advances in technology and medicine, has become much safer over time. As an intensive surgery, caesarean is not without risks, however, including increased risk of maternal and infant mortality in comparison to natural birth (OECD). There is also some evidence to caution against a marked rise in "unnecessary" or elective caesarean in many developed countries (WHO). If we take the United States as an example, nearly one in three births is now a cesarean (Fields and Moritz 56). Yet the US has one of the worst maternal mortality rates of developed countries, particularly for women of color who die in childbirth at rates around two and half times higher than white women (Faborode et al.) As the WHO report on global sexual reproductive health data notes, "timely access to caesarean section when needed is required for safe childbirth, but 'too little, too late,' or 'too many, too soon'" remains a problematic pattern in global birth statistics (WHO). As medicine, policy, and community activist groups work to curb maternal mortality rates and promote birthing justice, how we discuss, define, and legislate women's health—how we talk about birth and cesarean—matters. Perhaps, more importantly, how caesarean mothers talk about birth matters.

What can we learn from listening to caesarean mothers' stories? This is the question Amanda Fields and Rachel Moritz, both C-section mothers, posed to an online community several years ago as they endeavored to make sense of their own caesarean experiences. What started as a rich social media thread eventually turned into a larger political project to "widen the conversation around birth," intentionally embracing "the power of many voices" (xvi). The result is an edited collection that articulates a range of experiences and perspectives on caesarean often absent from broader public discourse and commonplace birthing talk. Readers of the *Community Literacy Journal* will be drawn to the collection's intimate series of first-person narratives, representing a range of authorial standpoints and identities, that explore C-section as a "potent symbol" of contemporary childbirth, and the opportunities and challenges therein (2). Reading at times like poetry, at other times like a series of meditations in the essayist tradition of Michel de Montaigne, contributing authors "spin trauma into beautiful scenes," helping readers better understand the caesarean experience one word, one scene at a time (134).

The book is organized in three sections across which essayists unpack how tropes and myths central to birthing talk impact caesarean mothers' sense of self-worth and health. Section one, "Birth Matters," explores birth as what Alicia Jo Rabins calls a foundational rite of "passage" (5). In this section especially, the twin tropes of control and failure frequently rear their heads. In "Pulled into brightness," co-editor Amanda Fields recounts how her birth plan, which originally involved a natural birth assisted by a midwife in a women's center, changed suddenly to an emergency caesarean in a hospital. Such change of plans forced Fields to confront how the "thread of control . . . is a powerful root in birthing narratives that pits 'natural' against 'medical intervention'" (26). The result is often feelings of failure. "Whenever prompted about my daughter's birth," writes Fields, "I recounted the caesarean in an embarrassed apology. Everything I said was geared toward my body's failure" (26) because "my body had failed to do a thing [it] was engineered to do" (33). Fields is not alone in these feelings. Jacinda Townsend's essay "On Becoming a Mother" recalls how, despite "split open like a hog" (11), she still "did not actually feel that [she] had become a mother" (12). Perhaps, muses Townsend, it's because she had been "handed down a cosmology of mothering that did not include one's body *failing* to do its natural job" (12); or perhaps it's because "we fetishize the birth experience" (17), creating impossible standards and reducing birth to clichés that ignore the lived realities and complexities of the scene.

And while there is grief, there is also gratitude woven into the tapestry of section one. In "My Unnatural Birth Stories," Rabins notes how it's "[i]mportant to be grateful for the knife and the anesthesia when they can save your baby's life, or your own" (6–7). After surviving the trauma of having lost her first son during childbirth because "a doctor tiptoes around the 'caesarean' word until there is no chance" (42), Robin Schoenthaler's essay "Wounds" rejoices at having given birth to her second son, Kenzie, by a caesarean that she describes as "stately, majestic, simple" (44). "Wounds," among other essays in the collection, is a reminder that "[a] C-section for us meant life. His life. My life" (Schoenthaler 42).

In part two of the collection, "At the Threshold," essayists explore how "intersecting webs of identity, culture, and meaning" inform experiencing caesarean (57). As a preface to the section, Fields and Moritz recount important statistics around caesarean, helping readers understand the necessity of the practice even as we may question its increasing prominence in Western medicine. Essays in this section help readers see that sometimes C-section is the best and only choice; often this is accomplished by problematizing tropes of martyrdom and self-sacrifice tied to birthing lore. In "I Didn't Dream of Pregnancy," Tyrese Coleman asks readers to consider why "we birthing parents feel we have to sacrifice ourselves and our bodies for the sake of our children? . . . A vaginal birth says, 'Here, I give myself up for you.' Just the beginning of such sacrifices that will happen throughout the course of our lives with our children" (84). Resisting such sacrificial rhetoric, however, Coleman forwards the "unpopular opinions" that "C-section is an act of empowerment" (84), and "childbirth is trauma" (86). Likewise, in her daring essay "A Thin Blue Wall," Jen Fitzgerald, a survivor of child abuse, notes how her own childhood trauma leads her to resist notions of motherly martyrdom. Echoing Fields' critique of the illusion of control and Coleman's insight that birth can be traumatic, Fitzgerald recounts how she asked her husband to choose her over the baby. "It was the last bit of control I had to relinquish," she writes (79). This too is a threshold, one about family and loyalty and femininity and martyrdom; and it is taboo terrain, turning notions of feminine virtue and sacrificial birth on their heads as Fitzgerald invites readers to see the caesarean mother as more than just a womb, a vehicle for delivering another life into the world. It is a challenging, but necessary, read.

Along with critiques of self-sacrifice are equally challenging acknowledgements of loss in section two. For Daniela Montoya-Barthelemy, her emergency caesarean birth—as a result of a rare disease—meant confronting suddenly and violently the "whitewash[ing]" of birth that explained for her how she "could be so ignorant" of her own "Latinx family's traditions in the birth room" (121). This confrontation left Montoya-Barthelemy feeling "blessed and cursed" and "still holding grief" (128). Likewise, co-editor Rachel Moritz, in recounting her birthing story as a queer parent whose son spent his first days in a NICU as a result of a lung infection from a delayed caesarean, notes how she is "struck by how much of Finn's birth story still resonates with loss. The loss I encountered while trying to bring someone new into the world, which was ultimately a gain. How some losses continue; they're part of the story" (Moritz 142).

Stories in the third section, "Beyond Postpartum," reflect on the extensive recovery, physical and psychological, that follows birth. Here, perhaps more than in other sections, essayists mine the metaphoric potential of the scar. For LaToya Jordan, her "zigzag scar" symbolizes how her "plans have changed" (161). In her essay "Zig Zag Mother," Jordan notes her alarm at reading "article after article about Black women dying at higher rates in childbirth" (162). For Jordan,

> These statistics and inequities and memories are life and death possibilities . . . So I asked myself, . . . Was bringing another life into this world that important to me that I would risk my own health and life? Was I willing to die for an imagined human being when I already had a family? The answer is a resounding *No*. But it's not an easy no. (163)

If Jordan's scar is about plans changed, for Lisa Solod, the scar is about plans confirmed and "evidence of [her] motherhood" (197). For Susan Hoffman, the scar represents a kind of roadmap to motherhood, which "began along those lines" (223).

Too, there are the psychological scars. Sara Bates' essay "When Expectations Go Up in Flames" is a frank look at the psychological wounds we tragically inflict on each other in the aftermath of birth. She warns of the dangers of digital mommy wars, "cheap shots and rarely face-to-face" that play out over the comment sections in online birthing articles that too easily demonize "C-section monsters," throwing gasoline on the flames of failure already burning for too many caesarean mothers (183). And in a timely essay about postpartum depression, Misty Urban's "C-section Blues" invites us to humanize all mothers, caesarean and otherwise, reminding readers that,

> The costs of pregnancy and motherhood to a women's physical, emotional, and mental well-being are rarely reckoned with in the broader public conversation, and, if glanced at, are expected to be cheerfully paid as fees for the Sacred Honor of Nourishing Life. . . . It's not one big long serotonin high for everybody. We make sacrifices. We emerge with scars. (211)

As a book focused on women's bodies and birth, *My Caesarean* broadly falls within the domain of body literacy and New Literacy Studies. The collection is interested in understanding body literacy as a social practice that occurs within situated discourse communities. *My Caesarean* is a roadmap to the intricacies of body literacy as a pivotal threshold in every mother's life, and the way birthing talk functions as a social practice with real consequences for mothers. Editors Fields and Moritz invite essayists to share their stories, without reservation, in ways that trouble the tropes that unnecessarily fuel the "mommy wars" endemic to birthing lore. Importantly, *My Caesarean* reads against the grain while expanding the boundaries of birthing talk and early parenthood.

To these ends, *My Caesarean* does a remarkable job in representing the diverse community of people that experience cesarean in diverse ways. Stories illuminate experiences of first-time caesarean mothers, second-time mothers with first-time caesareans; emergency and elective caesarean; Vbacs (vaginal births after cesarean), Cbacs (cesarean births after cesarean), and delayed caesarean. Contributing essayists also represent a diverse set of identities and standpoints from straight to queer mothers, single mothers to mothers in nuclear families, white mothers to multiracial mothers and mothers of color, adopted women-cum-mothers; mothers writing fresh from the wounds of birth and mothers reflecting with a vision that is tempered by time. Written with invaluable frankness and honesty, the stories, woven together, reveal a kaleidoscopic tapestry of cesarean. This feat should not be underestimated. The collection is remarkably balanced, which is one aspect of what makes *My Caesarean* so valuable: it refuses to commit to a singular narrative, argument, or judgment about the practice and its subjects. Instead, Fields and Moritz hold space for the essays to unfold alongside one another in uncomfortable contradiction and, at times, in a series of staggering points and counterpoints. If the intention of the collection is to offer salve to caesarean mothers, Fields and Moritz resist the temptation to prescribe a singular way to do so: there are moments when authors grieve laid next to essays where mothers rejoice in the empowerment afforded by C-section. All perspectives are given credence, and readers are invited to find their home within the collection's many potential meanings. It's a breathtaking range of experience and perspective that is done more to honestly capture the complexity of the topic of caesarean birth than to score diversity points. The result is a raw, honest, and nuanced exposition that renders our understanding of cesarean, its mothers, and motherhood in a more complex and interesting light.

As a collection that widens the field of how and why we talk about birth and women's bodies, *My Caesarean* makes for an informative addition to discussions of body literacy and women's health. Programs and departments of rhetoric, gender studies, and public health will find value in reading excerpts, essays, or the entire book in preparation for discussions of the relationship between birthing discussions and the judgments and policies that legislate women's health. The collection also prompts valuable discussions that interrogate the rhetorics of failure and sacrifice that all too often coexist alongside birth stories and make it too easy for judgment and misunderstanding to occur. Said differently, this collection supports readers to become, as Rabins says, "less preachy, more sensitive to the tone of conversation" (9).

In sum, *My Caesarean* is a beautifully measured look at the grace and grief that accompany cesarean as told from the diverse perspectives and identities of caesarean mothers themselves. Anchored in empathic and reflective narrative inquiry, the collection is deftly curated by two women who risk much in sharing their own stories in an effort to hold space for cesarean women to find community and healing one essay at a time.

Works Cited

Faborode, Oladeji, et al. "Reducing Maternal Mortality Among Women of Color." *Avalere Health*, 5 Jan. 2021, www.avalere.com/insights/reducing-maternal-mortality-among-women-of-color. Accessed 30 March 2021.

OECD. "Caesarean Sections." *Health at a Glance 2019*. https://www.oecd-ilibrary.org/sites/fa1f7281-en/index.html?itemId=/content/component/fa1f7281-en. Accessed 30 March 2021.

WHO. "Deaths from Caesarean Sections 100 Times Higher in Developing Countries: Global Study." *World Health Organization*, 29 Mar. 2019, www.who.int/reproductivehealth/death-from-caesarean-sections/en/. Accessed 26 March 2021.

Oral Literacies: When Adults Read Aloud

Sam Duncan
Routledge, 2021, pp. 212

Reviewed by Jamie D. I. Duncan
Lancaster University

This book is rare in that it focusses on an area of literacy studies that at first glance seems familiar, but which in fact has been remarkably under researched. Addressing this gap was thus one of the starting points of *Oral Literacies: When Adults Read Aloud*, according to its author, Sam Duncan, an adult education specialist, and literacy across the lifespan researcher, at University College London.

Over the last ten years, Duncan has published in adult reading development, reading for pleasure, and community reading circles, both in the UK and elsewhere. Along the way, she encountered the need for a book which theorized adult reading aloud as a part of people's everyday lives. Not finding one, the book *Oral Literacies* came into being with its broad scope and nuanced approach to adult reading aloud practices. Owing to these, this is a book which will interest a wide range of researchers, graduate students, and teaching practitioners, across the field of community writing.

So what exactly are oral literacies? How would one go about researching such a topic? And, indeed, how might this new term help us to understand contemporary literacy practices? Prior to answering these questions through an overview of the book, it is worth pointing out the period in which it was published—that is, one year into the global COVID-19 pandemic. Regarding this moment, Duncan states: "some of the ideas within the book became more obvious or acute in the new world of 'lockdown', [where] the powers of the voice and ear seemed particularly important as ways to be together while not together" (xi).

This latter sentiment perhaps makes sense to the many people who necessarily engaged in digitally mediated relationships, increasingly so, throughout the pandemic, and Duncan lists examples of online reading aloud and listening to reading which gained in prominence. Yet, long prior to lockdown, of course, both online, and offline, reading aloud has played many important roles across a wide range of personal, familial, educational, professional, leisure, cultural, political, and also religious interactions. *Oral Literacies* discusses reading aloud practices relating to each of these domains in detail.

Chapter one starts by describing what is referred to as the dominant view of adult reading in Anglophone and Western European settings—where contemporarily reading is most associated, societally, with being a silent, individual, and comprehension-focused activity. This idea then gets deconstructed and the argument of the book is forwarded, concerning how the dominant viewpoint does not depict the reading practices of adults holistically, what they actually do, and why—particularly, in relation to oral reading (or reading aloud) and aural aspects of listening to reading.

A literature review then follows, revolving around five main fields of research on reading: formal education, family studies, ethnography, literature, and history. Regarding the first two, Duncan highlights the breadth of work there has been on reading aloud, but how this centers mostly on children and a limited range of settings in which reading gets done. Relating to the next three, Duncan overviews situated and multimodal accounts of reading, as well as historical studies which challenge teleological accounts of a transition from reading aloud towards silent reading, as if one replaced the other. Hence, Duncan states two aims of the book as; first, "to challenge this dominant discourse of silent, individual adult reading and indeed to challenge the idea that oral reading is itself 'one thing'"; then secondly, to do this by examining as wide a range as possible of contemporary reading aloud practices which "adults perform or experience in the different contexts, communities, languages and phases of their lives" (4).

Chapter two details Reading Aloud in Britain Today (RABiT), a two-year funded study from 2017–2019, concerning, in short, how, what, and why adults read aloud and listen to others doing so. Duncan's book resulted from the RABiT project and its three main forms of data collection: a national questionnaire; a citizen commentary project; and interviews carried out across the UK. Chapter three outlines the design and data of the questionnaire. Across extensive examples readers get an initial the sense of, as Duncan puts it, how adult "reading aloud practices are ubiquitous and remarkably varied", and "important to personal or cultural identities" (47). An initial typology of reading aloud practices is also developed in chapter three, including multiple perspectives on their 'commonness'—from the socially pervasive to the hidden or invisible.

One of Duncan's most distinctive features in RABiT is the incorporation of a unique citizen commentary project called the Mass Observation Archive (MOA). The MOA emerged in the UK in the 1930s, where, in brief, realizing that the mainstream press at the time did not know what 'the masses' thought about contemporary issues, a group of social scientists, media producers, and artists, came together to start a part research project and part political movement, where among other activities, volunteers started to write about what they did and thought about particular topics. The MOA still continues today, basically functioning through a series of 'directives' that participants receive several times a year, which they then write about in a style characterized as combining a kind of autobiography and amateur sociology (Sheridan, Street, and Bloome). There have been many directives concerning literacy in society over the years, and as a part of RABiT, in 2017, a new directive was sent out that specifically concerned reading aloud in everyday life. This directive and responses to it are included in chapter four.

In chapter five Duncan discusses the recordings of interviews and examples of reading aloud. One point to note here regarding these is that, similarly to how participant responses to the MOA directive would become part of the UK Mass Observation Archive, so recordings for RABiT are integrated into the British Library Sound Archive—ultimately forming part of broader and ongoing social history projects made available to the public. Personally, here, reading about the researcher going off to the Shetland Islands in Scotland to record people's voices for national library archives reminded me of the work of Alan Lomax and others in the fields of folklore studies and ethnomusicology, or perhaps closer, linguistic anthropology and sociolinguistics (see, for example, Richard Bauman)—but I had not encountered this kind of archival recording directly before in the field of literacy studies.

Next, from chapters six through twelve, the book empirically and theoretically investigates six main themes that emerged through the questionnaires, MOA directive, and interviewing data. As the first of these, chapter six is entitled "Family, Friends, and Lovers" and it focusses on reading aloud as a way of being with others. In doing so, it discusses ideas of community, domesticity, and intimacy, as well as how oral reading practices serve to mediate between "inner and outer worlds, personal and political worlds, familial and global worlds" (Duncan 83). Beyond questions of power associated with social groups and respective contexts, this chapter also highlights different ways that participating in reading aloud practices can join people together physically and/or affectively, and how in particular, both the voice and shared texts can enact love.

Chapter seven discusses working life. Reading aloud is shown here as ubiquitous "in larger and smaller, more and less obvious, ways across our working lives and lives as citizens" (115). As in other studies of literacy practices we get the sense here of how reading aloud practices hold workplaces together, as it were, through the performing, mediating, and disseminating of social roles and relations. The chapter discusses ten specific areas of work in closer detail: editors, writers, actors, broadcasters, religious figures, magistrates, judges, registrars, librarians, and teachers. Across all examples, reading aloud practices are "slightly different in each case, as purposes, priorities and contexts vary, as do power relationships and the ways in which written documents are used" (Duncan 115). This point links to different subjectivities, as well as, ultimately, "the systems of organisation, law or administration that we deal with as citizens" (Duncan 114). Relating to the latter, the chapter ends by discussing two areas of social life where people are seen, first, being pushed away by, and second, pushing back against, systems of governance. The two examples Duncan gives concern the role of reading aloud and related literacy practices, in the prison system, and in protest movements.

Chapter eight concerns religion. In discussing multiple religions and related forms of oral reading, the chapter revolves around what it refers to as five areas of difference and three areas of commonalty. The former includes different religions, different systems of belief, formations (of activities), physicality (bodies, objects, and spaces), texts, and languages. In the latter, commonality is discussed through memory, meditation, and meaning. In contrast with reductionist understandings of rote learning, Duncan emphasizes here how "across different religious traditions memorisation and recitation are associated with forms of meditation, creativity and the accessing of deeper meanings or understandings" (127). One concept—from Myra Barrs—that follows is that of "reading aloud, and/or hearing, sacred texts" becoming "a meeting place for worshippers past, present and future" (127). Multiple roles of the body, the voice, and the ear are discussed in turn as are what Tuuli Lukkala calls the personal-cultural soundscapes of religious spaces—or "everything a person can hear in a given place and time", whereby "what people perceive and pay attention to as well as the meanings people give to different sounds var[ies]" (Duncan 122).

The next topic in chapter nine is literary life, and aspects of production, performance, and experience framed as being literary. One main argument of this chapter is that every human being can be thought of as having a literary life, once, that is, high-cultural notions of literature are deconstructed, and emphasis is placed on the central role that stories occupy in people's lives. Duncan summarizes that a literary life is "a creative and story-alive life, awake to the experiences of others, whether reading, writing, singing, hearing, watching or imagining them" (136). Notions of sound are central to this chapter once again, drawing on ideas including the auditory imagination from T.S. Eliot as the particular (and primal) place of the ear and voice, and of sound and rhythm, in experiences and meaning making through texts as poetic. We also get the profound reminder that when we take up texts through oral reading, such as through song, poetry, and drama, we lend the text, not only our conscious engagement, but also our bodies and our breath or life force. Drawing on dramaturgical theory, Duncan discusses role playing from Dorothy Heathcote throughout the chapter, both generally as a site in which creativity and coping strategies can develop, and more specifically, in terms of shifting roles in production processes, and a kind of oral-aural reflexivity, such as where writers, shift from, for example, writing, to reading and listening, to judging, and editing work.

Chapter ten focusses on solitude and reading aloud alone. The chapter opens by asking the question: do people actually read aloud alone, and if so, what and why? Besides issues relating to who is not there to listen; cognition, affect, and the voice itself are considered. Duncan makes the point that oral reading is most commonly thought of in communicational terms, as between people, but in this case, "if we consider someone reading aloud as she sits, completely alone, and writes a story, checks an index or enjoys . . . poetry, whatever her voice is doing, it is not serving or communicating with others" (152). The chapter then develops its argument around two overarching categorizations: thinking and feeling. In relation to the former, examples of oral reading are shown to form part of "individual thinking work" such as: "focusing or concentrating; memorising or learning; and understanding, picking or interpreting" (Duncan 154). The second overarching category of feeling interconnects overlapping notions of sensoriality and identity. People are shown reading alone in this case for reasons relating to personal and group needs and identities; spirituality and religion;

enjoyment and pleasure; as well as to invoke feelings of comfort and company; and, for some, to establish a sense of being present in the world.

Chapter eleven, lastly, discusses education and oral reading. Duncan reminds readers in this chapter that the main purpose of the book and RABiT research was not a directly pedagogical one. Nevertheless, owing to education being a common frame of reference for participants, this did become one of the life domains to which they referred. Chapter eleven consequently describes reading aloud within planned educational settings—early reading, reading development, and language teaching. Beyond these areas, however, Duncan highlights that, through the RABiT data, in fact, the majority of examples of reading aloud in education mentioned by participants actually referred to subjects not specifically concerning language or literacy (e.g. biology, technology, math). Duncan discusses more generalized uses of oral reading, where, for instance, "participants speak of reading aloud to give instructions and share information. . . to bring learners together in a shared listening activity, to focus on a text being studied. . . to share and celebrate students' work, or to quieten or raise the mood" (166). This list thus becomes another example of the broader ethnographic observation throughout the book, where oral reading practices weave together broader social practices and contexts, in this case, principally, pedagogical, and educational ones. What chapter eleven, and the book on the whole suggest, then, and successfully so, is the need for an expanded sense of "what is understood by [oral] 'reading' in the first place"—as part of people's daily lives—and with this then supporting an improved understanding of how the doing, learning, and teaching of oral reading takes place (Duncan 176).

Works Cited

Barrs, Myra. "The reader in the Writer." *Reading*, vol. 34, no. 2, 2000, pp. 54–60.
Bauman, Richard, ed. *Folklore, Cultural Performances, and Popular Entertainments: A Communications-Centered Handbook*. Oxford University Press, 1992.
Duncan, Sam. *Oral Literacies: When Adults Read Aloud*. Routledge, 2020.
Eliot, T.S. *The Uses of Poetry and the Use of Criticism*. Faber and Faber, 1964.
Heathcote, Dorothy. "How Does Drama Serve Thinking, Talking and Writing?" *Elementary English*, vol. 47, no. 8, 1970, pp. 1077–81.
Lukkala, Tuuli. "The Soundscape of Orthodox Christian Worship." *Music and the Sacred*, vol. 41, no. 2, 2019, pp. 286–92.
Sheridan, Dorothy, Street, Brian V., and Bloome, David. *Writing Ourselves: Mass-Observation and Literacy Practices*. Hampton Press, 2000.

Coda: Community Writing and Creative Work

A Word from Coda's Editors

Kefaya Diab, Leah Falk, Chad Seader, Alison Turner, Kate Vieira, and Stephanie Wade

Just as musical codas persist beyond the end of musical work, Coda—a new section of the *Community Literacy Journal* devoted to creative writing—offers space for the representation of the lingering effects of community engagement, public engagement, and activism. Beginning with this, our inaugural effort, Coda will publish creative writing in a range of genres and voices in a move to expand conversations about writing studies, to document and preserve the work of community writing, and to encourage more creative writing. We invite readers and writers who are eager to create knowledge in new ways to join us in enacting writing as a form of communion.

We develop this section as a collective of editors with interests and experience in transnational literacy, peace building, creative writing with children and youth, collaborative exhibitions, poetry and archives, harm reduction, community building, arts administration, archiving and archives as spaces of community literacy, writing groups as forms of community building, language justice, garden-based writing, environmental writing, and anti-racism. We hope that our commitment to the foundational work of process building is reflected in a creative section that is inclusive, challenging, and nourishing. We believe that scholarly and creative work in writing studies should be in conversation, and that such conversations deepen our understanding of, appreciation of, and use of writing to meet the pressing social and moral issues of our time.

Following the tradition of rigorous generosity enacted by Veronica House and Paul Feigenbaum, the Coda Editorial Collective aims to ensure that the writers with whom we work are heard. We commit to community listening by striving to apprehend various, divergent aesthetics and ways of knowing. We recognize our responsibility toward authors, readers of Coda, and the larger community writing project. As a collective, we are engaged in evolving discussions about mission, vision, and of course submissions, and we invite you to join these discussions.

We welcome submissions of poetry, creative nonfiction, short stories, and multigenre work on any topics that have ensued from community writing projects. This may be work about community writing projects, and this may be expressed in ways we have yet to imagine. We ask authors to include a personal reflection about the submission itself—information about your community writing group (if you belong to one); your personal journey as a writer; what inspired you to write your piece; and anything else you'd care to share about your life—as an invitation for the author and Coda's readers to consider writing and activism as intertwined.

In our inaugural issue, we are honored to present four pieces: a short collaboratively-authored anthology from a university-based community partnership; a series of poems from a collective peace project in Columbia; a solo-authored narrative; and a solo-authored poem. We are grateful to the writers who have trusted us with their work, work that illustrates the possibilities Coda holds and that illustrates the power of the word. In the poems published through the Colombian EncantaPalabras collective, the youth voices present a clear call for justice, peace, and integration with the earth. That these poems are also being used as testimonios in Colombia's Commission for Truth, as part of the peace process, speaks to the power of expressive writing for social change. Mary Kovaleski Byrnes's and Livia Meneghin's piece, which introduces an anthology of poems and nonfiction by students in Boston's EmersonWRITES program, pairs reflection on program vision, methodology, and growth with the centering and celebration of students' formal and linguistic innovation, as well as students' contributions to topics ranging from the poetry of Kendrick Lamar to the ways racial injustice forces Black teenagers out of childhood. In "Moments," Jessica Pisano shares her experiences teaching writing to people who are incarcerated as part of her university's prison education program. Pisano's narrative brings readers into the ongoing tensions that occur when writers and instructors are located in multiple systems (in this case, prison systems and academia), and when systems set limitations to the relationships that writing can make possible. Eli Goldblatt's poem, "Side Streets," conjures the loneliness of the pandemic and evokes the hope of community in a changed world.

Coda will be published each spring. We encourage readers to look for future calls for submissions and share them widely with writers you know. In the meantime, happy reading.

Poesía para la Paz: Voces de Jóvenes Colombianos

Introducción y comentarios por Juana María Echeverri Escobar y Rodrigo Aicardo Rojas Ospina

EncantaPalabras, es un colectivo colombiano que agencia experiencias pedagógicas y artísticas enfocadas a la construcción de cultura de paz en comunidades educativas vulnerables y territorios afectados por el conflicto armado. A través de procesos dialógicos, simbólicos y otras acciones artísticas nos adentramos a la esencial y expresiva magia de las palabras, entre versos, poemas…nos reencontramos, nos liberamos del miedo y sanamos la memoria individual y colectiva; queremos volver a escuchar-nos después de los gritos de las balas, para recuperar el sentido de la conversación con ese otro, otra, que quiere comunicarnos, hacernos partícipes de su ser interior, que nos regala sus luchas y tesoros en las propias palabras…

Nuestro proyecto lúdico-pedagógico *Poesía para la Paz* es la manera afirmativa que trabajamos para descolonizar el lenguaje y transformar la cultura distorsionada por la violencia, después de años y años de conflicto armado, de injusticias y traumas. Proponemos re-encantar el lenguaje, permitir que tintineen y resuenen desde la poesía palabras como: empatía, arcoíris, reconciliación, alteridad, familia, sueños, amigos, nubes, raíces, respeto y diversidad. Lenguaje donde es posible instalar una ideología de paz con nuevas imágenes, sonidos, sensaciones, emociones para ampliar el mapa del mundo, para expandirlo con nuevos sentidos. Trabajo colaborativo que requiere de coraje para innovar en prácticas y acciones de resistencia pacífica, que implica sumarnos a experiencias humanas y resiliencias comunitarias susceptibles de transformarse en aprendizajes.

Desde hace once años, junto a las comunidades venimos sumando voces alrededor de la poesía y la escritura; explorando nuevos territorios semánticos donde se pronuncian palabras de la Paz, de las Paces, en plural, porque somos muchos y son muchas las posibilidades de escribir las Páginas de la Paz de Colombia.

En el 2021 *Poesía para la Paz* hace parte del proyecto "**Baúl de la Esperanza**" de la COMISIÓN DE LA VERDAD, Eje Cafetero—entidad que surge en el marco del acuerdo de paz—firmado en el 2016, entre el estado en cabeza del gobierno de la época y la guerrilla de las FARC-EP. La comisión de la verdad hace parte del Sistema Integral de Verdad, Justicia, Reparación y Garantías de no Repetición—y en cumplimiento de su mandato ha desarrollado mesas de diálogo social en la Territorial Eje Cafetero; una de ellas es la que trabaja el enfoque de Curso de Vida que comprende el reconocimiento de los impactos del conflicto en niños, niñas y adolescentes. Desde esta mesa se ha posibilitado un lugar de encuentro para que esta población aporte sus poemas publicados en las cartillas—memoria del proyecto y entregadas junto a otras iniciativas comunitarias, artísticas y pedagógicas a modo de aprendizajes para el presente y futuro de nuestra sociedad colombiana. Los poemarios de *Poesía para* *la Paz* publicados por EncantaPalabras y la Secretaría de Educación del Departamento de Caldas durante 7 años, contienen en sus textos además de realidades, sueños, anhelos, *recomendaciones para la no repetición y/o la no continuidad del conflicto, en clave poética:* son voces sobrevivientes, sujetos históricos, políticos, éticos y se alzan para contar sobre la dignidad, sobre la convivencia e inclusión, sobre su propio presente y futuro; sobre la escritura como experiencia de imaginación, auto-afirmación y sanación. Todo ello para contribuir a la construcción de una cultura de paz. Y que ningún colombiano o colombiana viva otra vez el dolor y desamparo del conflicto armado.

Poemas por Danna Samira Pérez Ramírez, María Fernanda Montoya Trujillo, Mariana Ospina López

Danna Samira Pérez Ramirez
Institución Educativa Fundadores INELFU, 6° grado secundaria
Municipio Riosucio, Departamento de Caldas, Colombia
Memorias del Proyecto "Cartilla VII Poesía para la Paz y la Inclusión en Tiempos de Pandemia"

VIVE LA PAZ
Vamos a pensar
en aquellas palabras
que nos hacen reflexionar
cumplir con buenas obras

La paz nos lleva a la justicia
la justicia nos llena de amor
el amor llena nuestros sueños
de alegría y libertad
deja la guerra
vive la paz
deja la guerra
vamos a cantar.

Contexto y comentarios del poema **VIVE LA PAZ:**

Danna Samira, niña autora del poema, vive y estudia en las montañas de la cordillera central de Colombia, en Riosucio, rica y diversa región del occidente de Caldas, territorio ancestral poblado por campesinos indígenas, afrodescendientes y mestizos, en donde las huellas del conflicto armado aún se sienten. Ella, una niña de 11 años, invita a pensar en la paz e intuitivamente descubre que las palabras hacen parte esencial del mundo que habitamos... *Vamos a pensar en la paz/en aquellas palabras/ que nos hacen reflexionar.* Ella con su poema juega y construye Paz, su texto nos remite como lectores a su escala de valores, que comparte como categoría vital: *deja la guerra/ vive la paz/ deja la guerra/ vamos a cantar.*

María Fernanda Montoya Trujillo

Institución Educativa Nuestra Señora de la Candelaria, 7° grado secundaria
Municipio Marquetalia, Departamento de Caldas, Colombia
Memorias del Proyecto "Cartilla VII Poesía para la Paz y la inclusión en tiempos de pandemia"

EL CAOS DE LO INESPERADO

De repente, anuncios y noticias,
que crean conmoción.
El sentir generacional
redunda la confusión,
aparece un virus, se destruye lo habitual.
Todo cambia, todo es caos
no existe una realidad,
o talvez, no la queremos aceptar.
El mundo evita, el mundo prohíbe, el mundo sugiere,
y solo el virus que acontece
se convierte en nuestro actuar.
Proliferan los contagios,
proliferan los miedos,
prolifera el estrés, prolifera el hambre,
y cada situación se halla en un vagón,
en un viaje sin rumbo.
El tren del dolor y la tristeza
hace su parada,
no elige la estación,
no elige la familia,
no elige condición.
Y el caos inesperado, provoca la desesperación.
El terror de la muerte circunda por doquier,
y ha tocado de tu ser las fibras más profundas.
La persona amada se diluye y ha dudado,
estará contigo en un nuevo amanecer
y nuevamente ocurre el caos de lo inesperado.
Los demonios con sus miedos, en su obra maestra,
lloras, gritas desesperado,
tu rostro perfilado, no desea escuchar,
aquella fatal noticia que te hará desgarrar,
ya no estará contigo aquel ser amado.
Se acabaron los abrazos y se acabaron los besos,
y no podrás ver aquel féretro yerto,
y solo queda entender,
que no esperarás su regreso
y quedarán los recuerdos de lo que para ti no ha muerto.

Contexto y comentarios del poema **EL CAOS DE LO INESPERADO**

Escribe la estudiante María Fernanda, experimentando su adolescencia en el municipio de Marquetalia también al oriente del departamento de caldas, una reflexión conmovedora sobre cómo ve y siente la actual crisis de la pandemia global; recrea la confusión a la que se ha visto abocado el sistema educativo colombiano que como la autora lo indica en su texto, le ha tocado vivir la experiencia del virus en sus vidas cotidianas. Hace un recorrido por diferentes aspectos que su inquietud juvenil observa, los efectos psicológicos y emocionales que han padecido millones de estudiantes como ella.

Mariana Ospina López

Institución Educativa Manzanares, 10° grado secundaria
Municipio Manzanares, Departamento de Caldas, Colombia
Memorias del Proyecto "Cartilla VII Poesía para la Paz y la inclusión en tiempos de pandemia"

WANÔPO

Inspirado en los animales que murieron incinerados en las selvas amazónicas, en honor a ellos.

Hoy redacto con ira llena de una tétrica y negra realidad podrida.
Mi tristeza la reflejaré mediante una metáfora llena de melancólicas sombras caídas.
Ya no hay humedad, al contrario, hay sequedad.
Mi oxigeno se extingue en medio de la brevedad.
Creo que pequé al nacer siendo un animal
y sin pensar mi subsistencia depende de un irracional.
Mi libertad ya no es del todo vivencial
al contario es un infierno en forma literal
ahora mi inocencia es una deficiencia
y mi débil deferencia se convierte en preeminencia.
Su antagonismo contiguo y continuo me perturba
y su irreverencia me repudia,
pido que por favor nos excluyan de su disputa,
su indolencia nos afecta y su inconciencia nos irrespeta.
Son mis últimas palabras, pues mi existencia se incinera
mi mente se desespera y mi alma se despeja.
Me voy teniendo una profunda tristeza.
Y una gran duda en forma de inconformidad
¿Es tan valioso su extraño objeto de metal?
Bueno, creo que su codicia es de interés general
y su actitud tiene demasiada voracidad.

Contexto y comentarios del poema WANÔPO:

Mariana Ospina adolescente, quien vive en Manzanares municipio del oriente del Departamento de Caldas, zona cafetera montañosa, afectada por el conflicto armado y por conflictos socioeconómicos y ambientales. En su poema utiliza la Personificación: les da voz y autoridad a los animales, sitúa al lector ante un problema ético actual la crisis medioambiental...*Pido que por favor nos excluyan de su disputa*...Aboga por las relaciones inter-especies; plantea la necesidad de desplazarnos del antropocentrismo hacia el biocentrismo; reivindica el valor primordial de la vida de todos los seres. Mariana es implacable utilizando sus palabras como amonestación frente a hombres depredadores, negligentes e inconscientes para co-habitar en el planeta tierra.

Colectivo Cultural y Pedagógico EncantaPalabras
Juana Echeverri & Rodrigo Rojas
2encantapalabras@gmail.com

Author Bios

Juana María Echeverri Escobar nació el 1° de julio de 1971 en Manizales, Caldas. Poeta, activista-feminista, constructora de paz y profesora en comunidades. Trabaja proyectos educativos y culturales con la Secretaría de Educación del departamento de Caldas y la Universidad de Manizales, entre otros.

Rodrigo Aicardo Rojas Ospina nació el 4 de marzo de 1967 en Manzanares, Caldas. Activista, constructor de paz, profesor en comunidades y escritor. Trabaja proyectos educativos y culturales con la Secretaría de Educación del departamento de Caldas y la Universidad de Manizales, entre otros.

Danna Samira Pérez Ramírez nació el 1° de mayo de 2008 en Riosucio, Caldas, donde también reside. Estudiante de grado 7°. Es una niña que ama el canto, el baile y el estudio del idioma inglés. Sueña con ser cantante y profesional en ciencias forenses.

María Fernanda Montoya Trujillo nació el 23 de junio de 2008, en Marquetalia. Caldas, donde reside actualmente. Estudiante de grado 8°. Le gusta la actividad física en especial el baloncesto. También le agrada escribir, inclinándose por las obras narrativas.

Mariana Ospina López nació el 13 de mayo de 2005 en Manzanares, Caldas, un hermoso pueblito de Colombia y allí mismo reside. Estudiante de grado 10°. Con tan sólo 16 años, su amor por la literatura y la escritura es inmenso, redacta al son de la sinfonía de su alma.

Persistence and Creativity: EmersonWRITES Celebrates 11 Years with Young Poets and Writers of Boston

Introduction by Mary Kovaleski Byrnes and Livia Meneghin

Essays and poems by Rejeila Firmin, Star Igbinosa, Ebony Smith, Essence Smith, Winter Jones, Yaritza Santana, Paola Ruiz Manrique, Madison Lucchesi, and Zaryah Qareeb

EmersonWRITES is a free creative writing program for students in Greater Boston public and charter schools, co-sponsored by the Offices of Enrollment and Student Success and the First-Year Writing Program at Emerson College. EmersonWRITES is guided by the principle that writing is essential to intellectual engagement, self-representation, and access to opportunity. Students in the EmersonWRITES program engage in college-style creative writing classes on campus at Emerson College, where courses are structured to build writing and critical thinking and to guide students toward negotiating a range of writing genres and rhetorical situations. EmersonWRITES seeks to foster individual voice and engagement with the world through the written word.

On a Sunday afternoon in February, EmersonWRITES hosts a celebration of creative writing for our local high school students. While these celebrations have occurred for over a decade, when we reflect on the last eleven celebrations, our minds are drawn to the stark contrasts between February 2020, when we gathered with over 100 people and shared a meal in a boisterous auditorium, and this past February in 2021, when that same supportive group was seen through a screen of rectangles. Like so many aspects of our lives, our community writing program had to adjust to the demands of this ruthless virus. In recognition of all losses of this past year, it may seem insensitive to seek out celebration. However, it would be a mistake to view our students and teachers as anything less than triumphant in the face of one of the biggest challenges any of us will ever encounter.

Prior to this year, when our courses shifted to a virtual model, the EmersonWRITES program offered free creative writing workshops and college-access programming to students in Boston public and charter schools on Emerson College's campus on Saturday mornings. Our students come from all over the city and identify as African American, Asian, Black, and Latinx; many speak multiple languages including Arabic, Haitian Creole, Spanish, and Somali. As the program's mission is grounded in pedagogies of anti-racism and multilingualism, it's important to recognize how teachers and students move within and against the challenges presented in our city and in our greater society from sexism to police brutality to ICE raids in their neighborhoods. In some ways, the work of the program was daunting and riddled with obstacles even before the pandemic hit, no matter how enriching the subject matter and mentoring, the friendships made, or the free lunch offered. Our students come from various neighborhoods on the T, which was often under construction or generally slow; the weather between October and February could be described as brutal; and our program runs on a weekend. Many of our students' lives are full of responsibilities and challenges that would feel overwhelming to any adult, let alone a teenager. Teachers juggled the demands of graduate school and work as Boston's exorbitant and continuously rising cost of living pushed teachers' housing options ever further from Emerson's downtown campus. And yet, even in the throes of the pandemic, students and teachers persisted.

Out of the eleven years of student work published in our annual anthology, *SPINE*, we have gathered nine pieces below. Some of the older pieces include Rejeila Firmin's essay "A Flower Bloomed in a Dark Room," which was part of a grant-awarded project that explored intergenerational narratives in families. There's Winter Jones's contrapuntal poem "Butterfly," which uses extended metaphor to connect ideas about place, identity, and strength to prompt multiple readings. Poet Yaritza Santana wrote "An Intruder," which uses narrative and code-meshing to share her commentary on the realities of immigration. Another poem, "Ode 2 Pac," written in 2017 by Essence Smith, mourns the continuous loss of Black lives to murder by police. Four years later, her twin sister Ebony Smith wrote "Millennial Voices Debate their Ancestors," a poem that embodies a sense of weariness in the face of such endless injustice. And there's Paola Andrea Ruiz Manrique's poem, "A Letter to My Neighbor," which reflects on the demands of being a teenager in today's society. In addition, there are three texts from this past year's virtual iteration of the program: sophomore Madison Lucchesi's poem "Salutary Neglect" responds to the January 2021 insurrection on the Capitol building; junior Zaryah Qareeb's memoir, "Wrinkles," is a reflection on self-criticism and mother-daughter relationships; and junior Star Igbinosa captured the sudden emptiness of pandemic life for teenagers in her poem "Dreams with No Substance with No Life."

When the students took the spotlight during our virtual Zoom showcase this past February and read the words from these and other stories and poems, they affirmed that their creativity and their labor with the written word would be a beacon for them and their audiences during the toughest of times. With the country slowly moving forward out of this difficult year, EmersonWRITES will continue to reshape and adjust to meet our students' needs and grow this community in ways we never anticipated before the pandemic. Knowing how much heart and talent these writers have brought to the program for over a decade, we look forward to reading more inspiring work from the creative and resilient teens in Boston for many years to come.

"A Flower Bloomed in a Dark Room" by Rejeila Firmin

I remember getting forehead wrinkles that I thought would be permanent from the amount of stank looks I gave that day. The cool breeze relaxed the humid air like a shoulder massage as I popped my headphones in, eyes closed. The city felt more and more like home with each passing block. I gazed at the corner stores, barber shops, and beauty supply stores, finally acknowledging their cultural significance. I thought about all of the cookout stories that took place there, like the one my uncle told that made us laugh until our stomachs hurt. And that's when it happened. Perfect timing, really. My playlist ended and Spotify automatically played "m.A.A.d city" by none other than Kendrick Lamar.

Kendrick Lamar Duckworth, 32. Born and raised in Compton. To some, he's an opportunity. To others, he's a rapper. To me, he's a reflection. What makes Kendrick so different from the rest? He is a lyricist. He puts words together like art. His delivery is a mixture of cultural metaphors, double entendres, history lessons, onomatopoeia, tongue-twisters, and modern-day allusions. He spits the kind of lyrics that make you stop and run the whole track back. Kendrick is on a different type of time.

Every set of lyrics is a poem. Every poem becomes a song. Every song tells a story. Every story carries a message. Every message pertains to the Black community in some way. I listen to Kendrick because he indulges in Black culture. He is Black, just like me. A fact as simple as that amplifies to speak volumes. His albums became learning opportunities for me, a chance for me to relate to someone for once.

Last year, I read *If Beale Street Could Talk* by James Baldwin and underwent a plethora of emotions. In the midst of all the tears, laughter, pride, and enchantment, I discovered a connection between Baldwin's novel and Kendrick Lamar's "m.A.A.d city." Baldwin's romance novel is told from the perspective of a young Black woman throughout her journey of discovering the gutting reality of what it means to be a Black man in America. The father of her unborn child, lifelong companion, and first love acts as her catalyst for discovery. The characters truly construct and drive the story. The purpose of the novel comes in the fact that the most complex character was the setting.

Throughout the novel, Baldwin gave the setting the ability to influence the characters, the ability to feel sorrow and inflict that sorrow upon others. Baldwin does this to pay homage to the communal bond between members of the minority. Baldwin's critics saw the novel as utopian, rather than providing an alternate ending to a common story. There is power in being Black, which is something that Baldwin's critics failed to realize, hence the subliminal comments on Baldwin's optimism. And that's where I drew the connection: optimism.

In "m.A.A.d city," Kendrick Lamar says, "Hope euphoria can slow dance with society." In an interview, Kendrick revealed, "So I always wanted to put that type of vulnerability out there where I have always been this dreamer. I am a realist, but at the same time what separates me from the rest of my homeboys is the fact that I can dream of this hope." Kendrick is aware of the dangers of being a dreamer, as is Baldwin who said, "Every poet is an optimist…but on the way to that optimism 'you have to reach a certain level of despair to deal with your life at all.'"

It takes courage to dream as a person of color with societal limits and expectations. But Baldwin wrote for the minority anyway, and Kendrick Lamar raps for the generations after him. Kendrick's optimism and pride are seemingly contagious, and I find it hard not to gain insight and inspiration from his words.

So back to that story that my uncle told. Nothing special. Honestly, I don't even remember it that well. He was a young Haitian immigrant, starting trouble outside of the laundromat. He tried to act tough with some older kids and they ran after him and my dad (who was carrying two big-ass laundry bags) until one of them ran right into a pole. Now, yes, the story itself is funny…but that's not what I'm getting at. It's the way we all laughed (or some of us got up and ran) and shared our happiness with each other. At that moment, our connection felt multidimensional, bigger than us. That's what optimism means to me.

"Dreams with No Substance with No Life" by Star Igbinosa

Without Free Enterprise
  I've planted my body on this cushioned chair
    In this room so bare
Neglecting the many deep green spiraling stems
      Flourishing from my indoor garden of flower paradise
  This large white canvas sits in front of me
      Mocking me
  Alluding that I will never be free of all its glorious natural space
     Is this space really natural?
  The focus is now on my crown
In the sun's eyes my kinky curls reach for limitless skies and radiate self-restoration
  In its golden-brown eyes, my trauma was nothing more than a
Compromise
  Irreplaceable pieces of me snatched by this merciless life
    With no regards as to how I would make it out in time
  Shrinkage
My crown begins to decrease in size until the not-so-natural space devours it
  Whole?
    No
  Just enough to leave me feeling empty
Wandering aimlessly in a world that requires nothing but direction and paper
  How am I supposed to conquer those systems if my self has
Dissociated
  Far from the point of restoration?
  So now I float above the bare room
    Of flower paradise
With the cushioned chair that my black body cannot escape from
  Staring at the white canvas
    With half of my soul gone

"Millennial Voices Debate their Ancestors" by Ebony Smith

Martin Luther King wasn't even mainstream

With a 75% disapproval rating in his lifetime.

This is useless.

Stop making me the spokesperson,
to be meticulous,
perfect,
to say the right things to the wrong crowds.

Why are you forcing me to be politically aware?

Like I don't see them walking on the other
side of the street.
Like I don't hear the underlying tone
in the white women's voice,
telling me that I need to buy something,
because it's illegal to loiter.

How can I forget that I'm Black
when they remind me every day?

I don't have an opinion to share.
I don't have a vote to cast.
I don't follow any social activists to repost.

Where's my childhood?
Did it get lost in my kinky hair?
Is my skin too dark for you to find it?

"Ode 2 Pac" by Essence Smith

Excuse me,   but it seems y'all still haven't learned
it's been exactly 20 years since my demise
but even from the shimmering, azure heaven above
Ms. Lady Liberty still cannot see
all the people want is the joy of being free
they want 2 live in glee
without having 2 flee every time
the red and blue lights shadow the streets
Liberty and Justice still hanging and banging on my homeboys,
doing us dirty

like we are not supposed 2 make noise
the cops still carrying their glocks blasting their rounds of blazing fiery
bullets into us

CLICK
        CLOCK
                BANG
                        SHOT

when will America wake up
it's like the alarm clock never went off
do they not hear our screaming?
 another brother that looks like me
lying in the dirt
lifeless
his crimson blood stained his ebony skin
the media will only show his story once
unless he was a criminal
or a Thug
or had a picture of himself, posing with a gun
because then it will seem like he deserved what was handed to him
like he was living in the fast lane, but karma still caught up
but
who asked the cop to play God?   now the family is dressed in black
gathered in the church, trying to remember someone who is already
forgotten
trying to get back
the one they lost
but even as the days pass
the mass of Black brothers and sisters
stand together
hand in hand
their strong voices shouting
 "NO JUSTICE, NO PEACE"
to fight against the ones who give out
cruel and unusual punishments

hope for the youth and the future may seem lost
but we are not hopeless
the fervent flames are still burning in our eyes
gasoline flows deep in our bloodstream
all we need is a match
                to set the crooked system in flames

"Butterfly" by Winter Jones

Breathe in. But I can't…
Breathe out. I can't understand why.
Move on. You won't do it, no balls.

They didn't mean it But they did
maybe they did mean it.

It's suffocating. It's gut wrenching
to understand to think
that words deeply embedded
with full trust, with genuine speech
With (un)requited love, with deep respect
with seemingly tantalizing truths that words can be so fragile,
can dance through the air and shatter at the slightest bit of doubt
oh so violently oh so crippling
that they immobilize. that they disenchant.
That they lose their dance They lose their purpose.

They drop the oils
of sorrow,
of self-doubt,
of trust issues,
of abhorrence,
unintentionally.

Stopping the butterfly from doing her own dance.
Stopping the butterfly from knowing her purpose.

"An Intruder" by Yaritza Santana

It's the Caribbean Sea that carries me home
On June 16, 2003, at Clinica Peravia in Bani
My culture is rich and its people diverse
The blood of my ancestors courses through my veins
You say that makes me an immigrant
I say that makes us one and the same
You are so quick to toss us aside
But you love our food, our music, and you study our language
But you don't know anything about our culture
So here is a quick lesson:
Mis ancestros levantan los puños debajo de nuestra Bandera
El Rojo representa la sangre de mis ancestros,
En la lucha por la Independencia.
El azul representa el cielo que se encuentra sobre nuestras cabezas.
Y simboliza a Dios y la protección que él nos da.
El Blanco representa la Paz, no rendición.
The tongue that I speak may be foreign and cause you fear
When I come knocking on your door
But it's because you can't decipher the code
You weren't meant to hear
I came to your country for the education at the age of two
My tongue became my enemy
As it didn't speak like you
I had to train it so that you could understand me more
Me adapte a tu idioma
But by doing so I chipped away at my tongue
And while it started to speak like yours it also bled,
It was never my intention to change who I am
But I had to learn to adapt if I wanted to rise
But assimilation is never what I had in mind
You seek to tie us down like a dog on a leash,
But I won't roll over so don't try to make me bark before I speak.
Don't try to give me a treat so I'll behave.
I don't follow your rules and I'll happily bite back any day.
You pick at my skin because it's mapped out,
But I bring the route of my home with me and an eraser won't brush it out.

"A Letter to My Neighbor" by Paola Ruiz Manrique

I am the neighbor of such a strong person.
I see what you go through every day.
I have seen how broken you were left. The pain you carry.
The way this society celebrates disorientation.
And the way it crashes you into panic and anxiety.
Silencing it with melodies of Romeo Santos and Drake.
Although you may see yourself as weak for being expressive,
I see you as strong because I lack the ability.
I have seen how much you searched for an anecdote to your hurt.
And through your pain you educate me.
Strength is a quality you have taught me.
You taught me wild love.
You taught me selflessness when you pose in front of
the Christmas tree to see a smile arise on my face.
You taught me to dedicate my time through hours on facetime.
You taught me to listen.
You taught me to be fearless when expressing myself.
You taught me how much I need to be cared for,
and how much I need to care for you.
You taught me strength.
I fantasize of being as strong as you are.
I see the way cultures clash and the segregation
in the way we pursue our daily life.
It leads back to disorientation.
Trying to attune your family traditions
with the American lifestyles of your teachers.
Your Salvadorian curls reshaping into waves
betraying your documentation.
Afraid to miss any more days of school
because your parents will end up in a court duel.
But school is teaching me to discriminate my own people.
You taught me to perform Maluma concerts in the hallways.
You taught me to enunciate parce instead of dude.
You taught me what strength is.
But I also find myself and you seeking love to refuel us of that strength
A fierce love
A wild love
A selfless love.
An expressive love.

"Salutary Neglect" by Madison Lucchesi

the act of a government turning a blind eye to the actions of its citizens

>When the Black Lives Matter movement marches through Chicago
>Join them or close your eyes, open your ears
>Absorb the mosaics of pain and then act on it
>
>Remember your manners
>When you see a woman in a hijab at the grocery store
>For her first amendment right is not a punchline
>
>Take your personal beliefs and throw them in a dumpster fire
>If you'd raise a sign against
>Free healthcare and a woman's choice
>
>Welcome your neighbors into your home
>That means the immigrants too
>For your blood is part immigrant
>
>Cover your arrogance in glitter and rhinestones
>Put the funding for Straight Pride in a rainbow box
>Gift it to the LGBTQ+ community
>
>But do not turn your cheek
>When the president of a leading nation
>Encourages his supporters to terrorize a federal building
>
>This is not a time for silence
>It is a time for screaming since
>Speaking has been overlooked for centuries
>
>We demand
>To be given the
>Tools to prosper
>
>And to truly have
>Life, liberty, and
>The pursuit of happiness

"Wrinkles" by Zaryah Qareeb

Her hand picks up the bulky metallic machine raging with hot air against the flimsy ironing board. I sit there studying the atmosphere around her, as she presses the steam iron onto the fabric with much determination. My eyes follow the trail of her arm, moving back and forth like a pendulum ball. "I hate wrinkled shirts," my mother murmurs.

She rushes, listening to the sound of the ticking clock taunting her. She corrects my lopsided pigtails and helps me to put on my black leather shoes. She stops to inspect me head to toe before leaving for the event. I can't recall the purpose of this event or why I was there. All I remember that day was my mother speaking highly of me and adults praising me in return. At the time, I never understood why she constantly emphasized looking polished. All I knew was that being close to perfect made Mom happy.

Growing up, Mom's motto in life was to always be prepared for anything, at any moment; "Those who prepare to face the unexpected, are the ones who succeed." This sentence echoed in my head as she buttoned up my shirt, dressing me up as if I were a doll sitting in the front window of a toy store.

You should always look presentable and be polite to make a good impression on others. Individuals with class must never wear a wrinkled shirt to convey the wrong message. A youthful white button up blouse will make you stand out amongst the rest. I was a representative of my family, and a symbol of my mother's hard work. Therefore, I took everything she said to heart; I desired her approval.

I began associating wrinkles with failure. One curve of a fold meant I failed. I failed to prepare myself for the day and for the opportunities ahead. Thinking about failing scared me, but the idea of disappointing my mother frightened me most.

As I grew older, I despised how time-consuming smoothing out my wrinkles was. Every second of going back and forth, thundering thoughts of disappointing my mother shook me.

One morning I forgot to iron my shirt. Looking down and seeing small creases on my clothing disturbed me. I felt as if everything depended on this shirt. I tried smoothing it out with my hands, but it didn't work. These wrinkles were a physical representation of my flaws. My guilt and shame magnified the longer I dwelled on it.

During moments like this, I pictured what younger me would say. I could see her face look up at me with eyes of confusion as the words "it's just a shirt" fall out between her lips. Younger me would be upset that I let little things like this make me feel like a failure. She would be disappointed that I put pressure on myself to be perfect all the time. I was always seeking approval from others but never from her.

In the end she was right, it was just a shirt, pieces of fabrics sewn together to create a whole. I remind myself that I'm not defined by it and it does not represent me as an individual. Giving up on the idea of being "perfect" made me feel renewed. Eventually, I found beauty in my wrinkles.

Author Bios

Mary Kovaleski Byrnes is a co-founder and Program Director of EmersonWRITES and Senior Lecturer in the Writing, Literature, and Publishing Department at Emerson College. She is the author of a book of poems, *So Long the Sky*, and her work has appeared in *Best of the Net*, *The Boston Globe*, *Guernica*, *Borderlands: Texas Poetry Review*, and more.

Livia Meneghin is the EmersonWRITES Program Coordinator and writing instructor at Emerson College. She is the author of the chapbook *Honey in My Hair*. Her individual poems and reviews have found homes in *The Academy of American Poets*, *Entropy Magazine*, *Tinderbox*, *Whale Road Review*, and elsewhere. She earned her MFA in Poetry at Emerson in Spring 2021.

Rejeila Firmin is a Black female writer and student at Emerson College. She is passionate about music, activism, and photography. Also known as Wordsbyrei, she has a blog and an Instagram account dedicated to sharing her writing. She participated in EmersonWRITES in her last two years of high school.

Star Igbinosa is a junior at the Academy of the Pacific Rim Charter Public School and has seriously enjoyed being able to write in ways she never has before. Her love for being able to read the works of so many talented young artists like herself runs deep. Star's favorite foods are plantains and avocados. She can't wait for what the future has in store.

Winter Jones, as a newly admitted student to Simmons University and recipient of acceptances to schools such as Spelman College and Emerson College, hopes to find plenty of opportunities like what EmersonWRITES offered. Outside of her time writing, Winter plays video games, builds her connections, and actively searches for more opportunities.

Madison Lucchesi is a sophomore at Revere High School where she leads the Feminist Empowerment Movement and the Inclusive Opportunity Club. Her writing can be found in Teen Blurb Magazine and on Instagram @eclipsingentries.

Zaryah Qareeb is a visual artist who recently discovered her passion for creative writing. Many of her works contain screenplays and short stories. Her interests include watching films, baking vegan snacks, and playing with her cat, Star.

Paola Ruiz Manrique grew up in East Boston and was raised by Colombian parents. She is a senior at East Boston High School. Next year she will attend college and hopes to double major in English and Communications and Media to further pursue her passion for writing.

Yaritza Santana is currently a senior at Boston Prep, and this is her third and final year at EmersonWRITES. She loves to do writing in her free time and is going to pursue screenwriting in college. Sidenote: she also loves streaming the Marvel series with her friends on Disney+.

Ebony Smith is a current undergraduate at Harvard College. She plans to concentrate in Government with a secondary in History & Literature. She has furthered her creative writing skills as an Editorial Writer for The Crimson journal at Harvard, and by starting up her own personal blog, titled "Black Girl Thoughts". Her sole purpose in writing remains: to address the racial inequities in this country through art.

Essence Smith is an upcoming sophomore at Trinity College double majoring in Political Science and History. At Trinity, Essence is involved in Trinity College Black Women's Organization, CONNPIRG, and Habitat for Humanity. In addition, Essence works in the Admissions Office and helps welcome incoming freshmen classes.

Moments

Jessica Pisano

Reflection: When I first learned I would have the opportunity to teach first-year writing through my university's prison education program, I challenged myself to chronicle and reflect on my experiences each week for the entire semester. As a full-time lecturer, writing program coordinator, and mother of two, it's hard to find time to write unless it's sanctioned like this, scheduled into my weekly routine. This piece emerged from the tenth of what ended up being twelve narrative reflections. In all honesty, I have mixed feelings about this project. While it has been personally fulfilling and revelatory, it also highlights the privilege with which I am able to write about the prison system from such a safe distance. This narrative is very much the story of my own growth, not the story of my students', as I could never begin to speak for them. I want to be cognizant of the ways in which I, like so much of our nation, profit from their incarceration, in my case through the publication of this piece. My purpose for publishing—and for continuing to teach reading and writing for almost twenty-three years—is rooted in a deep desire to promote understanding and foster conversation about important issues through the sharing of stories.

"It's a beautiful day," I said, walking from the gatehouse towards the prison entrance at noon last Thursday. "Too pretty to be inside all day." After weeks of teasing us, appearing here and there sporadically, spring had finally, as my dad would have said, decided to take off her coat and stay a while. The guard walking in with me, a man I'd never seen before, agreed, "Too pretty to be in *here* all day." He chuckled, and I wondered about his joke.

I had been teaching first-year college writing in a medium-security men's prison for almost three months, but I still found interactions with the staff more challenging than with the students. I couldn't help but think that my students were always in *here*, snow, rain, or shine. Perhaps that was the joke. I smiled and shrugged, excusing myself to the restroom labeled "Females."

I have to be honest, just thinking about the day ahead was exhausting: thirteen half-hour writing conferences were more than I would typically schedule in a single day on campus, but the hour-and-fifteen-minute drive out to the prison made it a necessity. And so, steeling myself for eight hours in prison, I finished in the bathroom, picked up my box of donated books, and headed through the double metal doors and up to the education wing.

The first seven conferences went well. The students were engaged, excited to talk about their projects, to tell me the stories that motivated their research. Before the end of the second conference, I knew there was no way I'd be able to stick to my thirty-minute limit. By the fourth conference, I was running half an hour late. The seventh conference ended only minutes before the hour-long "break" I'd scheduled myself should have been over. As Slate and I finished, I asked him to tell Barrington to come on up while I ran quickly to the bathroom.

As I buzzed to be let into the staff area, a maze that led past offices to a unisex bathroom whose door was perpetually propped open because it locked as soon as it closed, I heard a voice rumble over the loudspeaker. There were often garbled, almost unintelligible announcements during class. I knew there was a list of codes posted somewhere in the classroom, but typically I would just ask the students, "What was that?" And they'd let me know it was a code 3, code 4, whatever. "It just means we need to stay put," someone would tell me. "Not like we're going anywhere anyways," someone else would laugh. So I'd learned to ignore the announcements. I figured if it were something important, Johnson, the education wing guard, would let me know. I figured if something went wrong, we'd all know about it before long.

When I returned to the classroom, I was surprised to see Slate, still sitting there in his usual spot, grinning back at me. "Code 2," he explained. "We gotta stay here."

"Huh," I said. "What's code 2?"

"Count. They've gotta count everyone. Make sure they know where everyone is."

I nodded. While I might not know the codes, I did know that this wasn't the regularly scheduled evening count. Most nights, we'd see Johnson's face appear in the window of the classroom door around 6 p.m., silently counting the students. It startled me the first few weeks, but it had become routine. So many things about teaching in prison had become routine. The whole rigmarole in the gatehouse: clear-plastic bag, pockets emptied, metal detector, cell detector, pat-down, driver's license, sign-in. The invisible door guards hidden behind one-way glass windows, determining my every entrance and exit from on high. The weekly clearance by administration of every item I'd need to bring into the classroom. After a few weeks, I remember telling my husband who also taught at the prison that I'd started getting used to it all, that it wasn't as big of a deal as it had been the first week. "I know," he said. "But I don't want to get used to it. I don't want to accept that this is just the way it is."

But now, there was nothing to do but accept the moment. There was nowhere we could go, nothing we could do. I thought about the irony of the situation: after class, if a student needed to talk with me about an assignment, he'd ask a friend to hang back with him so we couldn't be accused of "undue familiarity," an accusation we all knew could jeopardize the program. But now, because administration had called count, Slate and I were supposed to sit in the classroom together for… how long? Who knew? And it was all fine, because they were calling the shots.

Slate had opened his laptop and was starting to work through the revisions I'd suggested on his research essay. I fumbled through my clear plastic bag, searching for something to occupy my time. If I only had my laptop, access to all the emails and grading piling up online. But of course, I had nothing other than what had been approved on this week's clearance list, and there was no internet. I found a piece of paper and started making a to-do list.

"What's your perspective on prisoners?"

I looked up and realized Slate must have stopped typing.

"What do you mean?" I asked.

"I mean, what do you think of us?" he asked.

Of course, I knew what he meant, but answering him would mean giving away a piece of myself, something I'd been told not to do. It's not like I'd been able to follow the advice we'd received from the prison administration during our training. I'd slipped so many times already. Once I'd said something about having kids. Another time I'd mentioned driving to a conference in Pittsburgh. The first time, I remember being worried. I'd fucked up. Given away too much. But then I realized the reality of the situation. There was no other faculty member with the same last name at my institution. If any one of my students wanted to learn my first name, where I lived, the names of family members, they could find out in a matter of days just by having someone on the outside do a quick Google search. In fact, I realized, they probably already knew.

So I took a deep breath. "I don't really have an opinion on prisoners in general," I started, "but I think there's a lot more people in prison than there should be. I think that if we really cared about rehabilitation rather than retribution, there'd be a lot more people in rehab and counseling and lot fewer behind bars." It felt good to say these things, things I wouldn't say to colleagues who would find them obvious, things I couldn't say to so many others without having to defend myself. "I think there's a problem when the majority of people in prison are people of color, people living in poverty, veterans. I think that points to something wrong with our country, that we'd rather pay to lock people up than make sure everyone has the support and opportunity to be productive members of society."

Slate nodded. "Yeah, I want to do something when I get out of here. I want to talk to people back in my community. Help them do something better." He smiled and shook his head. "You know, back when I was a kid, my step-mom, she used to try to keep me straight. She'd tell me what to do. I thought she was trying to change me, to make me different from who I was. Huh." He snorted and grimaced. "Man, I wish I'd listened to her."

I shrugged. "That's how most kids are."

"How old are your kids?" he asked. And there it was. I'd slipped once—he'd heard and remembered.

I tried not to skip a beat. "Twelve and nine," I admitted. "How old are yours?" Slate not only bragged about having nine children, but he'd covered the sides of his brown accordion folder with their pictures.

His grin widened to a smile. "My youngest is two and my oldest just turned ten. I got her a locket for her birthday. A locket with my picture inside." The smile faded as he looked down at his hands. "She doesn't have it yet. It's in the mail." A moment passed. "I hate being in here, not out there with them."

"I can't imagine how hard it must be," I offered.

He continued looking down. "Twelve..." he nodded. I realized he was talking about my son. "That's how old I was the first time I got locked up. Juvie. Been in and out ever since."

I couldn't help but think of my son, a kid who could get in his own share of trouble, locked up.

Slate broke through my thoughts. "This class," he said, "this is the first time I've really tried to do something different. Make a change. Man, it's hard. I never finished the seventh grade. But I'm really trying."

"I know you are."

Slate nodded, and returned to his laptop. I wasn't sure I could leave the classroom, but, even more worried about accusations of undue familiarity now that I'd just spent thirty minutes alone with a student, I decided to chance it.

"Hey, Johnson," I called, approaching his desk. "Any idea when this code might be lifted?"

"Nope," he said. "You never know."

I started doing the mental math. My conferences were close to an hour behind schedule. It would be at least nine o'clock before I finished. Then an hour-and-a-half before I made it home. And that's if I didn't stop and grab dinner. "Well, I guess I'm going to be here for a while tonight."

Johnson nodded slowly as he often did before responding. "I'm gonna make some coffee. You want some?" he offered.

"That would be amazing."

As I started back to the classroom, the loudspeaker came to life: "Code 2, cleared." Slate passed me at the door. "I'll tell Barrington to come on," he said.

Fifteen minutes later, I sat back down at my desk in the classroom, sipping black coffee from a Styrofoam cup. Still no Barrington. I walked back out to ask Johnson what was going on.

"I'm not really sure," he shrugged. "I called 'em."

I was starting to feel annoyed. Trapped. Caged. With a tinge of guilt I realized this was barely a taste of what my students must feel on a daily basis. I took another sip of coffee and tried to relax.

Suddenly, a soft melody drifted from the classroom next door. I thought I was hearing things, but no, a light, clear woman's voice sounded again, singing some old hymn I'd never heard. It was beautiful.

The prison chapel was at the other end of the education wing, and sometimes, towards the end of class, I would hear piano and voices lifted in praise and consider the contrasting redemption offered at opposite ends of the hall. But it was too early for evening service, and this music wasn't coming from the chapel, but from the classroom next door. Then I remembered the woman from the local community college who taught career exploration and whose class had just switched rooms.

"I hope we're not too loud," she'd laughed when she warned me about the move. "We can get pretty loud. Sometimes we even sing!"

But I hadn't heard her. Not until tonight. (My class could get pretty loud, too.) As I listened to her song, I wondered what her students thought of her, this tiny, middle-aged country woman, singing to them. I wondered if it felt patronizing.

Her song in the background, I scanned the classroom shelves now filling up with donated books. At the end of a long semester, all I wanted was an easy read, nothing I had to think too much or too deeply about. My students were devouring the books, every carefully crafted sentence, every intricate detail. Earlier, after describing himself as "you know, that little Chihuahua who's so excited to see you he pisses himself?", Samson told me that while he was enjoying all the books he'd read so far, his favorites were the ones by female authors from other countries. "I get to hear other perspectives, you know? Hear about experiences I'll never get to have. Visit places I'll never get to go."

Now, a mystery novel caught my eye. I remember bringing it out to the prison, placing it on the shelf and realizing that my mentor, a beloved friend and former professor now retired, had recommended the author. As I reached for the book, a new voice sounded through the wall. This was a slow, deep rendition of "Achy, Breaky Heart," a song I never could have imagined sounding this tragic, this pained, this beautiful. Perhaps my colleague's students didn't find her songs patronizing after all.

The novel hooked me right away. Mysteries have never been my favorite genre, but I was enjoying this one. Perhaps it was the moment. A few pages in, "Achy, Breaky Heart" dissolved and was replaced by "Amazing Grace," now swelling with the sound of multiple voices.

I closed the book and sat listening. Yes, it was a beautiful day outside, and yes, I had spent most of it inside a windowless prison classroom. I hadn't told Slate, but today was my son's birthday. Today he turned twelve, the age when Slate was first sent to juvie. I remember the days leading up to his birth. Storms raged outside the window of my hospital room. I watched the rains, the wind, the thunder and lightning from deep within a storm of my own, a storm my son must have been struggling through, too. Sometimes, as he and I continue to struggle together through this life, I wonder if that storm ever ceased. I remember someone delivering the newspaper under the door of my hospital room and seeing the headline: "Thirty-two Killed, Twenty-three Wounded in Virginia Tech Shooting." I remember being relieved when I realized he would be born after midnight. The next day. Not the day of the shooting or during the candle-lit vigil for those killed.

Earlier in the semester I joked about dragging some of my outside students towards the finish-line. This morning, in an impromptu meeting with the prison program's director, she suggested a more apt metaphor: "It's like giving birth," she laughed. "It's painful every time, but after it's over you forget, and you start a new semester, and every time you misremember just how hard it's going to be and do it all over again." I hoped that I could embody her metaphor. That I could exist in the moment with all of my students without the realities of our divergent realities, realities shaped by systems of power and control, ravaging those moments of connection.

Sometime after "Amazing Grace" had ended, after I'd returned to my novel and finished my now-cold coffee, Barrington burst into the classroom, followed by Hanson and Kellog. It was almost two hours past his scheduled 5 p.m. conference, and he was pissed. Johnson had called him as soon as the code was cleared, but the guards had laughed at him, told him it was almost time for shift change, and he'd just have to wait. He'd tried to explain that I was waiting, that I'd spent my whole day conferencing with students, that it wasn't fair to me. The guards wouldn't budge. And then it was shift change and scheduled count—absolutely no movement. As I sat peacefully in the classroom, my students had been frustrated, harassed, detained. Like so many times this semester, I felt helpless and useless. I questioned my effectiveness, the effectiveness of the program in the face of such blatant abuse of power, such disregard for human dignity. I questioned my ability to connect with my students, to even begin to understand the ways in which the institution of prison had shaped and was shaping their existence. But I had to try. I listened to Barrington. I told him I was sorry, that I'd report it to the program director. He showed me notes he'd taken, documenting the times Johnson had called him, the times he'd asked to leave.

By 7 p.m., he'd persevered, made it through the storm, and was reading me his essay. Separated by the mandated bulk of my instructor's desk, we leaned towards each other, discussing opportunities for revisions, losing ourselves in his ideas, his research. By the time we finished conferencing, Barrington had regained his usual demeanor, a relaxed awkwardness barely hiding a tendency towards serious intensity. Hanson joined me across the hulking desk next, then Kellog, each one of us struggling through our own storms, sometimes together, sometimes alone, always searching for those moments of calm and connection.

Author Bio

Jessica Pisano is a senior lecturer and the writing program coordinator for UNC Asheville's English department. She has taught for the past twenty-three years both in the public school system and higher education. She lives in Asheville with her husband and two children.

Side Streets

Eli Goldblatt

Reflection: Poems explore places not accessible to academic or even personal prose. Words in lines can sound interior depths at the same time as they can reflect, record or conjure external scenes. In the ancient Chinese Taoist/Buddhist poetic tradition known as "Rivers and Mountains," the poet or painter's long sorrow or momentary joy is always embedded in the larger landscape of cliffs and waterfalls, distances and heights that dwarf human action. The pandemic forced us all into greater solitude but also generated an acute awareness of the needs and struggles that neighbors and strangers were living through. In 2020 my wife, artist Wendy Osterweil, and I walked nearly every day in the Wissahickon Creek Park, a deeply wooded area in Philadelphia with 56 miles of trails. We also delivered for our food coop now and then to seniors who lived in food deserts and couldn't leave their apartments. Poems allow for inside and outside occurrences to exist without direct judgment or analysis. "Side Streets" comes from a series I wrote during this period called Walks & Dreams.

Snow on side streets narrows
        heart's arteries to alleys.
                Quarantined in two rooms

the knitter barely able to fit
        her walker thru a channel
                walled by magazines & news

moves from sitting room to
        bed, kidney bean cans &
                Ritz cracker packs

stacked on kitchen counter. *Set*
        the box anywhere, she says,
                do I know you? Roads

lead to store but she's
> not taking that trip anymore—
>> payment late, landlord

might lock her out, drop
> her things on pavement
>> tree roots jacked up.

Outside I watch robins
> feast on berries they find
>> in vines wrapping dead

oaks along old railroad
> tracks. Shoe shop shuttered
>> but next door they still

sell coffee & damp doughnuts.
> I listen to sparrows fuss & a
>> woodpecker searches for grubs.

Author Bio

Eli Goldblatt's poems have appeared in literary journals since 1972. His fourth poetry collection is *For Instance* (Chax P 2019). His 2020 book on literacy, co-written with David Jolliffe, is *Literacy as Conversation: Learning Networks in Philadelphia and Arkansas* (U of Pittsburgh P). He is Professor Emeritus of English at Temple University.

PARLOR PRESS
EQUIPMENT FOR LIVING

New Releases

Pedagogical Perspectives on Cognition and Writing, edited by J. Michael Rifenburg, Patricia Portanova, and Duane Roen

Running, Thinking, Writing: Embodied Cognition in Composition by Jackie Hoermann-Elliott

Collaborative Writing Playbook: An Instructor's Guide to Designing Writing Projects for Student Teams by Joe Moses and Jason Tham

The Best of the Journals in Rhetoric and Composition 2020

The Art of Public Writing by Zachary Michael Jack

MLA Mina Shaughnessy Prize and CCCC Best Book Award 2021!

Creole Composition: Academic Writing and Rhetoric in the Anglophone Caribbean, edited by Vivette Milson-Whyte, Raymond Oenbring, and Brianne Jaquette

Check Out Our New Website!

Discounts, blog, open access titles, instant downloads, and more.

And new series:

Comics and Graphic Narratives
Series Editors: Sergio Figueiredo, Jason Helms, and Anastasia Salter

Inkshed: Writing Studies in Canada
Series Editors: Heather Graves and Roger Graves

www.parlorpress.com

CLJ **Discount:** Use CLJ20 at checkout to receive a 20% discount on all titles not on sale through July 1, 2021.

www.ingramcontent.com/pod-product-compliance
Lightning Source LLC
Chambersburg PA
CBHW031321160426
43196CB00007B/618